INTUITIVE

KNOWING HER TRUTH

CONTENTS

INTRODUCTION

It is not that you don't have it, you just left it along the way.

Beliefs are a strange beast, they are learnt behaviours, observed patterns, socially and environment impacted and changed by who or where you hang out. What's your belief around intuition? Some people say they have had it since they can recall and some stop listening, some never knew it was there until a moment in time, that they can describe. Connecting and deepening your intuition can occur by choice, by an event, by trauma, by those around you, we all have the ability to connect within and we all can deepen our intuition.

Described in many ways, Intuition is a thought, a knowing, a gut feeling and the list goes on. For me intuition is listening for that inner voice, it may not be a spoken word but a voice none the less and it is undeniable once you actually allow it to be. It is the ability to understand instinctively, without the need to have it validated.

I recall the day I was given the title of this book, it was granted to me after my morning of stillness, silence and solitude. A practice for me that strengthened and aligned me closer to my intuitive self.

INTUITIVE — Knowing Her Truth is a collection of stories from women who stand true to themselves and those they live and love through their power to be connected to themselves – connected to their intuition. Through the sharing of their stories, their one constant intention is to impact the life of another. Should you find you are impacted, touched, changed, connected to a story, to a writer that you tell them, the power of stories is so grand and must be celebrated!

As you read these chapters, be open, be receptive, be curios to the idea you too can connect to your own inner knowing, your own intuition. If you are already connected to your intuition, be inquisitive at the idea that there are lessons in this book for you and as you devour each one search for it intuitively!

The pleasure in working with like-minded women is evident in this book. The intuitive thought I had to become a publisher has definitely ignited a passion in my heart, I want you to find, through your intuition, your passion too. Enjoy the stories, take note from the lessons and let go as what is meant to be, will be.

B xx

ALETA O'MEARA

THE REBIRTHING OF ME

I write this as I look at my 5-year-old son, Toby, and always gaze at him in amazement. It's true! I am a registered nurse with 27 years' experience, and I went to the local emergency department in end-stage labour. My partner Rod and I had five hours' notice to prepare for the birth of our son, Toby.

You probably have many questions right now. How on earth could a nurse with my experience not know why she wasn't pregnant? How about I suggest that, in hindsight, it was part of the universe's divine plan beyond our control and putting me on the track I was meant to be living.

Rod and I know how we made Toby, der! It's okay; we've heard it all before. I'm the first to take the Mickey out of us. However, what is so amazing is that there were numerous layers of complexities to this little fella coming into the world that makes him pretty cool. He also has excellent energy levels, endurance, and stubbornness, which means it takes all of our efforts to get through the toughest day. Thankfully, there are few.

Let me take you back to 2009, when I completed my Masters in Advanced Practice Nursing. I had a passion for End-Stage Liver Disease. My now late mother, Maria, and I had a problematic relationship because she felt that my studies distracted me from being a reliable and dependable family member. If something was wrong or needed fixing, I was the go-to. I was the eldest daughter, and there were unspoken expectations of me. Studying was about doing something for myself—something I thought I loved. Little did I know at the time where this expertise I developed would take me.

Mum was diagnosed with bowel cancer and liver metastases in around 2011. She frightfully went to the hospital to have a bowel resection and partial hepatectomy, removal of some liver. She came home with a colostomy bag and the early onset of liver failure. Did I tell you that she was only 58 when diagnosed? My mum experienced body image issues, relentless bouts of unwellness, and a concerning delay in post-operative recovery. This became the time when I could step in and provide support and advocacy as she had intermittently lost her ability to make decisions about her health care and lifestyle choices. To see my mother vulnerable and a shade of her former vibrant, bubbly self was devastating. But I would put my big girl pants on and have a wedgy to push through. It required a lot of strength and courage to have conversations about death and dying and her wishes afterlife. This was not a foreign conversation for me to have as I have been so privileged many times with others who have passed, whether it was making sure they wore a leopard designed G-string to their grave, took their driver's licence, took a quilt, I would respectfully do it.

I had separated from my ex-husband eight years ago. Little did I know that I would find love and friendship soon after with my dear old friend Rod. We met at his school bus stop in year 11. We united together with children from previous relationships. They are all adults now and are just amazing, humble, and admirable people for different reasons. We spent a significant time supporting Mum to access services and create and activate her end-of-life plan. There were many orders from her. She was an arranger, quite bossy when it came to organising experiences important to her. She was quite funny as her intensity grew when she was in a mindset. I feel my exposure to these was the most important lesson. They are not palatable to everyone; therefore, I tend to speak conservatively.

My mum experienced severe complications from decompensated liver disease. Now and then, we would titter so that she had some quality of life, but then it didn't take much for the wheels to fall off, and she'd be in the hospital gravely ill. Bowel obstruction hepatic encephalopathy were the top two favourites for admission. I had educated her friends that if she said anything downright bizarre, they should consider calling an ambulance. Her friends were very diligent and supportive of this and reported nice stories also.

Before April 2015, I participated in paintball, enjoyed an alcoholic beverage, camembert cheese and son. I wanted to live and enjoy myself when Mum was well. My responsibilities were fewer at those times. After leaving a toxic marriage, I was definitely going to have a bit of fun. My partner was on cytotoxic medications for a chronic health condition. I had an Implanon rod inserted. I learnt later that there was no rod to be found. I had had these before, so there was a lot of scarring. The doctor said it migrated, but it wasn't to be seen actually as the X-ray showed nothing. Painting an interesting picture, right?

I always wanted to have a tummy tuck. A few unappealing things were going on because of my first natural birth. I did this in April 2015. One of the post-operative side effects is temporary or permanent loss of sensation. I felt *nothing* in my lower abdomen. I resigned myself to never being a supermodel, but a tidy up here and there would be just fine by me. I was going to have a breast reduction six months after, but then that idea went down the toilet when Toby came along! I had my tummy tuck in April 2015. I had problems with being anaesthetised, an interesting, colourful recovery with insidious post-operative complications. I did everything right and surprised the surgical team with my excellent progress.

In June/July 2015, I reported the presence of cankles to my surgeon. I pointed to this weird movement in my upper right tummy. I even joked, saying, 'I think I have aliens in my stomach!' Thankfully, he told me the symptoms would subside—what a relief to have this reassurance. He had an excellent poker face and later conceded he had no idea what was wrong with me. I had developed chest pain, shortness of breath, and a feeling of lethargy. I went to the local medical officer for advice, where they found me to have iron deficiency anaemia. I took iron injections, which were a pain in the arse, but began to feel improved. I continued working full time and was committed to my role in the workplace until Friday, August 7 in 2015.

I had a chest infection and was on oral antibiotics, my throat was so sore that I demanded my partner go and buy a spicy bourbon for a hot toddy. The night before the grand arrival, my daughter, 11 at the time, begged me to go to the hospital for help. I had other plans. She was pressing the red siren alarm, and I still wasn't going to listen! I was going to work, sign off on the pays, etc. I assured her that I had an appointment with the medical officer again. I had these crippling lower abdominal cramps from five in the morning. I was in agony. I was thinking, *Holy shit, what's happened?* I went and had a bath. My daughter found me and again insisted that I go to the hospital, as they would be the only ones that could help me. She demanded I be in the hospital by the time she got home from school. Well, at that point, I caved in and said, 'okay.' I just had to make her lunch, get her ready for school, and put her on the bus! My partner remained asleep. Bless, he must have known that the shit would hit the fan later!

Off to emergency, we went. The staff was so lovely. I waited patiently. I took this lovely quilted bag that my mum's friend made. I had a bottle of water, my phone, and my wallet in it. I didn't think I would need much. I carried on a bit with cramping and enjoyed the intermittent administration of morphine to keep me quiet. I waited a few hours for the doctor to see me since I was triaged non-urgent. I was embarrassed to be there, really, but I knew there something out of sorts. My daughter went on about how the doctor at emergency was the only one who could fix me. Thank God I listened to her, a natural empath and intuitive right there!

I was on a bed in a corner, quite naive and bemused by the way I felt. It baffled us as we had had children before. The doctor came in and told me, 'you're pregnant,' to which I replied, 'fuck off and come back with something different.' The pathology tests confirmed it. I was given a wide berth—no pun intended—for a while. Rod and I had reached the scariest moment in our lives, and we were all alone. The fear of the risks for this little person confronted and overwhelmed us right away. They took me to have an ultrasound to see the baby's position. His head was engaged; I was dilated, and he was keen as mustard to get into the world. I asked the sonographer if she could go and bring my partner. He could not come with me at the time because there was not enough space in the room for him. We soon demonstrated you could fit six people in there, not only fast but also easily.

While the midwifery team ferried me to the labour ward, they asked about my birthing plan. I thought having more morphine and getting the baby out was comprehensive enough. We were welcomed to the birthing suite by the obstetrician/gynaecologist. He had been sipping his tea, thinking that he would wait because he knew something would happen and there would be a need for him. I had contacted my best friend's husband to see if he could find my daughter and take her to my mother before she could be brought to see that we were okay, but there was some news. My mum later rang the hospital, and they put her through to the labour room. She asked if I was having a baby, to which I replied, 'Not at the bloody moment, mum! Far out! Like, what a thing to say!'

My mum and her partner arrived with my daughter. My daughter walked in and saw the enormity of where her intuition led us and immediately departed; I saw her three days later. My mum walked and stated to the effect, 'I'm dying! You can't play those jokes on me!' We had an awesome midwife who was fiercely protective of us in our vulnerabilities. Mum had cognitive impairment, anyway, so it would take her a while to process this information. She followed doctors and nurses and soon realised she was to be a grandmother again! She came into us and sat, holding my hand as long as she could. She was amazing and so supportive of us. Then, she needed to go home to rest. An hour later, we welcomed our son into the world. He was healthy and adorable and looked like Elma Fudd's love child. My step-children came to see us. It was a very confronting situation for everyone involved. They were incredible and embraced the moment. My partner's eldest daughter was there for Toby's birth and cut his cord.

Could you imagine how Mum's best friend felt when she received a text saying: 'Aleta had a healthy baby boy last night, all is well?' They called me to see if they needed to call an ambulance, of course! It was hilarious. We were so blessed to have this perfect baby and to be unscathed by all that had happened to our bodies prior. Our feeling of shock was mutual with our visitors, who offered kindness and beautiful gifts for our son. Rod made three trips home with baby stuff before he could take us home. I did only take a quilted bag to the hospital, remember?

My partner and I were so pleased with the names chosen for our son. We named him Toby Giovanni after my father and my grandfather. We only had to tell mum, and the outcome of that conversation was fairly unpredictable. She was delighted with Toby's middle name, but she sure tapped off when we mentioned his first name. She demanded to know why and then spoke of her unresolved regret and resentment for my father. She wanted a meaningful and adventurous life with Dad, but end-stage multiple sclerosis at 59 shortened his life. We assured her that he came back to spend time with her and that she could hold and cuddle him all she liked. At this point, she realised why she was still alive: to see her first grandson. He helped her to find peace within and understand why she was still with us. She was difficult to keep away from. I was allowed to breastfeed and handed him over. I knew not to obstruct this special union. The sad truth was that she would not be with us for much longer. This crossing of worlds was not about my partner and I; it was about reconnecting my parents' spirits, bringing peace and contentment to them.

We had Toby for two weeks. One evening my mum called and asked bizarre questions. We packed up the kids and went to see what was actually happening. She whispered to me, 'I need to go, Leety.' We placed Toby in bed with her for cuddles, and we called the ambulance for her maiden voyage.

Since Mum wasn't cognitively present, she was admitted to hospital. I would put Toby in her arms and feed her while she gazed into his eyes. Those moments were beyond words. I knew they were important and that I was the conduit for this to occur. I felt all alone, but I wasn't. Toby was with me all the time. There were such amazing and kind healthcare workers who supported me. They were not given the easiest situation to muddle through.

After a multidisciplinary team meeting, I began to remove Mum's supportive measures. Her oxygen and IV fluids all went and I reduced the pill burden to keep it to essentials for her comfort. This was her plan and she trusted me to implement it to the letter. Heaven forbid if I did, because I'd know about it in her afterlife! My mum had organised for my cousins to bring Toby's baby chain—a gold chain with the crucifix on it—from Italy. Her end of life plan had two tasks left on it: to be anointed for the last time and to put Toby's blessed chain around his neck. She was unconscious for some days. I honestly never would have thought that she would be sitting upright, lethargic, and greeting everyone! OMG! I could not believe it. Relatives from near, far and Italy were there for this moment. She was so proud to have placed Toby's chain around his neck. We blessed her and farewelled her. An hour later, she returned to unconsciousness and never woke again.

I had resigned myself because I would not be present for her last breath as I was recovering from major surgery, giving birth, and being a prize Jersey Cow. My partner would give me alone time with Mum and bring Toby down for a feed and then take him home. Watching mum change as she approached her end of life was quite tiring emotionally. I realised nothing was in my control after having Toby. There was some bloody method in the madness surely. September 3, 2015 came round—it was also the anniversary of my mother-in-law's passing. Rod had been secretly hoping this would not be, how could it be? As I spoke with the nurses in the corridor, the curtain blew gently towards mum's bed. I finished the conversation politely and encouraged everyone to go home and grab some lunch. I sat with mum and fed Toby. I knew I had to clear the way and that it wouldn't take her long. Twenty minutes in fact. Our mothers passed the same day, five years apart.

My mum always thought it would be funny to bequeath her quilting machine to me. She had a quilt on it before she died with three rows left. It was Toby's baby quilt. It took six months to find someone who could help me finish it and teach me how to use the machine. Nearly six years on, I can say I love quilting. I feel this mindful connection with my mum. I initially struggled with purpose and have found beautiful ways of keeping her memory. I have made quilts for friends and family across the world and share her legacy with them.

I have learnt so much about myself, who I am and what I'm about. I have an unenviable skillset to support others to find this within themselves. We are so blessed to have been chosen to be custodians of our divine gift. Everything makes sense now. I equate this to a rebirthing of the true authentic me. The universe has aligned us on the right path. We were so brave and are being richer for finding beauty in light, chaos and darkness. Together, my partner and I shined a big bloody flashlight light on it and found ourselves.

ABOUT THE AUTHOR

Aleta O'Meara is 47 years old, really 21, to her youngest son. She is a nurse, mother, stepmother, partner to Rod, joker, carer, counsellor, friend, machine quilter, traveller, go-to for hard conversations around end-of-life care for friends and family, cheesemaker, and home cook. Aleta has many life experiences of adversity, trauma, and hardship. These led her to the key events when the universe turned everything on its head with her son's surprise birth and her mother's passing. She has become the accidental death doula to several, machine quilter and an authentic version of herself. Aleta is interested in developing her knowledge and skills in being a death doula, motivational speaking, and ongoing quilting. Aleta has eloquently and respectfully articulated a story that will form part of her personal and evolving quilt.

Email: *aleta.omeara@gmail.com*
Facebook: *www.facebook.com/aleta.omeara6*
Mobile: *0497946032*

BARBARA BRANGAN

DISCOVERING HOW I AM INTUITIVELY
DESIGNED

T he producer turned and said, "OK! We'll go live in an hour!" My
body froze, and my brain tried to compute what he had just said.
I was on the set of Psychic TV, a live TV show where people phoned
psychics for advice, and I was about to go live as one of the psychics. I
thought I had come along to meet some people to check it out, not go
live tonight!

Instead of panicking, I had a conversation in my mind with my Spirit Guides.
They replied with: "You are precisely where you are meant to be. Trust us!" I listened
to them, as I had full faith in them. Technically I could finish my story there, sharing
how my intuition had led me to be on Psychic TV. The End. Only it was the beginning of a wild ride.

About 18 months before this night, I had no clue I was intuitive. A friend had
said to me that she was going to a meditation class. I was baffled that she could meditate, as she was relatively high energy like me, so I thought if she could meditate,
maybe so could I? I also secretly loved how the class was at 7 pm, so it meant I
skipped bed and bathtime for my young daughters, which at times was like
Groundhog Day. I was seeking something. However, I didn't actually know what. I
attended the class, not yet realising that it was a Spiritual Meditation class. Over time,
I learnt to meditate, strengthen my intuition and read energy for others and myself.

I was in awe that this whole Spirit world existed, and how could I have not known about it? I had so much fun on that journey; it was a great joy to connect to intuition and share love and trust messages. I started doing psychic readings and psychic fairs, which led me to the night on Psychic TV.

So why then wasn't I happy when I was doing Psychic TV? There were a few reasons. I couldn't place the feelings into the words back then, but what I felt from the other psychics and mediums was incongruence. Something was off. I sat next to men and women with 20 years' experience, who were highly skilled in channelling energy, as I heard them in sessions as we sat next to each other. Yet, when the camera was off, there were gaps between the 'love and light' messages they shared with clients and with what they felt about their lives. Like everyone, they were insecure in aspects of their lives. I kind of expected them to be on a pedestal of 'having found the light!.'

Then I noticed the same clients coming back repeatedly. People, mostly women, sought advice about their romantic or family relationships, seeking options and assurance that it was all going to be OK. The thing is that messages from Spirit, no matter who they come through, are always loving and full of hope. I could often read into someone's energy field and show them their options or the path they were being guided towards. However, I didn't realise then that we have free will at all times and it's up to us to choose to embody the wisdom. But I couldn't figure out why someone wouldn't choose the easier path instead of the hard one. So, I was baffled to see the same client back asking the same questions, receiving the same wisdom. It didn't feel right to accept their money.

I also was exhausted working in the world of Psychic TV. My daughters were both very young then, under the age of four, and the TV show started at 11 pm and ended at 2 am. The Psychic fairs were long days; you could easily see 10-15 people back-to-back. I loved being in session, the time flew by, but my body and energy suffered as it took me days to recover. The sad part is the people who suffered in that process were my kids and my husband, as they saw the tired and cranky side of me.

Then it dawned on me that the incongruent person was I. Here I was sharing messages of love and intuition, and I wasn't embodying it myself. Everyone I saw in my world who showed me this, industry colleagues and clients, were a mirror of me. We are all interconnected and co-dependent on each other on our journey of trusting and loving ourselves. So then, with perfect timing, my meditation teacher, whom I had grown to trust deeply, invited me to take part in this personal development program called Landmark. At first, I was dubious; who wants to go to a three-day-long seminar? But again, my intuition nudged me to accept, and that was a pivotal part of my deep dive into my personal development, growth, and exploration of my subconscious.

The journey I went on, understanding who I am and why I make the choices I make, showed me that we indeed are what we think and how so much of our thoughts are unconscious thoughts. These thoughts were formed into beliefs and filed away in the first seven years of our lives. It taught me to recognise how highly intuitive, highly empathetic, and sensitive I was as a child. I could feel the truth of the emotions of people that were around me. I could, and still can, feel the unconscious beliefs of people I meet. However, as a child, I struggled to let go of others' emotions and pain, often believing them to be my emotions. My parents have always been fantastic; however, looking back, they weren't given the insights into how to support a sensitive kid. It was simply the era we were in. We know better now (every generation does); however, adults didn't have information surrounding sensitive kids back then. When I was younger, being so sensitive to others' feelings hurt me, and my journey through Landmark showed me how I chose to ditch that identity and instead become a strong and independent person so that no one could hurt me. When I shared this awakening with my best friend, she laughed and reminded me that I used to say, 'I'll do what I want, when I want, with whoever I want!' all the time as a teenager.

I had an epiphany after this deep dive into the fact that I am not broken and that the approach of choosing to be 'strong and independent' was a mask when I am sensitive and intuitive. People mistakenly assume I am invincible, as I have portrayed this for years when I am strong on the outside and soft and fragile on the inside.

I decided to identify myself as a psychic no longer. I didn't want people coming to me for my gifts when they have direct dial access to their intuition and Spirit Guides themselves. I shifted into intuitive guidance sessions with a focus on connecting women to their intuition. At this point, I entered the world of women in business in the wellness industry. It was like being a kid in a candy shop. I had an ache to express my Soul Purpose, and these women offered me courses and programs to show me for sure how to do it. I wanted that candy, and I was willing to pay top dollar for it.

Enrolling in all these programs was one of the repeating arguments my husband and I had. I remember once getting mad at him for not letting me enrol in a $20,000 program. I used to question what he knew, how could he understand? Sometimes I listened to him; often, I didn't. I joke now that I should get a t-shirt that says 'Frankie knows best!' I should have listened to him. He has excellent business wisdom and is the one person who knows me the best, not the strangers on the internet. I learnt a lot in those programs, and I don't regret my journey, yet I certainly spent a lot more money than I got in return on revenue. There are many amazing programs available. However, it is also an industry (like many others) where it is a known fact that women enrol in business programs that will never receive the outcomes promised. Aspects of this 'high vibe' industry lack integrity, as many 'Soulpreuneurs' are racing towards the $100k revenue goal for their business. I have reconciled and recognised that one of my Soul gifts is sharing past wisdom to help others avoid making similar mistakes. To authentically embody this gift, I first had to make mistakes and take risks myself.

I have an insatiable thirst for wisdom, which led me (back) to Human Design in 2019. I had initially come across it probably three years before, and like many when I looked up my human design, which you can do for free. I was confused by the weird chart, and the language attached just baffled me (as it's quite old English). Human Design is a relatively new way to help us understand how unique we are. It combines profoundly esoteric and scientific systems. I popped in my birth details and discovered that I was a Projector, and there was something mentioned about 'wait for an invitation' as a strategy for my life. I was in a program that I had just paid about $3,000 for that was anything but wait for the invite. It was promoting how to go hustle, create your funnel, create your signature program, create your Facebook ads to get people to sign up so that you can make $100k. It was all go and no wait. So, I ignored my Human Design and kept going.

I realised my return to Human Design reflected a conscious choice to honour my truth and self-worth. It also occurred at the time I chose to take a leap of faith to become fully self-employed, I was listening to a podcast (with Jenna Zoe) that shared Human Design in simple English. I began to fall in love with Human Design, and I am still falling in love with it to this day. I truly began to understand the beauty of my aura as a Projector, a natural intuitive guide, and how my intuition speaks to me and shows me what others are truly feeling. I truly recognised that my soul chose this life —to be me and no one else.

My soul chose to be sensitive. It chose to be empathetic and intuitive. I am designed perfectly to be me. There is nothing wrong with me. The feeling of being broken occurs when I try and shapeshift into being someone else. It is safe to love myself exactly as I am. My only real soul quest is to explore: 'can I become the sensitive and intuitive adult my soul intended me to be?'

I began to see that I am not designed to go out and hustle for clients (not many of us are!). I am more successful when I find something I love and share it from a place of full intuitive trust. When I do this, I radiate energy that brings me the right people, who subsequently invite me to work with them. Some days I am great at remembering this; other days I am not. Being a human is an experiment for each of our souls; some days it's perfect, other days it flops—it's all part of the experiment and evolution of who we are.

Understanding myself so deeply allowed me to reconcile that many of the programs I enrolled in were not right for me. The programs I learnt to trust my intuition were experiences to help me remember my intuition, as it's always been there. Always. Yours is too. Realising this truth has led me on a massive journey of forgiveness, of myself for giving my power away and blindly believing amazing marketing. I can now see how the women delivering these programs were sharing what they loved and that just because it worked for them doesn't mean it works for everyone. We are all unique. A big piece of forgiveness I did recently was forgiving myself, my ego, for wanting the power and adoring followers that come with a $100k+ business. I secretly wanted others to put me on a pedestal (who doesn't?). I have reconciled that within me lies extremes of the shadow of my ego and light and my soul. I am accepting of that.

Before I chose to learn from someone, now I ask myself, 'Am I attracted to this opportunity as I love the energy of this person?' The vibration, or emotional resonance, we each feel from others as they share the spark of their Soul, is incredibly attractive. However, this attraction does not have to mean that I need to enrol in their program. I now learn and grow as I love to learn, not because I am learning to fix something wrong with me.

Human Design is one of the first things I began to experiment with, in my client sessions. I witnessed how understanding their Human Design gave my clients enormous personal power, confidence, clarity, and real permission to know and accept themselves. The power came when they began to say no where they previously would have felt the pressure to say yes (even when they didn't want to!). I won't lie, I was tempted to do a 'certification' in Human Design. Many $10,000 programs can offer this, but for once, I am genuinely at peace with not being formally certified. I believe the age of the Guru is over for many industries. I trust instead that my energy, passion, and authenticity speak for me, not my certificates. I continue to study and invest in developing my knowledge of Human Design and carefully choose the mentors I learn from. That in itself is so liberating for my Soul.

After the initial pause that COVID-19 gave 2020, it turned into a phenomenal year for my business. After the initial shock of what happened, people pondered, 'Who am I?' and 'What is my purpose?' and Human Design is a great map to explore these questions. I offered short programs and private mentoring to align women to their unique identities, as per their Human Design, and it was so much fun. My ego would love to tell you that this was the magic pill, and I had a $100k year, but that's not the case. I have been very successful (and super happy) and truly feel this is the foundation upon which everything is coming together, so watch this space. I am proudly self-employed doing my Soul's work, reminding people how freaking amazing they are, and I am magnetic doing it.

I am also very much an everyday human. I still have subconscious fears that trip me up. I can be cranky and irritable like lots of people. I feel that our Soul call is an invitation to be both Human and Divine at the same time. The time of separation is over. There are days we will have full trust in our intuition, and they are fun and carefree, and there are days we'll be in our heads and worrying about all that could go wrong because we aren't good enough. That too is OK. The only thing our Soul asks of us is to narrow the gap between the extremes and to be super compassionate and forgiving of ourselves when we forget how amazing we are. This is how we evolve and embody our divine light.

I do three things to help me stay in a place of trust and surrender; they may help you.

1. CONNECTING WITH MY INTUITION

It is remembering that I am not alone. So often, I fall back into the old habits of putting myself under pressure to do everything myself. Bringing myself back to my truth that I have immediate access to my Spiritual support team soothes and relieves this pressure. I can simply ask for guidance and listen. When I practice this, life is always more comfortable, and when I feel like I am meeting resistance, I have often stopped having these intuitive conversations. I connect with my intuition in a few ways from conversations while I walk, journaling, (guided) meditations, or sitting in

Circle with other women. Every time I have been at my peak of success directly correlates to meditating at least five days a week.

2. BREAKING THE PEOPLE-PLEASING HABIT AND CHOOSING ME

Before I choose, I ask myself, "Is this true for me?" and "Is this best for me?" I filter everything through my unique human design (you will have a process unique to you too). I check that the choice suits my aura type and that I have considered my strategy and inner authority, which is 'have I been invited?' and 'have I had a chance to talk this through to see if it feels right for me?.' The most significant gift is permitting myself to say no when I often say yes because of the people pleaser and empath in me wanting everyone else to be happy. Now I recognise that perhaps me saying no is part of God's plan for the other person and me. It is safe to say no.

3. EXPLORING AND REWIRING MY SUBCONSCIOUS

The more I dive in here, the more fascinated I am. I often think I am this 44-year-old woman who has got it all together when in fact, at times, it is my 3-year-old self or my 10-year-old self who is running the show. I have learnt the power we have to rewire our subconscious with neuroplasticity and energy. I connect with my inner child through meditation, compassionate inquiry, and journaling. I curate my news-feed and social circles to reflect my values, my truth, and my dreams. I connect with my inner child and remind her that it is safe to be sensitive and intuitive, and everything has worked out great for me and that I am safe.

If I were to go back to chat to myself on that night of starting Psychic TV, knowing what I know now, I would tell her, "Discovering you are intuitive is not the end of the ride; it's the start, and it's going to be a wild and fun ride. The more you can let go of trying to control and instruct the universe and instead choose to surrender and trust the journey, the easier it will be. You are a Divine Being in a human body. Embrace the contrast and be kind to yourself in the process. Ultimately, you will discover that you are not broken. No one is. You were never broken. You are amazing; your Human Design will mirror that back to you. Embrace being how unique you are and the universe will reward you for it."

ABOUT THE AUTHOR

Barbara Brangan is an Intuitive Mentor skilled at guiding women to find clarity and purpose by remembering and reclaiming their unique gifts, attributes, and wisdom. For many years, Barbara suppressed her intuitiveness and sensitivity. Within 12 months of reconnecting with her intuition, she appeared regularly on Psychic TV, offering channelled messages from Spirit. Through this, she noticed a gap in the messages of how amazing we each are, which Spirit & Source consistently share with us, and what we believe to be true of ourselves; we easily underestimate ourselves and waste our power.

Barbara is an avid learner who began her deep dive into understanding emotional intelligence, energy science, subconscious fears, and the art of intuitive mentoring over the last six years. This led her to Human Design, a system that expresses how unique and amazing we are and how the universe responds in support when we stand in the gloriousness of being different. Her passion is to witness women fall in love with themselves through experimenting with living their Human Design in all parts of life. She advocates that as we do this, we collectively create a positive ripple effect.

Barbara is proudly intuitive, empathetic, sensitive, and different. She was born in Ireland however now calls Sydney home. The beach is her happy place. She has a quirky sense of humour which she infuses into all of her work.

Barbara offers free Human Design reports. Request yours at her website listed below.

Website: www.barbarabrangan.com/humandesign

CARLA SCHWITALLIK

BIG GIRLS DON'T CRY - A STORY OF DEEP DESPAIR AND POWERFUL TRANSFORMATION

"Please, come back. I know it is all my fault. Please accept my apologies; I am such an awful person. Please, I am begging you."

There was nothing more than silence on the other side of the call before it was hung up.

I called again but only got as far as voicemail. I repeatedly called, my despair increasing, tears welling, panicking. How could I reach him? How would I make him come back?

It had happened again—I had said something, did something, put on the wrong face, made the wrong gesture...

The times when I had still been questioning and arguing what exactly it was and justified myself were over.

The only way out was to get through to him and beg him to accept my apologies. I didn't know why I was apologising, but I did it anyway. I had learned that questioning and discussing my "mistakes" made everything worse. When it first began, I had been stunned, but I was way beyond that by now.

I did everything I could to be a good partner and take care of everything, but nothing was ever good enough. My life was similar to living in a minefield where every time you clear a mine, new ones came from nowhere.

I was desperate and exhausted but highly committed.

I was committed to making this relationship work—committed to show my love and compassion for this man who always doubted it. I would prove that I was a good person, an empathic wife, and a kind mother. Whatever it takes.

When I was on the end of that phone, desperately calling with no answer, I had just given birth to a beautiful baby girl a week before and expected a dear friend and her husband to come over.

My partner had left our apartment once again. In a dramatic scene, he rushed out, announcing to drive to his hometown, abandoning the baby and me.

Like many times before, I felt as if my life was out of my hands. Full crisis mode. My body hurt from the tension it was enduring. I prayed for the baby to stay asleep as I was on the mission to bring him back. Calling and calling him again.

Thoughts raced in my head: What would I tell the visitors? How could I explain this?

It did not even cross my mind to tell them the truth. The truth of the hell I was living. Speaking of that truth would only be for very much later. There was no way I would admit to anyone that everything was going very, very wrong.

At that time, I was ready to do almost anything to hold up an illusion. An illusion that we were a happy couple with well-paying jobs, living in a lovely flat, having just welcomed a beautiful baby together.

Everything was perfect. At least it could and should have been. That's what I sold to everyone. Most importantly to myself.

Yes, the man I lived with was not easy. He couldn't control his temper or his emotions. Everything could change within seconds: plans, moods, and our relationship status. Without warning, our plans to move in together crashed as he could no longer imagine living with me. Within a split second, the man who had just said he loved me would pack his stuff and drive away because I had said something upsetting, he wouldn't tell me.

He would leave the room and refuse to speak to me or explain what I did wrong. When he answered, he told me that my lack of knowledge of my wrongdoing confirmed what an awful empathy-lacking person I was. Every wrong guess from my side was only a further demonstration of my incapacity to understand his needs. All of this proved that I was mentally unwell and incapable of considering anyone but myself. He was suffering, and it was all my fault.

Sometimes he would freak out and scream, throw plates of food against the wall, sometimes hit me, cover me with allegations, insult me, humiliate me. However, the silent treatment was worse—not knowing what was going on, being shut out and ignored as punishment. The pain and desperation rising within me were almost unbearable.

I would often wake up at night and stare into the dark. What had I done? What was I missing?

However, I was also in charge. This was merely about me understanding what was going on and navigating the ship differently than I used to.

Put all my wishes and needs aside? No problem, I did not need them anyway. No compassion for me being pregnant working in an international law firm with long working hours and immense client pressure? Big girls don't cry. Being frequently criticized and blamed for everything? Yes, exaggerated, but if that helped him to calm down, why make a fuss?

How difficult could it be to make him happy? I was confident that I had this. I would make this work.

Rewind to a year before:

I was a 31-year-old independent, happy and healthy woman living in the tiny country of Luxembourg in the heart of Europe and successfully working as a lawyer in the financial industry. For a while, I was single and enjoying my life, going out, making friends, travelling the world, etc.

On a New Year's Eve, I received a strong knowing. I would fall pregnant in the new year and have a baby. I even told a friend and toasted to it.

A short time after that, the man who had been my high school love and soon-to-be father of that child contacted me out of nowhere. After many years of doubting whether commitment, family, and children were for me, here I was: Ready! Oh, yes, I was so ready.

I ignored my brother's concerns, who could not be happy for me as he remembered how things had gone ten years before. How I had been unhappy and heartbroken. How this man had been jealous of everything, including my good relationship with my brother. He hadn't forgotten how this man had been controlling and unjust with me and everyone else.

I preferred to remember the first months together—how much in love we were, how amazing everything was.

Ten years before, my intuition had told me one night that it needed to stop, that I needed to leave, that I needed to say No to him to be *me*. I received a clear message after an ugly fight and endless discussion. *Leave.* You need to leave him. *Now.*

And I did it. I amazed myself. No one could believe it when I announced my decision without a doubt the next morning. My heart was breaking, but I was true to myself. I left.

Yet ten years later, I decided to pretend as if all of that had never happened.

And of course, it happened all over again:

Fairy-tale-like first weeks together, feeling amazing, adored, loved, and appreciated.

I had everything planned out. I, who always lived in fear of commitment for so long, would prove everybody wrong, notably, my mother—she had warned me about marriage, losing my independence, and giving away my freedom.

Only six months later, I lived a personal hell I told no one about; in constant anticipation of what would happen next. There was almost no safe space, no time to relax.

I learned to become incredibly careful of what I said or did.

There were times I wished I could disappear to avoid other people looking at or speaking to me as any little attention I attracted could trigger massive jealousy scenes.

Everything made him suspicious. I got used to FBI-like investigative interviews as he was constantly checking and controlling where I went, with whom I had lunch, which friend I phoned, and searching for proof that I was lying and betraying him.

When we were together but even more important when he was in another room or at work,

I referred more and more to my intuitive knowing to navigate through this situation. I felt him shift from a good mood to a bad one. I left conference calls at work to check in with him, and rushed home to prevent the worst.

Managing his emotional rollercoaster became my main task. All my focus laid on making sure that I would be attentive enough to avoid the next drama. The better I got at it, the more I could increase periods of calm in our life. I could then convince myself at least for a few hours—when I got lucky, for a week—that everything was fine in my picture-perfect world.

Of course, only to face the next challenge when his anger and frustration would erupt even more violently than before, leaving me shattered and full of guilt and shame as he was constantly blaming me for being incapable of creating peace and calm for him.

I was beating myself up: had I paid more attention, had I anticipated better, had I been less selfish and narcissistic, less focused on myself, I could have prevented the derailment.

Instead of seeking help from family and friends, I isolated myself and avoided speaking to them. Being pregnant, often tired and exhausted, was a perfect cover-up.

I was unwilling to see what was happening even though the universe was doing its best to present the message in flashing red lights around me.

In retrospect, my life then feels like a movie with a highly absurd script. The situation deteriorated massively after the birth of my daughter triggering heavy emotional reactions of her father. Blaming and shaming me for everything increased, threats to leaving were back, and humiliation was my daily bread.

The climax of absurdity peaked when my daughter was only three weeks old. He gave me one day's notice to pack and dropped me off at my parents' house after a three-hour night drive where I was supposed to live with the baby for the next few months while he moved back in with his mother, supposedly because he needed to study for an exam.

I refused to see how all of this was unacceptable. My parents and friends questioned what was going on, trying to break it to me that he was dumping me.

The worse it got, the less I questioned it, and the more I held on. I was capable of tuning in and knowing what he needed, and I was strong enough to control and suppress my needs and emotions.

I had learned to do that in many ways before I met him, and this situation simply meant that I was to become excellent at doing so.

Now that it had become more difficult to hold up the facade, I tried to persuade everybody that he was suffering from depression and burnout. We all just needed to support him to get better. Everything would be fine. I was fine. Absolutely. In full denial but fine.

Because my parents started heavily protesting his behaviour, I very carefully shared a few details of how my life had been the past year.

I see myself sitting in the kitchen with my mother urging me to open my eyes—nothing I could have done justified the blame for everything and this behaviour. My father telling me that I had been brainwashed, that he was the one being egocentric and cruel.

I still had difficulties grasping the truth I felt they were speaking. I just needed to get it back under control and make this work. I still thought I knew better!

It was only until my baby was three months old and even more sadistic drama occurred on a daily basis that I would find myself in a situation where I finally surrendered.

Another ugly late night conversation, a "wrong" answer from my side, full anger and blame covering me: "I have enough, I need peace and calm, it is all your fault, you are such a failure, I hate you, I am leaving for good." Silence as he hung up the phone.

Immediately I was back in my downward spiral: Despair. Panic. Calling. No answer.

It was 2 am, sitting in the dark, in front of the computer, and like many times before, I wrote this email: "It's all my fault, please forgive me. Please give me another chance. I beg you!"

Like on autopilot, I kept writing, and then there was this message. *This stops now.*

The first time in over a year, I listened, trusted, and acted. I pressed the delete key. I would not send this email.

I knew that I had let go. I knew that there was nothing more that I could do. I knew this was the end.

I cannot remember how I fell asleep. But a long-missed calm came over me.

The next day the pain was so intense, I could hardly breathe. This sensation would be around a lot the following months and years. I was devastated and heart-broken—my life in pieces.

But I also felt a sense of profound relief that I would never forget. It was the first day of returning to myself.

Gradually, I started living my life again, meeting friends, going out. Without controlling what I said or did, where I looked, when I called, or how I answered a message.

I used to explain back then that I could not open up and tell others about this ridiculous situation I got myself in because I loved him too much to end the relationship and that I needed to be there for him.

It was only until much later that I understood that I had not been ready to let go of control.

To accept that I could not control him nor anything or anybody else. To accept myself as I was. To accept that life was not going according to my plan. To allow the pain of having been deceived, the grief of having been so wrong. To admit my shame and guilt. To feel the fear of being judged.

Yes, I had been massively manipulated, but in retrospect, I could have seen it coming. I could not bring up the courage to face the truth about this man and about myself. I was not ready to let go of my plan but kept fighting a pointless battle.

What this deeply troubled man did then and since then is his responsibility he is to assume.

However, it was my decision to constantly look the other way: he was emotionally and mentally unable to actually be who I wished him to be. I was emotionally unable to love myself enough to accept that.

I used my intuition to (try to) control the situation instead of recognising the clear message that it was not good for either of us. I had not yet learned that the Universe was actually caring for me but my ego thought it knew better and wanted to argue with God.

It took a lot of work through pain and guilt to understand that I was not the victim of the circumstances but that I always had a choice:

I had been to one to chose to prolong my suffering by trying to bring him back instead of letting him leave. I believed that suffering for love was necessary, and I needed to prove worthy of it. I chose to ignore that I was giving myself up completely to please someone who had set the conditions in a way that I could only fail.

The victim's role is easy to fall into in such a situation, and I would be lying if I had not sat with this shadow.

However, over time, I understood my role in this story. My healing from it depended on me taking responsibility for my (re-)actions and feelings.

My heart opened to the help and wisdom of my spiritual teachers who took my hand and guided my along this path. I learned how energy works and to think in terms of vibration. I cut more and more of those energetic ties that kept me hostage.

This meant being radically honest with myself and facing how little I could communicate or even formulate my needs.

I had to unlearn that I was only safe when I was everybody's darling. That only, in that case, I was worthy of being loved.

I had to grasp that I had no room for weakness or vulnerability, that I had no space for sadness and grief within myself.

I had to become aware that I was incapable of feeling the emotions of anger or rage. That I was instead entirely consumed by shame and guilt.

I had to allow the realisation that I had mastered perfectly to suppress who I truly was when not feeling safe. That I was my worst enemy.

Our life does not just happen to us. We have a choice how we think, feel and react. Every single time.

Today, I am not only in a healthy relationship with a fully supportive partner but, even more important, I fully support myself.

I chose to be accountable for my reality. I chose to master my intuitive skills in alignment with my purpose instead of arguing against it.

Today, I teach and guide other women how to think in terms of energy, frequency and vibration. I have found my life's role as a sacred leader with the mission to share with other women what I have learned.

We are all intuitive, it is part of our biology, but we have often been told to ignore it. We were taught that we are small and powerless, victim of our fate. The moment we understand that we are the creator of our reality, that we always have a choice, we take our power back.

I have changed my mind about myself and I share this wisdom through my work with other women inviting them to do the same.

My work is for women who may feel powerless as I used to but sense there is something else out there, an urge, a calling from deep inside. I guide them to find the courage to take responsibility for their reality and hold the vision of being the fully empowered creator of their lives. To do so we must face our demons, our deepest fears, as these are limitations we have created.

Because the journey of life is not to seek for love but to find all the barriers inside ourselves that we have built against it.

ABOUT THE AUTHOR

Carla Schwitallik grew up in Asia and Germany while her maternal roots lie in Austria. She is a mother of three beautiful girls, married to a French husband and living and working in the financial industry in the polygott and international community of the tiny country of Luxembourg in Europe.

She has always been intuitive and a spiritual seeker. After many years of being in the student role, she has stepped up to be a spiritual teacher and leader.

She is kind, generous, enthusiastic and inspiring. She is fun to be with but she will also speak up against injustice and discrimination.

She is passionate about intuition in her work as trainer, guide and teacher of Intuitive Intelligence. Her vision is to inspire and empower others to be their authentic Self. In her service, she offers guidance and teachings focusing on recon-nection to our intuition, clearing of limiting beliefs and taking responsibility for our own vibration.

www.facebook.com/carlaschwitallikintuitiveintelligencetrainer

DANIELLE PREISER

THROUGH DARKNESS, WE FIND TRUE LIGHT

I am three years old. My mom went to visit her dying mother. My dad is working. My brother is safely tucked in his bed. It's dark. I feel imminent danger. I know who's coming up the stairs: Tanya. She gets on her knees to look me in the eyes. Tanya squeezes my small arms and starts shaking me, cursing at me, yelling.

I tell my parents what is happening.

They don't believe me.

No one does.

So, *Survivor Dani* comes out: I start ripping and ravaging clothes out of my closet; running up and down the block, nakedly; screaming, crying, peeing on floors; stealing from friends.

For years, I was ashamed of this 'crazy' child.

Now, I am proud of her.

She knew.

She knew the *truth.*

What she didn't know at the time was this:

My mom and dad were true lovebirds who once shared a romance worth writing about. Mom inspired Dad to let go of his hippie days and complete ten years of night school as he worked full-time. He became a CPA. Mom was a power woman, the head of sales, the youngest in such a position.

My dad was an 'oops' child of the 60s in Brooklyn. He came from a home with a lot of unspoken love. He frequently searched for words and ways to feel this unspoken affection—so he experimented with drugs. He also found joy in basketball. He was a huge-hearted, no-nonsense protector. His life changed when he was nineteen; he was in a critical car accident. The nurses called him *Miracle Boy* for surviving over-night. My dad pulled through. Carl Preiser, my dad, embodied what it means to be a *Preiser Survivor.*

My mom, Leslie, also grew up in Brooklyn. She was a gorgeous Jack LaLanne fitness instructor and model. She had an extra sweetness and cuteness about her that was all her own. She is the middle of three girls. Her dad was fun-loving and hard-working. Her mom was a renaissance woman. My mom grew up quickly—she graduated high school early and began her own life.

My mom and dad met on a blind date and were married shy of 40 years.

Months before the two wed, my dad's mom passed of a sudden heart attack. When my dad heard the news, he passed out and his tongue turned black.

Grief is indescribable.
Death is the deepest shock to the heart and body.
No matter how much we know death is inevitable, it seems impossible.
Unless you're Ram Dass, death kills the living, too.

My grandma's death was the foreshadow of life's unexpectedness.

The marriage was very different from their romance's heydays.

I can hear my dad's words: "I never knew life would be this hard." And his phrase: "While I'm still around…"

On July 9, 1989, my angel brother, Jonathan Ross Preiser, was born. After 24 hours of back labor, you better believe my mom cried of sheer overjoy when he c-sectioned out!

My dad, who watched the whole birth, was in bliss.

This baby was their co-creation of magic.

As the two watched Jonathan from the nursery window, my dad couldn't help but ask the nurse if she could please put Johnny's hat back on to cover his conehead.

My mom laughed, knowing my dad innocently wanted everything to be *perfect.*

In time, truth is always revealed.

Jonathan developed slower than his peers. He enjoyed knocking down the Legos rather than building them up. He laughed and clapped at inappropriate times. He could not fathom why anyone would use a toilet!

My mom and dad took Jonathan to a neurologist. The neurologist tested Jonathan for a few different genetic disorders. She told my mom and dad that Fragile X was the worst, but not to worry because she didn't think their baby had it.

For six weeks, my parents prayed and prayed.

Then came the day:

March 19, 1991, the phone rang.

The secretary called to speak with my mom.

Without much care, she delivered the news.

My mom was in hysterics.

She waited until my dad got home from work and school to bear the news.

My dad opened the front door, and his eyes met my mom's eyes. She told him their baby, Jonathan, had Fragile X.

He fell to the sidewall — leaning on the lasting of his arm's weighted limb.

He couldn't hold it.

Two years later, the two courageously decided to have another child, me. They knew I had a 50/50 chance of having Fragile X, too, yet they went through.

Bravery.

I was born on November 15, 1993. I neither have Fragile X, nor am I a carrier. I do not have any mental illnesses, substance abuse, financial strife, or genetic health issues that plagued my home. I was born to break the chain.

At six years old, I began to see Johnny's *truth.* My wide-eyed angel brother was different from our peers. People looked at us, at him, in public. They made fun of his mannerisms. Everything came more difficult to him.

So, I created *DP Schooling,* a cardboard box, with a hanging flashlight, Harry Potter themed, to teach him all I was learning in school.

We would figure this out!

At first, Johnny loved school and was, I must say, a star student. In time, he began to make excuses and no longer wanted to attend.

The gap widened.

The work became more challenging.

I, egoically, was not happy that he missed my class! However, my soul knew and cried for Johnny, for my parents, for everyone's dream of limitless life and potential.

As Johnny and I played Legos and K'NEX, 6-year-old me said I would build him a home one day. My heart wanted him close and safe, and my soul knew that my parents were not in a position to ensure his future.

Jonathan is my greatest gift from Source. He is love, joy, and appreciation. He has a magic about him: the second I see him, I smile. He is simply divine—he is raw, real, and true. He impacts all in seconds. His laughter is contagious. His eyes are pure. His heart is visible. Jonathan is my teacher, my inspiration, and my *why*. I am his protector, advocate, and his *how*.

As I grew, I became an advocate for all who were "different." In kindergarten, I was the messenger for my classmate who was selectively mute. In 6th grade, I told my whole class to stop making fun of our classmate upon her absence. I went out of my way to be a safe space for people to share their truths without judgment.

My soulful need to protect began to leak into a need to save. I became codependent. I compulsively needed to help, fix, or heal others to feel loved and valid.

I soon found myself morphing to be accepted, lying to be loved, saving to feel enough. This pattern became so deeply embedded that I could not see it when I looked in the mirror.

At fifteen and a half, I woke up paralyzed below my knee on my right side. My body quickly became emaciated. My brain felt foggy. I was bruising.

Doctors tested me for MS, MD, cancer, and a slew of other diagnoses.

Nothing.

I was eventually diagnosed with Celiac and went gluten-free, but the medical anomaly continued. I thought this medical mystery would last a week, a month, and it turned into over seven years. I ended up having my large intestine removed, unlocalized internal bleeding, nerve surgery, mitochondrial issues, amenorrhea, disordered eating, and more.

What I didn't know at the time, that I know now, is:

I had manifested an incurable, unnamable illness.

At seven years old, I broke my first bone. It was amazing. My dad carried me in from our front yard. My mom baked for me. People in school carried my books and gave me extra love.

This bone break happened naturally; however, I began to break bones purposely for the years following, throwing myself off our front porch, praying for the X-rays to show the breaks that ensure love.

And so, it was: I had "fragile bones."

For years, I broke bones and bones.

One of the best days of my childhood was when I broke my ankle. I had gotten a pink and blue swirled cast, and my mom and I went to see the Lizzie McGuire movie.

The body keeps the score.
It is impossible to repress our emotions forever without them surfacing in some capacity.

I taught my body that I needed to self-harm in order to put the world's weight down and receive love, attention, and validation.

I kept this secret for years. I was ashamed of the lies behind my casts. In fact, I felt safest in casts since they hid and held everything together.

At the time of my 7+ year medical mystery, I had no clue what was happening to my body. Top doctors and surgeons had no explanation for what was going on.

The Mayo Clinic rejected me.

I took matters into my own hands and went vegan. I became Dr. Dan. I would not eat a morsel of food that did not nourish my body. I began practicing yoga meditation. I moved out of my childhood home and couch surfed until I found a safe space for my healing.

I saved my own life—which is the only way to survive.

I appreciate what doctors, medications, surgeons, and eastern modalities do, but at the end of the day, it's me and you who choose, save, and live our own lives.

I could not hold onto my discoveries without sharing.

People pass away daily, some by their own hands, some by illness, and some by slow suicides.

So, I became a health coach and taught people how to choose their own medicines in food, fitness, and mindset.

I kept trying to go back to school, and my body kept saying "No." After five different colleges and six different rounds, I graduated. My senior year, as I worked a few jobs and finished up my courses, I was ready to continue the faux western "race" of life: I applied to graduate school for social work as I ordered books to prepare for

The GRE and apply for psychology. When decisions were in, I would choose what to study, where to go, how to take out more loans, and serve and bartend my booty off.

Piece of gluten-free cake!

After I began to submit my applications, I woke up.

I said, "No."

This was one of the first 'No's' in my self-induced people-pleasing dictionary.

I emailed each of the schools I had applied to and rescinded my applications.

I felt as though I were dying long enough. It was time to LIVE.

Post-graduation, I bought a one-way ticket to San Diego.

A couple I knew from middle school happened to be out there. I had no job, no rent, and no community and felt evermore freedom and aliveness.

I ended up watching their angel pup as the two got married and traveled.

I knew this time was for me, a gap year, to be, to see, to meet Dani. With her Pacific waters and mountainous dynamic terrain, California was the perfect place for me to unlearn, de-condition, and present Dani, without any labels of story, strife, or triumph.

I ended up working at Café Gratitude, my second home, a space where I met some of my dearest friends and most profound spiritual truths. I walked dogs. I was a companion for an elderly woman. I worked jobs I loved and began saving for my pilgrimage to India.

I felt single for the first time in my life. Previously, I had casually dated but was too afraid to burden anyone to truly partner. After years of doctors picking, prodding, invading my sacred space, I was closed off sexually.

Now, I was ready. I brought all of Dani to California.

Dani California *bay-be*!

I went on dates with all types of people—even considered going on a date with a woman. Although she had asked for my number, she never texted me.

Anyway,

I was full-body *free*.

I ended up meeting Rich. At the time, I had zero interest in him. Eventually, Rich won me over. He was a man-child in a way that freed my mind from the chatter of day-to-day depth, analysis, and consciousnesses.

For our first date, he took me to the fair on the back of his Ducati.

We were like little kids, laughing, skipping, playing...

On the way home, he told me to hold on and revved up to 135mph!

I didn't see this lack of consent as a red flag; I love adrenaline.

I was sky-high from the oxygen that rushed up my helmet and the speed of the wind against my skin. I felt this sense of childhood lightness that I may have never felt before.

We ended up dating, and in time, I was ready to lose my virginity. For years, I was very open about being a virgin. I had put myself on an untouchable pedestal, appearing to be ever so confident and "too busy" for boys. The *truth* was I was scared. I was scared to share my body, my temple, a home I didn't trust, with anyone. If I couldn't even trust my body, how could I trust *someone else's* body?

I shared all of this with Rich, and he seemed ever so patient. He said he wanted to marry me. I told him I didn't see us that way and was prepping to travel the world. He still wanted to date. I still wanted to have fun with him and felt ready to have sex with him. All seemed great.

On his own accord, Rich said he would get tested for STDs, knowing the importance of new health in my body. He seemed excited to prepare a special way for the big day.

Rich ended up atypically violating me. I remember looking him in the eye and hearing two voices in my head. The one that said, "No, he didn't, he couldn't!" and the other that said, "Dani, go, it's time to go."

I left. I am so proud of myself for leaving. I know how hard it is to look at an abuser and *believe what you see rather than what you feel.*

We were supposed to go to Santa Cruz the next day.

Instead, I took off from work and solo-traveled up and down the Cali coast.

It was medicine.

I cried of self-love.

I hugged my body so tightly.

I said, "I love you, Dani," and kissed both my shoulders before I went to bed.

I started to come home to myself.

It took months of healing and trauma therapy, but in a wild way, I can say this happened for me.

After a year and a half in Cali, I bought my one-way ticket to India.

It was time.

I thought it would be intimate time with Dani. I would shave my head, go into an ashram, and process my past.

It sure was a tale of intimacy, a romance novel.

I shaved my head to cleanse all the energy my long, healthy hair held. I told a few people, and word spread. As I sit in a silent secular Buddhist retreat, two reactions were birthed: some of my friends said, "Fuck, Dani, right on," throwing up a shaka, while others were quite concerned and said, "What the fuck Dani?" and phoned me to check in. My phone was off, and I was in deep meditation.

Oops, thank goodness I had prepared my parents.

In time, all could contact me, and the panic cleared.

During my travels, I met a magical man. We were on opposite sides of similar wounds. We made love before we even had sex. I met him soul-to-soul instead of body-shell-to-body-shell. We ended up sharing our shadows and feeling their light.

Fast forward months of magic and mystic, we fell in love. I flew to Argentina, his homeland, where I stayed with him and his family, and even extended my trip. The two of us drove out to his childhood farm, where we galloped on horses and played house. It was a real-life Nicholas Sparks' novel. It was just the land, the animals, and us. I found heaven as I sipped my coffee in a rocking chair, watching the horses run wild. I cried with appreciation as we spent time in the dunes. I felt so safe with his warm fires. When we returned to Buenos Aires, his mom invited all his aunts, uncles, and cousins to meet me.

They showered me in *besos, abrazos, Danielitas,* and gluten-free goodness. I felt so loved, seen, appreciated. As I looked at him, my love, I found bliss.

But

I knew it was coming to a close.

I had a premonition that my dad would soon die.

No one agreed.

But I, she, my intuition, *knew.*

We said goodbye at the airport, hugging, crying, exploding into one another's' arms. We said we would meet again. He was going to do whatever it took to meet me back in California-

Maybe we would do van life!

However, our souls knew

that day wasn't about to come.

The night I returned to the states, my dad told me he was re-diagnosed with cancer.

As I flew to California, I knew I couldn't stay. I gave all my stuff away. My aunt generously shipped my car to New York, and I flew back.

I got to spend my dad's last five and a half weeks with him.

A few days after his invasive glass-blast radiation, my dear dad had a stroke, fell, and had a brain bleed.

I was the first call.

As I chased the ambulance, I felt the imminence of his death. I stayed the night and spent countless hours watching him as he lay in a coma, his eyes closed. He was incoherent, paralyzed on his right side, crying, making confused faces, trying to pull the ventilator out with reflexive movements, and was eventually restrained. I have no clue what he was thinking or feeling. I could only imagine the pressure inside his head and his heart. I knew the brain drain could not relieve the weight he shouldered.

I bent down, whispered in his ear, calmly saying I loved him, that he fell and that all would be okay. I rubbed his feet, made a shrine, and brought crystals, lavender oil, a card. I nourished him in all my warm love and told him how he was my hero and that this was his time to be in peace, to let it all go.

Two weeks later, his huge heart took its last beat.

Be free, Daddio. I love you forever.

At the time, I stayed in my pseudo family's home. However, upon my return from California, I didn't feel welcome. I looked for places to live. I ended up staying in an elderly woman's dollhouse while she was in Florida. I wasn't allowed to have anyone over and fell into isolation.

For months, I was in deep dark waters. I was crying and screaming on hardwood floors, punching the air, blanketing the world with ample covers.

I was reliving all 26 years of my trauma.

I felt victim to it, cumulatively: our family's substance abuse, mental illness, cognitive diagnosis, extreme debt, my violation, my near-death experiences, my 7.5-year medical mystery, the totality, and weight, compounded.

I felt as though I were bleeding pain, and anyone who would encounter me would bleed, too, so I stayed inside, under my covers, hiding from my *truth*, shielding from humanity, from life.

I was the closest I have ever been to suicide.

I thought I had lost my mind—after a night I lay entirely awake, I brought myself to an emergency walk-in clinic and started medication.

March 16, 2020, my car was packed, the route was ready, my sublet over, from New York to California, I go.

That Day: Covid-19 lockdown in California started.

Wildly, I moved back into my childhood home, my first time entering this space for more than 20 minutes, in short of a decade.

I stepped in and stepped up as I helped take care of my angel brother. I re-met my mom. We had been distanced for years. Out of such darkness came light. I accepted her for who she was, rather than resenting her for who she wasn't.

Acceptance is key to healing.

I now remember the golden moments, too. I remember our late-night laughs, marathon-shopping days, and her ample calls and accompaniments to my doctors.

I can see the sadness in her story too.

My heart beats for all she has been through.

In the past ten months together, we have laughed, loved, cried, and bonded.

We healed.

I healed.

I healed here, in my trauma vortex.

Nothing changed, but I have.

I found *I*, Danielle Nicole Preiser—my essence, my *truth*, my smile, my light, my fight.

You can, too.

What I didn't know in my darkest days—that I do know now—is that *by reliving my pain, I was relieving it.*

I felt it and freed it from my mind, body, and soul.

This darkness happened for me, through me and consciousness, not to me.

It was and is a gift.

Our bodies need to release the trauma that is stuck.

In the depth of my core, I believe we are all human, and we are more the same than we are different. I know what grief, fear, abandonment, and trauma feel like.

Although I do not know what those emotions feel like embodied inside of you, I know there is hope.

Because of the arc of my story and all human experience, I know you can pull through.

I know you can do it, too.

My prayer is that my words are a beacon of resilience, compassion, and proof that you can step into your *truth*.

You are your medicine.

You are your healer.

You are your guru.

Just as I am my medicine, healer, and teacher, too.

Welcome back to the realization of *True You*.

27 Lessons from my 27 Years:

1. All emotions are allowed. There are no "bad" emotions. Emotions are energy in motion. They need to be seen, heard, validated, and felt to move out of our bodies.
2. You are enough. You never need to prove your worth nor your *truth*.
3. Everyone is entitled to their own beliefs. Just because someone feels differently from you does not mean either of you is wrong. We each have our own experiences and perspectives.
4. You always have the answer. Even if you cannot cognitively think it, your body feels it. Close your eyes, breathe deeply, and let your body speak.
5. Believe actions over words.
6. Acceptance is key to healing.
7. You are your own soulmate. You are bound neither to anyone nor anything but your soul.
8. You must get to know your sense of self; you can do so by asking: "What do I think? What do I feel? What do I need? What do I want? What is one loving way I can show up for myself today?" Even if the answers don't appear right away, they will come.
9. Intuition speaks to us, through us, in inspiration, insight, synchronicity, meditation, and magic. Keep your eyes and heart open.
10. People-pleasing is a disservice to the world. It leads to self-abandonment, resentment, inauthentic connection, and manipulation.

11. Boundaries are beautiful! Create a safe space for you to be *you* and others to be themselves.
12. The best validation is intrinsic.
13. Do not minimize nor compare trauma.
14. You are not your thoughts. You are not your emotions. You are the observer who sees, hears, and witnesses them. Detachment creates enough space to let them go.
15. Self-talk matters: listen to your thoughts, get to know your subconscious mind, and learn how to re-pattern it.
16. We have no clue what others are experiencing—be kind.
17. The universe is always listening—be mindful with what you say, do, and allow.
18. Your energy is precious. Your time is irreplaceable.
19. Part of healing is letting people go.
20. Surround yourself with people who love you, who let down their masks and allow you to do the same. Vulnerability breeds genuine connection.
21. You are meant to belong, not to morph and fit-in.
22. Travel: experience the world and get to know the locals.
23. Be a forever student.
24. Share your gifts and speak your *truth*—there will never be another you.
25. Your mind is an instrument—learn how to use it, so it doesn't use you; Your body is a miracle, appreciate it; Your soul is your greatest gift, shine it.
26. Empathy and compassion are the key ingredients to true connection.
27. I am *you*. You are *me*. We are humanity.

I am grateful to have touched the many crevices and hues of this physical life. May the above be in service to and for the highest and greatest good.

I see you. I hear you. There's a part of me that already knows you. I love you. Thank you for taking the time and energy to read the above.

With all my love,
   Danielle Nicole Preiser

ABOUT THE AUTHOR

Danielle Nicole Preiser is a source and force of resilience and compassion. She embodies true heart. Danielle is a transformational life coach and yoga meditation instructor. She is a safe space for people to share, offering pure love and zero judgment. She has such a soothing voice and a strong, energetic presence. Danielle is also The President and Founder of *One Special World*, a nonprofit for special needs advocacy.

Danielle graduated from Binghamton University with her Bachelor's in Psychology, Health & Wellness, and Education. She is passionate and purposed by human connection, communal healing, world travel, volunteerism, writing, learning, dancing, and yoga. Some of her most sacred moments include laughing with her brother and having deep conversations over cups of coffee around the globe.

She is a fighter and a healer. She hopes her words land on your heart with hope.

Enjoy the pages that follow and use the below to connect with Danielle:

> *Email: daniellenicolepreiser@gmail.com*
> *Instagram: www.instagram.com/daniellenicolepreiser*
> *and www.instagram.com/lethealthheal*
> *Nonprofit: www.onespecialworld.org*
> *and www.instagram.com/onespecialworld*

GEORGIA HANSEN

FINDING MAGIC IN THE TRAGIC

We are made of energy first and matter second. We are tiny little particles of water in a gigantic ocean. We are specks of stardust in a cosmic explosion.

We are so small.

We are so much smaller than the greatness out there.

There is something far bigger than we are. It is the Infinite that created us, the cosmos that houses us, the benevolent universe that is *always* working on our behalf.

I'll always remember the words my best friend shared with me from the day of my daughter's funeral. In the moments where her coffin was being carried out to the hearse by four solemn soldiers (my husband, his father, and two sisters), this friend turned to her mother, a wave of rage suddenly pulsing through her veins and said, "Why is this happening? It's not fair!" Her mother, ever so wise, turned to my friend and calmly stated, "My darling, we are so small."

This profound knowing brings instant relief to even the smallest bit of anxiety. It spreads calmness and bliss through to the core of my being. It brings wholeness to my fragile, vulnerable, courageous heart. I now live by the knowing that there is something much bigger than us working for us always.

I didn't always know or live by this. One life-altering event brought me home to myself, to realise I am part of an infinite cosmos far bigger than my human self. I was already on a deep awakening journey, perhaps in preparation for what was to come or perhaps accelerated because of it. Is it the chicken or the egg that comes first? Does it really matter?

Where to begin on the single most profound, soul-shifting event of my life.

Our daughter was baby number four, following three little boys. She was so long-awaited, her Daddy, brothers and I were beyond excited for her arrival. After all, we had known of her existence since I first dreamed of her eight years earlier. In that dream, I was clearly shown her name, Amelia Jade, written out in chalk on a driveway.

I would then "see" her in random little girls with curly blonde hair. Often when out, my head would turn involuntarily to see a little girl standing with her family, often smiling and staring back at me, she would go on with her day, and I'd be left with this notion that the universe was handing me a signal. Funnily, these little girls would often come up to me and hug me or just start talking. I'm like a magnet to curly blonde-haired girls.

We knew she was coming; it was a matter of when. I was convinced my third son would be her, but instead, we were gifted his amazing soul that I didn't know how much we needed to be part of our family.

Finally, after eight years of waiting, in October 2016, my intuition firmly declared that now was the time. I told my husband she was ready to come. He knew by now to trust me because of various circumstances in our life where my intuition had guided us. That same cycle we conceived her.

Ten weeks later, at 10 pm on a Friday, I sat in the doctor's office after finding out my blood results were ready, determining the gender and if there were any of the main chromosomal anomalies. After what felt like a year-long 20-minute wait, the doctor called me in. I sat nervously and told her how important this news was. I asked her to print it on a piece of paper and put it in an envelope, so I could take it home to share the news with my husband. I had packed a little box with a pink onesie saying, "Daddy's princess," in the car because I knew what the result would be. I also knew that I couldn't wait to open the envelope with him.

My hands trembled as I pulled out the piece of paper. Time stood still. Tears ran down my face as I read the words: "female" and "no detected abnormalities."

Fast forward the most glorious, joyous six months of waiting and preparing for our lives to change, it was 27th July 2017, and I was now one day overdue. Around 9 am I developed cramps, but as I had had Braxton Hicks regularly for weeks, I didn't overthink it at first. This time they were coming regularly, started at 20 minutes apart, and progressed to 13 minutes, ten minutes, and within a couple of hours, they were seven minutes. I was in no rush, my previous labours were quite long, and the early labours were always fairly drawn out. I was out, so I headed home around lunchtime and finished packing the last few things in my bags. By the time I picked my eldest child up from school at 3 pm, contractions were five minutes and regular, still just like period type cramps and not too painful. The next couple of hours I spent running around getting the boys sorted, feeding them dinner, showering them, packing their bags to stay with their grandparents, and generally making sure everything was done to make everyone else's life easier. This is my single biggest regret.

We were finally on the way to the hospital, in very active labour, ready to meet the soul we had waited so long for. In hindsight, the memory of this drive was nothing like it should have been. I should have felt excited about our dream finally coming true. The only way I can describe it is just blank with a feeling of doom. Up until the few weeks leading up to her birth, there was so much excitement, then suddenly I couldn't see her in the capsule or her bassinet. I just couldn't imagine her in our life past her birth.

There was a stillness, an eerie sense of knowing that our world was about to change.

We pulled up and rushed into the Pregnancy Assessment Unit. As we were taken into the consultation room, I contracted with only 10-to-30-second breaks in between. Leading up to the birth, I prepared myself for a much more sacred birth than I experienced with my sons. I had participated in a Sacred Birthing Program with a woman who has gone on to become one of my greatest mentors and supporters. I felt fully prepared for a divine and powerful birth, complete with soothing music, meditation, crystals, and a powerful mindset to face anything that came my way, so at this stage, I told the midwife I was hoping for a water birth. She started working on getting that ready with the birth suite staff.

She came back in with a Doppler, and while I fully focused on breathing through the intensity of the contractions, she put the machine on my bump to look for a heartbeat. I was standing and contracting powerfully, so after a few minutes of not finding anything, I wasn't really concerned. She got me to lay down on the bed and tried with the Doppler again. After a few minutes, she decided to call in the registrar doctor with a scanner. The doctor came, the midwife stood to my left, the doctor to my right, and the scanner facing both of them and my husband who sat on a chair next to me. All three displayed meek poker faces.

Another few seconds of silence passed, and the registrar said she would get a more senior doctor. The next doctor came in and started scanning; I was still strangely calm. I looked at the first doctor who stood at the foot of the bed, and I remember so clearly, she slowly pulled out what looked like a walky-talky and held it close to her face. That was when I knew something was wrong, and everything slowed to a standstill. Time, space, the air in the room seemed to disappear. The excruciating pain seemed invisible for those few seconds. I blurted out, "What's going on!" That's when the second doctor put her hand on my knee and told me, "I'm so sorry, there is no heartbeat."

This moment changed my life forever. "I'm so sorry, darling; she's gone."

"What! Do! You! Mean! She's right there. Look at my belly, she's right there. Find her," as if they were talking about something they had lost in the forest.

Now there was another doctor in the room. A man this time. *Maybe he can find her*, I thought. His words to me were soft, gentle, and kind but very firm. I begged him to cut her out of me, and he told me he was the most senior doctor in the maternity hospital that night. He outlined why he had never failed to convince a birthing mother to continue with a natural childbirth in his 17 years of obstetrics. At this point, I didn't care.

You hear stories of primal screams when a mother loses her young in the wild. I have come to learn humans are no different. Even in the confines of the pristine human-made settings, we are, in essence, wild, free, animals. In those first moments, I made sounds I had never heard come out of my mouth or body, or from any other human, and I hope I never hear them again.

The most extraordinary experience of my life followed those raging, primitive noises. A vibration entered my body. I now know it to be the highest vibration there is, Universal Source Energy, or God. It reverberated through every cell in my being. *Loud*, it still echoes in my ear when I recall it saying, "*Everything is actually going to be ok*." Somehow, I trusted it to be the truth.

We were then moved to the birth suite, and although there was a bustle of people, the mood and atmosphere were quiet, sombre, and dim. There were doctors, midwives, and an anaesthetist already waiting. I remember looking directly at one of the midwives who had a head full of big dark curls. I grabbed her by the arm and pleaded with her: "why is this happening?" She looked me straight in the eye with tears in hers and said, "I don't know, my darling." I took a huge suck on the happy gas, and I never saw her again after that moment.

Once the epidural was in, there was suddenly only one midwife, plus a student midwife and the anaesthetist. The pain was still extraordinarily intense, and after an hour, I demanded to know why the drugs didn't seem to be working. Apparently, when your body is in shock, even something as strong as an epidural doesn't work properly.

After that hour, though, I started to feel calmer, I could breathe through contractions again, and although I could still feel them, it was bearable. This was when my husband made the devastating calls to my mother and his father to tell them what had happened. I called my closest friends and explained through muttered words that my baby girl was dead and I was still to birth her. I don't think any of those people slept a wink that night as they made other calls to other important people in our lives and wept for us. It felt like the world had stopped spinning, and I felt every tear from every person who cried that night.

This was when I felt divine energy surround me, and I called upon my Guides and Angels to be there and support me. I wasn't sure how I would birth a baby who wasn't alive, and I knew I couldn't do it on my own in my human form. That I needed help from the Light.

The midwife assigned to me in the birth suite that night was an Earth Angel. Her voice was the most soothing I had ever heard, and she knew exactly what I needed in every moment. We had only been in the room for just over an hour and a half, and she informed me I was fully dilated. I told her I was scared and didn't know what to expect. Was it going to be harder to birth a still baby? "Yes," she said, "quite possibly, but we would get through it together." The midwife, her student, my husband, my angel inside me, and all others who had descended to be part of my support circle— my dad (who passed when I was 6), Archangels, Brotherhood of Light, God.

I felt so much presence from Light, and in my heart, I told this support crew, "I can't do this. You will have to take over." All of a sudden, my body pushed. I heard the midwife say, "Ok, honey, stop pushing and just breathe," and I exclaimed, "What? Can you nearly see her head already?" She said, "Darling, her head is out, in one push!"

My husband and both midwives busily grabbed wipe after wipe to remove the meconium that covered her. One more push and she was born. I felt every ounce of her tiny perfect body leave mine, and it was the saddest, most divinely sacred experience of my life. She was born on 28th July at 12.40 am at a solid 8 lbs 8 oz.

Our baby girl was perfect. She was blonde with the most beautiful lips and round cheeks. Everything about her was divinity in human form. I birthed the most beautiful angel. She was grace, beauty, and magic all rolled into one.

We got to spend the next few hours holding her, crying together, loving every inch of her body. My husband bathed her with the midwife, and the midwife dressed her in the first of two outfits she wore in her entire existence in this human body. Holding my baby girl, I stared in wonder at her perfection, wept, wondered why, and questioned everything, including what I possibly could have done to cause this. It was so surreal wanting to hold this baby forever but at the same time wanting to be so far away.

Every moment of every hour that followed for the next 24 hours is forever imprinted on my mind, but by far, the hardest part was telling our three sons. We went straight from the hospital to my parents' place. My mum was out collecting them from day-care and school. We sat and waited on the balcony, and I will never forget them bounding out of the car and bolting up the stairs to see us, with so much anticipation and excitement to meet their new baby sister. And the moment they got to the top of the stairs and saw our faces, their little faces dropped into sadness, and my 3-year-old came running over to me, sat on my lap, and said, "Don't be sad, mummy, I love you *shhooooo* much." Some moments in life will never leave you, and that was one of them.

The following days, weeks, months, and years following Amelia's birth and death, my husband, my children, and I have dealt with things that are just not natural. An autopsy, deciding whether to allow her brain to be removed, planning a funeral, and writing a eulogy for your child. Saying goodbye to her body forever and watching your other children deal with death in a way they shouldn't have to but seeing how strong it has made them.

One thing that happened around 2 am, the morning after she was born is a moment that shifted my perspective and gave me a distinct knowing and vision into the future, and a reason *why*. I was sitting glare-eyed, wide awake, yet exhausted, having had no sleep for 48 hours but in no way able to. I looked online to see if there was anyone to talk to, and strangely one of the only women on messenger was someone I hadn't spoken to in years, but I had known she had lost a baby. I sent her a message, and it was during this conversation I had the confirmation that our Amelia would return to us, in another body, not the same, not a replacement, but the same essence of her soul. I didn't know why she couldn't just have stayed, but I knew there was a reason far bigger than I could comprehend. So this is what I held onto.

There was so much light the day of her funeral. Loved ones, old and new friends, and swarms of butterflies surrounded us. It was perfect. I was able to stand up in front of 70 of our closest people and speak the words no mother should ever have to. I wasn't sure I would be able to, but I did, through tears, and through the tears and cries and weeping of those who were watching me. As her coffin was carried out, we played the song *Love You 'til the End* by The Pogues, and I remember seeing the hearse adorned with teddies and soft toys and all the things you would normally see in a nursery, not the back of a funeral car. I wanted so desperately to climb in there and go with her. As a mother, you always want to keep your children safe and it suddenly hit me that I had no idea where she was going or if she would be ok. In that moment, I would have given up my life to escort her. Then I remembered my boys; they needed me too.

I have since learned how to live with my heart expanded between heaven and earth.

Grief is a funny thing. You don't know how you will deal with it until you are facing it head-on. Finding grace in grief is an extraordinary thing—a task set for extraordinary people.

I want others facing a loss of this magnitude to know that it is possible to not only survive after an event like this but also to thrive. This journey has shown me power, strength, and magic beyond what I ever thought I was capable of. It has changed me and my family and numerous people around me, as well as my perception of life, and all of it is for the better. I can see the beauty surrounding us in every moment, and I choose every day to show up. To show up for the lows and to feel them; not to quash those intense and raw emotions, and to move through them. Once you move through those lows, you feel the highs.

I heard a saying as a child that always resonated with me, and even more so now. Those who have suffered can see the stars shine much brighter in the night.

Every second, minute, hour, and day of my life ever since has been the reaction to the catalyst that altered the course of my life. I vow to live a life of grace, reverence, and beauty in honour of my daughter. To teach and be the exemplar that there is magic in absolutely everything, even, and especially, in the tragic.

My trauma and grief recovery didn't include a single antidepressant drug (even though I have used them in the past) and not one appointment with a counsellor or psychologist (even though I have previously been in psychiatric therapy for OCD). I did the work on the inside. I found what I needed within myself. I'm not saying my way is the way for others but for me, I knew that no counsellor or trauma expert could have met me in the depths I'd been, so I knew I had to do the damn work myself. I used and continue to use my cosmic connection to Amelia and the Infinite Greatness, my non-local intuition, to guide every micro and macro decision I make. I used my own torch to light my way through the darkness.

In this darkness, I had a deep faith there would be light, six months after Amelia was born, I fell pregnant. I knew her soul would return. I kept seeing a vision of standing on stage in a packed arena with my grown daughter, inspiring and impacting thousands.

It was the hardest nine months of my life. I had severe anxiety and rushed to the hospital every time I didn't feel her move. The only way I survived was by allowing it all, throwing myself into full surrender to the Divine, and my trust in that Bigness. I spent my days outside grounded on Mother Earth and staring up to Father Sky, praying to God to bring her home safely. Leaning deeper and deeper into my intuition and knowing that *everything was actually going to be ok*.

It has been a fiercely wild and intense journey, fine-tuning my potent connection, learning about the complex quantum sciences and immutable laws that govern our universe, discovering powerful tools to shift through deep anxiety and fear, and how to use my innate wisdom to flow through all aspects of my life. For the duration of the entire 2020, the year of the pandemic, I trained in the Third Level with the Institute for Intuitive Intelligence, where I met myself, and found myself right where I was always meant to be. It is now my message to share there is so much grace in grief, and magic in the tragic. These are my taglines and my mission.

I am in the process of creating a platform, partnering with a dear friend, and collaborating with extraordinary women. It will be a Hub to showcase extraordinary stories, share intuitive wisdom, and tools for living a connected, soul-led life. A place to guide others how to find their grace and magic, just as my angel has shown me how to find mine.

I am constantly told how strong I am and how gracefully I am dealing with my grief, but the truth is I believe the universe doesn't give us these experiences to punish or destroy us, rather it shows what we are capable of in service of our growth. Our Light. Our ability to love unconditionally, no matter how broken our heart is. To trust in our knowing, and surrender all else to the divine. For when we know this power, we know the blessing of what it's truly like to be alive and I will never ever take that for granted. Life is a miracle. And I am so grateful to my daughter for showing me.

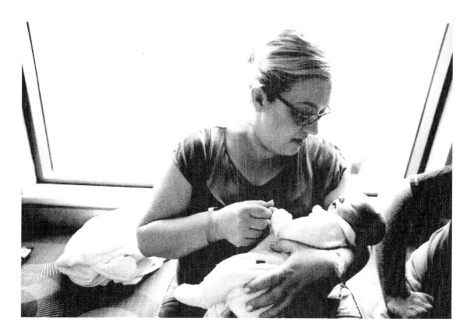

ABOUT THE AUTHOR

Georgia Hansen is an eclectic mix of marketing communications savvy and intuitive based wisdom. She is a priestess of non-local consciousness, a wife, and mother.

She started her career in PR and marketing 15 years ago. She is experienced in various sectors and industries, leading teams in non-profit, agency, and in-house environments.

She has spent the last ten years on an awakening journey, exploring all about intuition, the Universal Laws, and how to tune into the infinite. She is an Intuitive Intelligence Trainer, but her life experience has been the most prominent teacher.

Her life's trajectory changed in a single moment. On July 27, 2017, she arrived at the labour ward at 40-weeks-1-day, expecting a baby girl. After medical checks, her world crumbled when she heard: "we're so sorry, there is no heartbeat."

She went on to deliver a beautiful baby girl born perfect but without breath, and so began her life as the same woman existing in a completely new world.

Her purpose is to shift the paradigm around loss and grief. She embodies her tagline, "finding grace in grief and magic in the tragic."

Georgia is a writer, an intuitive marketer, soul mentor, and Angel Mama Advocate. She is a freelance creative director, running a company with her husband, and has just started her own company, teaching about intuition, how to tune into the infinite and guiding women to find their grace and magic in every part of life, especially in grief and tragedy.

Instagram: www.instagram.com/georgia.m.hansen
Facebook: www.facebook.com/georgiamhansen
Website: www.harkerose.com
Email: Georgia@harkerose.com

JAYCEE HUDSON

TO HEAL, EXPRESS AND RELEASE

M y residual panic remains. Am I revealing too much? I know
we live our lives behind a smokescreen of nonsense, and to
deal with it I have to peel off the layers but exposing what happened to
me is...frightening.

This is my final draft: the other tried to pretty it up but the result was something
—and someone—I didn't recognize. Having alienated my family by telling them, it's
time to bring it all to the light.

In the beginning was my Dad. The abuse I suffered at his hands was the root of
every experience of mine from that point on. I've run a traumatised life ever since.
Maybe it was me – my soul – that downloaded this life's journey but now I've run
that course. The need to tell my story burns in me. Any resistance I feel, I release.
That moves me closer to being healed. It's time for me to heal, to overcome my
addictions and conditions, and that means speaking out, and speaking the truth, the
whole truth. After I decided this, it wasn't long before the art of grace publishing
house popped up in my Facebook feed. The universe at work and my time to speak.

I loved my father. He brought me up but abused at me every chance he could,
sadistically so. He used objects and choking. It was hideous. Many, many rounds of
abuse that I've managed to drown out by creating alternative narratives. It lasted
from when I was seven years old until I was fourteen. Two babies were terminated as

I result. I loved him throughout, because I never knew not to. He was the only person close to me, apart from my beautiful gran. I relied upon him for everything.

When he died, I told my mum about the abuse I suffered. She said only "when could that have happened?" It's denial, I know that now. I said nothing more. She could have asked for more. I wondered what it must be like to hear that about your dead husband, how I would have reacted in her shoes if my daughter told me that my husband abused her every chance he could? I know I would be shocked, disbelieving, enraged but I would also be curious, at the very least. No, nothing.

The next time I spoke to her she told me she wasn't upset with me. Long before I had given up expecting sympathy and understanding, but the implication of blame was difficult to take. a long while ago being incredulous to statements as these. My Mum has a huge heart and is full of kindness, but she was never present with us: my Gran said she lived in a Walter Mitty world, with no morals when it came to money. I don't think that is true though.

I didn't know who Walter Mitty was. I saw the film and watched the wild imaginings of Ben Stiller in wonder: maybe that's what she did, envision a tropical paradise of beauty and light while the abuse went on under her nose. I really don't know if she knew, but it's difficult for me to believe she didn't. In her way she was broken, and preferred to look away from anything unsettling, to keep an outward veneer of respectability. She must have known, even if she couldn't accept it within her narrative.

We had regular novelty parties: vicars and tarts, vol-au-vents, jump suits, cheese and pineapple cubes on sticks. I looked very much like my mum. I dressed up on those nights: exaggerated rouge, short skirt. I loved getting dressed up and painting my face, playing an adult. I felt so far away from children of my own age. They seemed so light and carefree, and we did not have the same concerns. I was quiet and strange, a disconnected child. Afterwards, I dreaded my bedroom door opening. It was the door, then the light, and the shadow. The horror of it opening slowly, like in those Bella Lugosi vampire films. The dreaded chink of light played a film in my head —at least now I look back I can treat it like bad fiction. The shadows continue though.

* * *

I STILL LOVED HIM THEN. He was the father who tousled my hair and did fun things. He was a perfect father on the surface. Only the hidden truth was horrible. Incest: love, the love of a child imprinted with fear, guilt, and shame. Late night rides with all my teddies in the back, I felt like I tainted them to do the act on top with my face pushed in the plush.

The area we lived was safe, we had a bursary to a private school, my sister and brother and I. Dad had a respectable job and kept us in comfort. I idolised my older siblings and obsessed about becoming eighteen. I daydreamed. I wished my time away a lot. My beautiful Gran would always say 'Don't wish your time away' but I wanted to project forward, into a better place and time. Those words of hers would have stuck in her throat if she knew, but she never did. She would have stood up for me. I spent every day with her. We did crafts at the table, ate bun rounds and I practically wore out that little music box ballerina in the spare bedroom. The twinkling song and the spin hypnotised me. Yes, those times with Gran were my happiest, purest times.

The other best times were in the garden. The garden was my kingdom to create. Those quiet hours spent making grass camps were my connection to the sacred. I see that now. I loved it down there, after you passed the shed it changed into a wild, enchanted wood. I imagined the trees stood guard in protection. I didn't mind no one ever came down. It was my place and I'd fashion all sorts out of grass, flowers and rocks. I'd take them back to the house and try and sell them for a penny for the fairy garden fund. I actually kept the money though.

Mum was a free spirit and built walls while failing to deal with her own traumas – like losing her first baby. To this day she is blind to herself and surrounds herself with stuff to create comfort and security. Hoarding, drowning herself with things she cannot let go of. Years of unexpressed pain illustrated in Vogue collections and random newspapers from the eighties. Each dogeared paper so diligently sorted. We all deal with pain in different ways, she will let go when the pain of holding on is more than the pain of letting go. As long as she allows herself to see.

I always wished to be older. Since the age of seven I felt the heaviness and quietness of the world on my shoulders. Stuck in a silent numbing pain that became my normal. That's where my health conditions started. A trauma that seeped deep into memory and expressed itself in harmful patterns and programmes, self-harming. Now I see clearly the parts of me that split off, soul fragments I lost and have since retrieved. It's taken a long time to regather the pieces of me. We are always putting our humanness together. Because of the depth of my pain, I learnt to do it from a quiet place of the soul and as a distanced observer.

Why am I telling this story now? I hope you understand why I withdrew. Anaesthetisation was easier than facing the truth. After my Dad so many more followed. They liked playing with little girls. I see the pattern clearly now: it was like a smell or a target painted on my head. I was inside the story so could not read it: too close and too busy replacing my pain with need. I started a career in losing myself. I was a true professional, thorough and unrelenting. A career forged on the rough wooden floor of my bedroom and bathroom. I remember the ceiling so well. That's where I learnt to lose myself. I became expert at hiding, layering fear upon fear and anxiety on anxiety. They were hardwired into my nervous system.

By the time I was twelve I smoked, drank, everything, then straight to LSD. Little bits of cardboard blotted with acid. But the worst addiction was being chained to the chemist, and the beautiful, coloured pills they gave out like sweets. I was on happy pills at fourteen, nothing like chemically suppressing the system for healing.

When I was twelve Mum moved out. She met a lovely triathlete, very young, twenty-five if I remember. He wore extremely short, shorts, loud shirts and spat when he talked. So, then it was just us. My Dad, my sister and brother.

I idolised my sister, but my brother was a torturous little bastard. He used to heat pennies up in the fire and make me pick them up. I locked myself in the bathroom when I was alone with him. They're family, so I hold compassion for their trauma and wish that we will see each other again with different eyes and no blame or venom. I won't carry that anymore.

My Dad soon dated my mums' boyfriend's sister. We all had Christmas dinner with our paper hats and awkward smiles. Dad moved out to live with her when I was sixteen. Lucky escape for me but not for him: she humiliated him until the day he died, terrible alcohol addiction part of his karma I believe. Oddly enough, there was always whisperings that not entirely appropriate things went on in her childhood. We all have trauma, but she was very cruel with it. If your sensitive to energy and you walk into a room and feel immediately drained, that's what it was like with her, complete vampire.

I kept myself highly medicated at all times, but my worst addiction was to the doctor and the prescription pad. I floated from one relationship to another, from one humiliating situation to another. Jobs here and there, music, acting, cleaning planes at Heathrow, giving out free things, looking pretty. Participation without drugs and medication would not have been possible. I was functional in the most dysfunctional way. I manifested everything in the lost soul and energy vampire departments. I was the fixer, people pleaser. A chameleon who lived on the fringe. By the time I married, he and I were on state-provided opiates.

I was a checklist for functional, dysfunction 101. Incestual abuse, check. Detachment of person, check. Habitually abuse pharmaceuticals and any state altering thing, check. Seek any and all destructive and life force draining people and activities. And that's a big check. I got everything I wanted. I was always a master manifestor!

Living a toxic lifestyle, I picked up many health conditions. I was in hospital so much I would feel a weird comfort there. I had back problems and knee problems when I was young. I wasn't born with a curvature of the spine; it was made that way. That in turn through my knees out and my pelvis was twisted. There are endless physical anomalies with abuse. Endless infections and sores. No doctor ever asked any questions. We were not poor so we escaped all intrusion and scrutiny.

THE MEDICAL ESTABLISHMENTS model and methods suited me. Here, take more pills, be passive. Nothing you know about your body is valid because you are not a doctor. Lung disease, heart attack, an unidentified neuro disorder: the list grew. I was a walking, talking diagnosis. I needed a change of perception. Believe me, I sank. Under a tsunami of symptoms. I couldn't walk or even move. Most days and I had fits and absences five times a day. My beautiful teenage daughter had to look after my youngest Alyssa. She had to cook, clean, take her to school. She didn't qualify for carers allowance, I never understood why not. She has so much strength. Both my amazing kids have been through so much in one way or another, I want to hand them the world.

It was the lumps in my throat that first drove me to write this. I knew if I was to ever get well, I had to express every part of the shadow within me to mend what was broken. Facing my fear of exposure was where my healing lay, but it needed some amazing synchronicities to wake me to the way the universe truly works.

When I met Robert, I was gingerly putting my feet on the path to something new: energy medicine, Ayurveda herbal remedies. I felt something was changing and shifting in my life. I felt as though I could still access stillness, somehow. It was fate. Our car broke down on the way back from Dad's funeral. We explored and then the car wouldn't start. He stopped to help. He was wearing a bracelet with lovability on it. Walking away, he turned around and took the bracelet off. I said thanks. 'something tells me you are supposed to be here' he said. I felt his presence. Mum inquisitive nature got the best of her.

'You're not Robert Holden, are you?' she had his books. I had never heard of him but there was such an energy to him, I wanted to find out who he was. We swapped emails and he sent me and my mum some books.

I'd been away from drugs for a while and I ceased clogging myself up with painkillers, I was still raw though. Still being ravaged by all these conditions and bizarre symptoms. I knew I'd rather die than go forward with that old story of addiction. I found a video on you tube with Robert talking about coping with his father's drink addiction. I felt called to reach out, things were so fresh and I never wanted to be controlled by anything or anyone again.

Not long after that day I was laying on the sofa, I was still on a crutch and the fits and strange absences were plaguing me I woke up to a guitar note being plucked. I rolled over. For the briefest second there was an electric-blue aura that disappeared as soon as I focused my eyes on it.I believe it was my Gran, but a friend of mine Stephen said what I described was more angelic.Either way the energy I felt was amazing. I never had that operation.

By this time, I had begun exploring a group Robert and Hollie Holden run examining A course in miracles text. They allowed me a bursary but what the support of that group gave me was priceless, pure treasures for the heart. Beautiful souls. Something really began awakening in me then.

I felt renewed and, on a mission, to find out as much about health as I could. I had given up taking pills, but I was still in pain and still on a crutch. I'd fallen fowl of the medical system and after many complaints, negligent treatment. I just began to step back. I found fighting for treatment and recognition really out of alignment with actually health care.

* * *

I RESEARCHED and found scenar therapy and the beautiful Tony. Within five sessions I was off the crutch. Apparently, astronauts use these technologies. The spark was ignited and this was the path I wanted. Along with my reiki, I was doing more for myself then I ever had. I realized after a while I was playing a new role: the wounded healer. I ran community, donation-based clinics to help others. Not many turned up and the guys that came were not there for the healing experience I was prepared to give! I've seen other healers do it: I realized that running those clinics was another way for me to avoid my own healing process. Curing others is a pretence. There really is no escape from facing your own trauma.

Expressing my past by writing this is a massive healing upward curve for me. I'm still in that process. As I learnt to liberate each part of me from those past stories, I fuel my future growth. It releases the energy I have put towards feeling bad. My quantum flow practice was instrumental in that clearing process. Each bit that comes to us makes sense when it needs to.

I recently had an interview with the amazing lady who owns the publishing house, I realised as I was speaking words to her that I had never been myself. She asked me to do an interview in the group about my health journey. I wasn't keen, but I was flattered. And it's good to expose the ego. During the interview all the beautiful ladies there held space for me, but there was still the very smallest part of me which asked 'what for?' The past really is gone and done. Past stories are not us. We might loop in them, possibly for as long as thirty-five years but If we keep aiming out and choose with conscious intent, we can release ourselves from these patterns. That's what I've learnt.

Life changes magically when you are grateful and have faith in things that you cannot yet see. The more you have faith, the more that comes into your life. Knowing this is our medicine, it's how we let go of our traumas. trauma. Knowledge of how our bodies, and I don't mean more than just our physical body, truly work is the key to releasing our learnt and acquired limitations.

We experience all possibilities when we're in harmony with our heart intelligence. Our brain waves change, and work in coherence. I was so out of tune for years. I've found out that disconnecting from any outside source for validation is the way forward. My illness has been a gift because when the pills stopped, I heard my body talking in a different way and I responded to that. When I'm ready, I'm looking forward to showing people how on my own journey I've made many shifts. I've used several different modalities, including quantum flow. The modalities all seek the same thing. We can all shift into our highest being if we face all our own truths, internally.

I have always felt abused. You could describe my life as the suffering from abuse as a child led me to carry on that, as if it was my normal. But I've come to realise that I kept choosing abuse. The patterns repeated because I felt comfortable in them. I finally realised I had to break out of that cycle. I look around and see that we are all repeating patterns. Only when we recognise that and we break our patterns can we really step into our truth, our own truth.

* * *

THE MORE I trust in my guidance and my intuition, the more I connect to the natural flow of moving energy. I work with my body and mind to heal every day. I'm still healing but I know that sharing my journey can help others. I am stepping fully into guiding people to and through the practices that have helped me. The wellness network I'm building will expand and share many practises, different modalities, and with workshops focussed on healing through overcoming trauma. It's a long road but self-healing is the biggest gift you can give yourself and the world. And it's one the medical world knows nothing, or next to nothing of.

My mistake, both as a child and as an adult, was not to know that we do not have to sacrifice ourselves to keep the peace, within our own families or anywhere. We are all in our own process, on our own journey. We direct that journey, and we control it. If people are not part of our journey, they do not serve our purpose or wellbeing, we must lose them. Or we eventually lose ourselves. My journey lay in becoming my weakest, literally leading myself into an early grave, before a fire ignited within me.

Each and every day I continue to build myself back together, and I continue on with my journey. I gather more and more pieces of information, lost fragments that I am able to integrate. Build them into the whole of my person, rather than put together pieces of my ego. I more and more identify with being a soul first and foremost. And I realise that the biggest part of my healing process lies in ignoring my physical manifestation, to reconnect to my true self.

Being a healer does not mean we have to divorce ourselves from our own healing. Sharing my story, creating the wellness channel and podcasts and being able to highlight all the ways we heal are part of my journey. The more I move forward in those projects, the more I allow myself to speak out and the braver I feel when revealing my uncomfortable truths. I feel the healing potential in me so strongly it has unfolded and gains momentum every day.

Starting the expression project podcast has been incredible. I allow the words that channel through me to have a platform, validating them for myself at the same time as they emerge through me. Fear is never a friend and never has anything to do with keeping us safe. It's only purpose for me was to constrict me, to prevent me from moving forward and facing my trauma. I'd never allowed myself to truly see it for what it was, and fear allowed it to permeate every area of my life. Every step toward facing fear is another step toward being whole. For the longest time I built on foundations of shattered glass and a shattered psyche, crying out for recognition and remembrance. That fear is now gone.

To move forward I've had to unlearn every perception I ever had about what it meant to be me. It has been an unlearning of the humanness we are taught. One full of limitations, a script that we play out personally and collectively every day. Until it punches us in the face so hard, it's impossible to ignore. We must stand firm and rooted and face the litany of unpleasant things that have imposed on our life and experience of life. In unlearning everything we start freeing ourselves from the fear of our condition of humanness.

* * *

No matter who we are, we hold trauma in our cellular memory, we hold it and keep passing it down until we find the ability to face and clear it. This is our most important work.

I have seen many healers from all different modalities and the most potent thing ever said to me was 'Your head is going too fast for your breath'…

That statement right there sums it all up. Those crazy thoughts and feelings of inadequacy ran on a loop so fast for so long that my body forced a slowdown. Literally a shutdown of function. Until I started seeing what I needed to see and speaking to what I needed to speak. I had no heart and brain wave coherence. In the simplest terms, I was out of balance. I needed to tune back to our forgotten song, to our innate self where we truly all live, our highest self. Or, if you prefer our *divine archetype.*

There are so many of us to hold that note. The more of us that seek to do so, the more likely we are to all achieve that balance.

I hear our Goddesses now finding their warrior voice and the mamma bear's roar. Everywhere I look I see people stepping into true empowerment. It is such a beautiful thing to see. I'm full of gratitude that as I keep stepping into my own healing process and keep doing the work, that I can guide other souls with the tools, techniques and methods that I have gathered in my journey to wellness toolbox.

I'm so proud to be in this publication with twenty-eight ladies who stand strong in their truth and I am loving being able to stand in mine. When we drop our stories, we can really be free. I feel it in the air already, the breath of a new age of warrior souls not afraid to face the truth of themselves.

Moving forward choosing the strongest thing in the multiverse—Love.

We are all waking up to our infinite possibilities really quickly and right now. On my travels and from my personal experience I can say, those forged in pain who face it can stand firm against anything and stand strong for ourselves, our family, our wider human family.

No matter how deep trauma and abuse runs in our world, when we can lean into the stillness of who and what we are and see past the dark clouds of thoughts that hold our minds prisoner. That is the place where we make ourselves whole, where we find our connection to source and our intuition. We all have this, no matter what. We all have the ability to paint with different colours and create the world we want to see and take full responsibility for.

The time was so overdue to make a brand-new ending and every moment is a perfect time for a brand-new start. My purpose now is to keep peeling those layers, to keep using my design, writing and edits to make conscious statements. I am finally stepping into the world and I'm really passionate about healing our systems of health care, speaking to abuse and addiction and healing through our collective expression. Our powerful, potent individual expression that builds to the loudest roar in the most dynamic sea. We are all in it and we create together.

Every time I couldn't and didn't face my trauma, I kept feeding my lowest nature. I continued keeping myself safe as I walked deeper into the gaping jaws of a hungry lion. It is crazy what we are able to convince ourselves of as being the best for us. We are all so busy keeping ourselves safe and protected, we have denied ourselves the ability to see with true vision our safety is our fear. It is our limitation we put on ourselves.

* * *

I'M SO ready to stand up, step out of those jaws and roar for myself and those who have yet to find their voice. Let's shatter all the illusions we made together and step into the big I AM. It really is time, I feel it.

ABOUT THE AUTHOR

Jaycee Hudson is a committed warrior for natural health and empowerment of self by every means available. Through her channel, Zero to Freedom, and her podcast adventures in humanness, she highlights her journey with chronic health and deep-held childhood trauma to bring awareness and a grassroots approach to physical manifestations of health conditions stemming from unexpressed trauma.

Jaycee works with many modalities, and after enduring years of abuse and addiction, she is happy to share her processes and journey. Her mission is to bring awareness and highlight the importance of reconnection to the body's intuition, mind, and soul to align them to express our true healing potential.

She uses her experience as a reiki master and a quantum flow practitioner to move through her ongoing health journey. Her mission is to facilitate growth, knowledge, and empowerment for anyone challenged with chronic health and trauma patterns to their perception.

Jaycee is a grassroots love activist, who uses her platforms to bring people together in the common goal of healing and knowledge of how the body heals. Jaycee still is in her own healing process, and continues to bring awareness to these fields as she navigates them. She understands that healing like happiness is an inside job and is the most powerful gift that we can give ourselves.

Jaycee utilises the creative field as a poet, musician, designer, and art commissioner to shift consciousness and perceptions of limitation in the most amazing creation of all—the human being!

Facebook: *www.facebook.com/groups/303770367446265*
Email: *tribe2thrive@gmail.com*

JILLIAN LUTZ

RISE TO EMPOWERMENT

Have you ever felt as if you were a robot, just walking through life on autopilot? Sometimes devoid of emotion? Do you ever feel as if joy has been completely sucked out of your life? Irritable with things around you? Completely lost and alone, as if no one understands you or is willing to take the time to understand? Something inside just feels stuck or as if a puzzle piece is missing? Nothing you are doing seems good enough? Like you just want to give up?

This is exactly where I was about a year ago.

At 33 years old, I was in a very dark place inside. I tried really hard to hide these feelings from everyone in my life, especially those closest to me. I felt as though no one would understand, try to "fix" things only to leave me feeling worse, think I'm over-reacting, or ultimately not care. From the outside, it looked as though my life was going well. At the time, I had a great career, my own place, an adorable dog, supportive parents... I had a life some people could only dream of. Little did anyone know how upset, lonely, misunderstood, confused, and ultimately broken I felt inside.

I watched all those around me get married, have kids, or start beautiful long-term relationships. I thought that was my missing puzzle piece. I was missing that deep, meaningful, emotional connection. "If only I had a life partner, things would be perfect. Things will be better, and my life will make sense once I find *the one*," were thoughts that ran through my mind frequently.

Those thoughts would then trigger the next set of thoughts:

"I'm never going to be good enough."
"What is wrong with me? Why do they always leave?"
"Why do I keep falling for the guys that continue to hurt me?"
"Will I ever find someone, or am I going to be alone forever?"
"At some point, I must have done something wrong to keep getting mistreated."
"I'm not worthy of love."

All I continued to have were negative thoughts causing me to feel more disconnected from myself and those around me. I was not ok. I was in a dark place inside, but I knew I wanted and needed to get out. I refused to head back to another therapist because I got too good at that game. After sporadically seeing a therapist since I was a child, I knew what I needed to say to them and others to make it appear as if I were fine. There had to be more; something better for me that would help me move past this and just be happy again. Little did I know what the future had in store for me.

DIVINE TIMING

The universe connected me with a beautiful soul at a time in my life when I needed guidance the most. I didn't know it then, but this woman would have such an impact on my life in so many ways. After some resistance, I chose to work with her as my spiritual coach, allowing her to lead me to heal myself in ways I never thought possible. I was lost and needed to be shown the tools to help find my true self again, my soulful essence, my purpose in the world.

When I began my journey back to myself, I worked in public education for 12+ years, earned three consecutive college degrees, had been living on my own for 10+ years, and had a supportive family and loving friends. I considered myself independent, self-confident, successful, intelligent, and all those other positive words you would use to describe someone. In reality, I had just become excellent at playing the game and covering up my pain. In choosing to begin my spiritual journey, I was really just looking for guidance on recentering myself, controlling my anxiety, and finding a way to bring more happiness into my life. I was certainly not prepared for what was ahead of me. This journey released buried pain from deep within, stemming from being a child of divorced parents, other circumstances throughout my childhood, having suffered an abusive relationship in my 20s, and more.

THE JOURNEY

My *why*: "I want to truly feel myself again. I want to become the best version of myself and completely free from internal and external limitations. I want to finally be seen for who I really am."

To begin this journey, the first thing I needed to do was to relinquish control and to fully trust that something much greater than us all was supporting me. This proved challenging during some parts of my journey, but I continued to work at it. Becoming open, honest, and vulnerable with myself was also very important to do this work.

During one of my very first meditative exercises, I recall getting very upset and frustrated after being asked to identify who we were at the core. It was then that I realized I didn't know who I was aside from all the labels society placed on me. I struggled with identifying myself with anything outside of the confines of my career and who I was in terms of serving those around me. It was then that I realized I wasn't doing much in my life for myself. My entire life revolved around being there for others or fulfilling expectations set either by my parents or society. I had been living on autopilot. I lost my sense of self and my connection within. It's no wonder I felt lost!

"Who the hell am I? Who do I want to be?" ran through my head. This was my chance to decide and redefine who I was and wanted to be, which was foreign to me. One thing I knew for sure is that I wanted to be free from all that was holding me back and free from any past trauma that I was unknowingly still holding on to. I wanted to figure out my dreams and passions using my inner compass, my intuition. I wanted to stop allowing outside forces to dictate my life. I knew I wanted to be a strong, healthy, emotionally available partner; ready for a long, healthy, loving relationship. Most importantly, I knew I wanted to be someone who spreads positivity and light wherever they go.

My inner voice kept whispering, "Duh, these are all so simple. You've known you wanted to be all of these things the whole time. Haven't you been trying to become all of this already?"

For a few days, I was utterly frustrated. I knew those were the things I wanted to be, but I was just so mad at myself for not being there already. I was my own worst enemy. I allowed my anger and my frustration to get in the way. After a few days into practicing Kundalini yoga for the first time, focusing on my meditation practices and journaling, I finally released the negative emotions and saw clearly. I could now identify all that was holding me back: my anxiety, overthinking, comparing myself to others, living in my past trauma, being too guarded, allowing my negative emotions to consume me, my self-sabotage, allowing others' thoughts to question myself, thinking I'm too emotional, using work as a distraction, always seeking approval from those around me, lack of confidence, fear of making mistakes, and caring too much about what others think of me.

"Holy shit, was this *a lot* of shit to deal with! How did I get this bad? I thought I was good," I wrote in my journal. I continued to get further down on myself, and my inner thoughts just made things worse:

"When did I lose my way?"
"When did I stop being *me*?"
"What the hell went so wrong in my life to have gotten me here?"
"How the hell did I get like this?"
"What is wrong with me?"

I threw my hands up in defeat. I was embarrassed because I always tried to pretend everything was fine. I made a vow to myself that I would put in the work required to find myself again, to become my authentic self. I wanted to live a life with purpose, and that started with becoming open and vulnerable to try and get to the core to reconnect with my own intuition again.

As I gave control over to the universe to guide my healing journey, I kept revisiting scenes from my past. I would close my eyes, and I would see my little girl self, maybe six or seven.

It was a Saturday morning, and I was sitting in the living room waiting for my father to come pick me up. He was running late, as he would from time to time. I was used to this by now; after all, my parents got divorced before I was two years

66

old. As the clock struck 10 am, I opened the front door to watch for him impatiently out the window. With every car I saw in the distance, the anticipation grew as they approached, and when it wasn't him pulling in, I felt crushed a little more with each car. From the kitchen, I could hear my mother speaking to my stepdad. She was trying to be quiet, but they hadn't yet discovered what they would later call my "super-sonic hearing." Out of frustration, Mom said things acknowledging her anger for my dad not being on time, referencing his drinking habits, implying that he must not care enough. Otherwise, he would show up on time. Then the phone rang.

I don't remember if it was Dad calling to say he wasn't coming or he would be late, but that didn't matter to me. In this vision, what did matter to me was how my mother responded to that phone call. She got mad at my father and made her disappointment known. Meanwhile, here I was, a little girl who just heard her mother say that her father must not care about her. Otherwise, he would show up on time. Now, watching her get upset with him either being late or not showing up and paying mind to her own feelings. Sitting in the living room, all alone, wishing someone would have been there to comfort me. Sitting alone thinking: "Why doesn't my dad want to come see me? Why doesn't my mom care about how this is hurting me?" After all, it was me who was getting short-changed, not her. Sitting there wishing my mother could put aside her feelings and her animosity to console her child. If not comfort me, put your feelings aside and distract me at least by asking me to play a game or do something to pass the time.

Each time this vision came up during meditation, more and more pieces came with it. More and more clarity came each time. I recognized that this was the first point in my life where I was able to identify feeling unworthy, not good enough and as if my feelings didn't matter. I would then be joined by another vivid recurring step back in time.

I was a terrified little girl, about 7 or 8 years old, woken from a deep sleep by screaming in the kitchen just below her. I tried for as long as I could to ignore it, hoping it would go away soon, but it didn't. I crawled out of bed, tiptoed across my room, and slid as quietly as I could down the first few steps. Since my room was in the renovated attic, a wall covered half of the upper stairwell. Here I sat, on the first step where the wall ended, looking through the banisters around the wall and straight into the kitchen. My stepfather's back was towards me, and my mother's defeated and upset face was looking in my direction. I heard some more screaming back and forth. I could no longer see my stepdad and my mother's face changed from upset to terrified. That's when the kitchen chair went flying across the doorway towards my mother. I didn't even give it time to see if it had struck my mother before I was at the bottom of the stairs, on my way into the kitchen to protect my mother. I burst into the kitchen and went right after my stepdad as if some tiny little girl was going to stop the monster that the alcohol had turned him into. "My mother was in the corner terrified, and someone needed to stop him," I thought. I instead became my stepfather's new target for his screaming and physical aggression. It took my mother some time to register what was going on before trying her best to get him off me. He then screamed at my mother for protecting me and allowing me to attack him in the way that I did and stormed out of the house. Once my stepdad left, I waited for my mother to console me and show some appreciation for trying to protect her. Instead, I got yelled at for not only getting involved but also for attacking him and getting him angry enough that he left. She was more concerned that my stepdad left angry instead of how he had just treated her and her child, all while her newborn baby was sleeping only in the next room.

This wasn't the only time something like this happened in my childhood. Each time it did, I did what I felt I had to do to stand up for my mother and protect her because she never did. There were even times I argued with her because I couldn't understand why she stayed married to my stepdad since he mistreated her. Better yet, why would she stay married to a man who treated her child so badly? They had an up and down relationship for most of my impressionable years, and my relationship with my stepdad was rocky even longer because of that.

One evening, while practicing Kundalini, I was in a deep meditative state, then my phone rang. Instantly, I got aggravated for being interrupted. When I realized it was my mother calling, the feeling of rage that came over my whole body was indescribable. My heart was beating very fast, I felt my pulse pounding through my entire body, but my mind could not process why I felt so mad. It didn't make sense. After all, my mother called and interrupted me doing things all the time. Why did it bother me so much now? I sat in silence with these feelings for a while. I allowed these feelings without judgement. I asked the universe, "What is it that you're trying to tell me? What are you trying to show me?"

A few minutes later, it was clear. All the pieces came together, and it made sense like it never did before. The years I spent seeing therapists helped me overcome the surface level issues I suffered due to my parents' divorce, but underneath the surface was so much more. What I had witnessed in my childhood created patterns within my adult life that I had no idea could have been linked before now. The anger I had felt was not because my mother called and interrupted my meditation. At this exact moment, the universe allowed me to recognize that I had such strong, unconscious resentment towards my mother buried for all these years. The realisation began to explain so much, starting with why my mother and I seemed to fight over ridiculous things. I love my mother dearly and will be forever thankful for all that she has done and continues to do for me, but there are times we are just oil and water.

Not only did the things I witnessed and fell victim to as a child leave me with deep-seated, unconscious resentment towards my mother, but I also had no idea how that environment directly impacted my relationships with others or my relationship with myself. It was time for me to face my demons, what most would call my inner child wounds. After listening to the messages from the universe, I allowed my intuition to guide the way and spent the weeks that followed diving deep into shadow and inner child work, looking to find my way back to my true authentic self. During this time, I realized that my entire dating history through my 20s was a complete shit show; I chose all the wrong men, ended up in horrible, toxic, and abusive relationships, and pushed the good ones away. Like layers of paint on a wall that continues to be repainted—my childhood trauma remained hidden under the new layers of trauma from every failed relationship. My inner child wounds were hidden under so many other layers of other shit; it's no wonder it took this long to uncover them.

BREAKTHROUGH MOMENT

While beginning this healing journey and returning to my true authentic self, I had been dating someone—a very emotionally unavailable, avoidant man. I knew how to find them all! We had just spent time together, and I left there feeling pretty crappy. He had just spent our time together indirectly putting me down, making me feel less than and consequently triggering every aspect of my anxious behaviors. I couldn't help but think, "I was wrong. It was all my fault. I must have done something to set him off. What could I have done differently?"

On my drive home, I felt really defeated and unintentionally fully surrendered. It was in this moment that my intuition took over and guided my way. I received messages and downloads and had this compelling, yet clarifying experience. (Side note, this was the first I learned that the car is one of the two places I'm most connected to my intuition and open to receiving messages; the second being the shower.)

Images from flashbacks in my childhood kept popping into my head. Why? All this little girl, my little girl self, wants is to be loved, to be protected. She wants someone to hold her and tell her she is good enough and she deserves the world. Flashes to another scene: This little girl, me, just wants someone to stick up for her and to protect her. This girl wants to be cherished and made to feel special instead of being treated like a punching bag. She wants to be saved from all the fighting and wants someone to stand up for her. Next scene: This little girl wants to be held when she's crying and upset. After all, she's the child and should not be the one stuck defending herself. She wants to be told it's ok to express her emotions rather than be told to get over it, or everything is going to be fine. This little girl wants to live in a house where she feels like she belongs, where she feels safe, where she is treated fairly, doesn't get blamed for everything wrong or work her ass off to impress, and still barely get any recognition. The strongest feeling coming through was from this last little girl—me—asking to be part of a family that didn't fight, but one where they loved, supported, and encouraged each other. My adult self went to save her, but she curled into a ball out of fear. She was afraid to leave the chaos; she was comfortable here. She was afraid of what it would be like in the calm, but most of all, she was afraid of love. She was afraid no one would truly love her and afraid she wouldn't know how to accept proper love.

It clicked! My patterns now in my adult life, ESPECIALLY those in my dating life, reflect my childhood trauma. I continued to choose emotionally unavailable, avoidant men to be in relationships with because the chaos felt like home. I had been conditioned to think that this was normal and my inner worth had diminished, so I didn't think I deserved more. My deep-rooted resentment towards my mother is so fierce because this was her fault. She allowed this to happen. She didn't leave a household of fighting and chaos. She didn't protect me and comfort me the way I needed when things got messy. She allowed me to watch this, grow up around this and think in my subconscious that this was normal. WOW, WTF! But my mother loves me. She couldn't have done this on purpose. No. She, too, was going through her own shit and trauma because they didn't talk about that stuff back then. Not only had she been divorced from my father who was an alcoholic, but she married another man who was having issues with alcohol as well at that time. No doubt that had to have messed with her. Her childhood too! Oh, boy! This isn't her fault either. She didn't know any better.

As I parked my car, I decided to call my mother right from the car. If I waited, I would have lost my nerve. I took a few deep breaths to align with my heart space which allowed me to express myself vulnerably and intuitively. I told her about the inner growth work I had started and mentioned the shadows that came up revolving around her and my childhood. We spoke for some time about how this has affected me in my adult life and how I view myself. It was vital that I approached this conversation from a place of love and understanding because I wanted her to know that I recognized that this was not her fault and none of this was done maliciously. She, too, had suffered her own trauma, and because of this, she made her decisions because she felt they were the best at the time. After identifying her as a trigger, I informed her of my need to set boundaries with her. She was not happy about that and tried to lay on the guilt trip hard! If I didn't set boundaries with her, I would never be able to continue the work to better myself; work through this trauma, overcome my anxious behaviors, stop pushing good men away, avoid self-sabotaging behaviors, and overcome my limiting beliefs. I couldn't cave; I needed to stand my ground. I told her, "Either you respect the boundaries, or I'm going to have to cut you out of my life while I worked on myself because you're a trigger. If I want to be successful, I can't be around the triggers." She finally understood and agreed because being a part of my life with boundaries was better than not being in my life at all.

This moment truly cracked me open to the power of my intuition and all the magic inside that was waiting to be discovered. This is when I truly began my life-long journey of finding my inner peace and learning to love and support myself unconditionally. I committed myself to healing my inner child wounds, abandonment issues, limiting beliefs, and learning who I was at the core. While working with my coach, I learned how to take charge of my life and freed myself from everything I was ever taught that didn't align with who I wanted to be—my most authentic and best version of myself. My inner strength and intuition were always there; they just needed to be dusted off and repolished with a little hard work. I know now that I get to decide what no longer serves me. I get to rewrite my story, and that's exactly what I did! While becoming vulnerable and doing the hard inner work, I learned to listen to my intuition to give myself the things I need to be happy regardless of any stigmas.

ARE YOU READY TO ANSWER THE CALLING?

Close your eyes and reflect on these questions for a moment:

Do you ever feel out of place? As if you don't belong?
Do you sometimes have a hard time trusting yourself or doubt your emotions?

Now here's a tough one:

Who is your Inner Child? How would you describe the feelings and emotions of your Inner Child?

If any of your answers to these questions struck a chord with you, you have the power to change those answers just like I did. You, too, can do the hard work, go deep and shed the truths society, your parents, school, and everyone else has placed upon you, and find your core again. The first step is awareness, which is why I've shared my story. Without awareness, you cannot seek help to dig deep and do the work it takes to rewrite your story.

We all deserve to live in our greatness, so I leave you with one of my practices that helps me to shatter my limiting beliefs.

Write a limiting belief.
Turn it into a positive affirmation (I am worthy of...)
Commit to yourself (I will...)

Here is an example of one of mine:

I'm not good enough.

*I'm worthy of love.
*I will look into the mirror before bed each night and tell the beautiful woman I see something I am proud of her for accomplishing that day.

Just remember, everyone is worthy of love and greatness! There's always someone out there waiting to help guide you back to your true authentic self when you're ready.

ABOUT THE AUTHOR

Jillian Lutz lived most of her life how everyone else expected her to. She was made to believe that she needed to be completely independent, strong, and at her best to succeed. Her battle with depression and anxiety, leading into adulthood, made her feel ashamed and isolated.

In her 30s, Jillian hit a wall. She was no longer happy with herself. She reached out for help, and all the puzzle pieces started coming together. She sought inner peace, inner strength, and self-love. Through her spiritual journey, she found strength in her suffering, broke free of past trauma, and learned to be the author of her own story. She now spreads hope, positivity, and light wherever she goes.

Jillian has worked in public education for 12+ years and always felt a calling to step into her power, speak her truth, apply her open-heartedness to connect with others to help them in a more impactful way. As a result of her self-growth and facing her inner-child wounds, she uses her story and journey to support, and empower others to emerge into their authentic selves within her business, Jillian Ann Coaching.

As an Empowerment Mentor, in addition to one-on-one work, Jillian has used her personal self-healing journey, knowledge of Kundalini yoga, and expertise as a certified Reiki practitioner to develop her signature group coaching program to help others "Rise to Empowerment!"

Instagram: www.instagram.com/jillianann_coaching
Email: emerging.metamorphosis@gmail.com
Facebook: www.facebook.com/Jillian.Lutz9

JUSTINE PEACOCK

TRANSFORMING TRAUMA INTO TRUTH

W hat happens when you grow up in a world where everything looks perfect on the outside but is dysfunctional on the inside? When you are taught that what you create externally—money, influence, and achievement matters more than the truth of who you are? You create the same in your own life—external success and internal chaos ad confusion.

You can function like that as an adult for a while, but eventually, you will learn that the external means nothing if it is not created from a place of internal alignment. You need to cast aside your external referencing and journey deep within to your intuitive knowing and let that be the guide for your life.

Come with me as I share my journey from chaos and trauma to intuitive align-ment and knowing. A journey back to me. One that took me from a lost little girl in a woman's body with no self-esteem, poor boundaries, and little self-awareness, to an intuitive healer and coach with a global client base, a happy wife and mother. Someone who is kind, strong, and surrounded by healthy loving relationships and uses her intuition to guide her every step.

As a spiritual being, living from a place of intuition and seeking to fulfil your purpose for being there, your life will be filled with defining experiences—

opportunities for growth and the attainment of wisdom and love. The first part of
your life, as a child, will perhaps be the most potent shaping of your future
behaviours. As a child with a child's brain, you have limited resources and self-
awareness at this stage of development, and you will experience these defining
experiences from a place of powerlessness. You will have to accept what happens –
other people's opinions of you and your interpretation of events from a young
mind. In this place, we become who we need to so we can survive our childhood.

As children and as we progress into adulthood, we acquire beliefs and stories about life and who we are. These stories are NOT THE TRUTH. Our job as conscious humans and spiritual beings is to grow and learn and, when required, to revisit these events so we can release what no longer serves and step into our sovereignty and truth.

If you can look at a defining event from your past with acceptance and
detachment – not victimhood or blame—and clearly see why it happened or at
least what you learnt from it, then you have begun the work and gained the
wisdom that will further your journey to standing confidently in your own power.

Some people's formative years are idyllic; some appear idyllic but are laced with subtle traumatic experiences. Some are blatantly abusive, and the trauma is obvious even to the external observer. Whatever the journey or experience, whatever you have been exposed to, these patterns will emerge and require tending to if we are to live a fulfilling and congruent inner and outer life.

Come with me as I share my journey from an abusive childhood and the struggles that stemmed from that into reclaiming my inner wisdom and intuition and fulfilling my soul's purpose—as I share my discovery about transforming toxic and automated behaviours into awareness and agency over my life path for a truly fulfilling existence. In the process, I transform from compulsive overachievement, weight and self-worth battles, relationship woes, an unsatisfying law degree, to a life of intuition, deep self-love, a solid marriage, and a thriving career.

I was born in Canada in the mid-early to mid-1970s. My mum was a nurse and my father a surgeon. Both from Australia and had travelled to Canada for work and absolutely loved it. I have one brother who is 2.5 years older. Smart, quick-witted with a photographic memory, he never failed to entertain people, was praised for his academic successes and it seemed to me he could do no wrong. I always felt in his shadow. He always had more freedom than me and it seemed like he never really wanted me around.

I was a deeply intuitive and sensitive child. I never felt like I fitted into my family, and as you will see, they were not shy about letting me know that they felt that way about me, too. My childhood was marked by feeling alone and different.

I know now that souls who choose a path of growth often choose to be born into families where they do not feel seen or fit in. They experience themselves as the "black sheep" of the family. Their early years are often characterized by feeling different or alone. These conditions are chosen by you and for your growth. It might be to make sure that you do not follow the herd and learn to develop a deep inner strength, self-acceptance, and courage.

In Canada, we lived a privileged life. We lived in a gorgeous big house on an acre of land with a swimming pool and a pond that would freeze over in winter, and we would ice skate on it. I had good childhood friends at school, a happy school life, I did ballet and ice skating, enjoyed dressing up at Halloween and white Christmases – all the best elements of growing up in North America. And then, one unsuspecting day, my world fell apart, and the first rupture began.

My parents, originally from Australia, had decided that it was time to move back to Australia. We moved back when I was almost eight. I was distraught when I heard the news. I cried for hours and did not want to go from day one. But I was powerless to alter my fate.

It was a huge culture shock moving to Australia. My idyllic childhood shattered, and everything in my reality changed. I could not understand the Australian accent. The heat was unbearable, the sunlight was harsh, and the people were insular and unfriendly. Of course, as I was only eight, I decided the problem was me. I suddenly felt conscious of being different and truly alone in the world. Over time I settled into life in Australia, but it would take decades before I could even remotely identify with *being Australian.*

When we are young, we are dependent on our parents and our higher-order brains are not developed. This means that we cannot think rationally about it or see the bigger picture. Anything that happens in our lives, we make our fault and we see ourselves as the victim which, in a sense we are. In this way, many early belief patterns and stories of who we are, how life is, and our place in it develop. Many of these belief patterns are not helpful and untrue, but they will companion us for our whole lives if we don't stop and examine them.

Our family life continued normally in Australia until I was about 12. My dad – a brilliant, demanding surgeon who had been quite distant until then – became overly involved in my life. Triggered, I suspect, by his little girl going through puberty. An event perhaps that many grown men are not prepared for when it comes to their little girls? The emotional abuse started, and the turmoil began in earnest.

In the early years, it was because of my body size (I was sent to Weight Watchers at 13). Enforced fitness regimes – hours of criticism for my weight and the promise that no one would ever want to marry me because "boys don't like fat girls, Justine." Sometimes I would resist; sometimes I would embrace a fitness regime with gusto – but over time, I realized that Dad was never, ever happy with any efforts – it was never enough.

Dad's intense physical and emotional regime was tough to live under. He had rigid views on everything; not only my weight and eating habits but my friends, schoolwork, music tastes, clothing, everything that made up the fabric of the person I was trying to become and the identity I was trying to forge. He was never backward in coming forward, and my mother was either his companion chiming in with her views or offering silent witnessing and acquiescence. Rarely did she step in to stand up for me until I was a broken and blubbering mess. In their eyes, they were permissive parents, but nothing went uncriticized.

It is difficult to identify as an individual or think of yourself as worthy when your parents are in your space and face all of the time criticizing you and tearing you down.

As I got older, my parents' behaviour escalated into intense verbal abuse several nights a week for hours. A classic abuse cycle of build-up, abuse, remorse (but letting me know if I was different then would not "have" to abuse me like this). It is one thing to experience emotional abuse as a conscious adult; however, as a child, the deep wounding and patterning can profoundly affect a life journey.

Even as a little girl, I became skilled at reading his mood. From the moment he came in from work – exhausted and worried about his patients, I knew in my gut whether he was going to come after me. These nights in my early to late teen years were pure torture. He would start with nitpicking, but it always escalated. He would say the most horrifically damaging things over and over:

"You're a loser and a failure who will never amount to anything." "You're fat and will never get a husband as boys don't like fat girls." "You will end up dead in a ditch somewhere, a drug addict."

On and on. Over and over. For hours. At least weekly, sometimes more frequently. For years. I felt so trapped. As a child, reliant on her family home and caregivers, with no one to speak to and nowhere to go. My brother, referred to as the "Golden Child" in jest and there was truth in this statement. He was always upstairs studying. Seldom would he be seen during these times, although he heard it all. Why would he want to enter into a volatile and abusive situation voluntarily? Although I wish he would have, I suspect he carried his share of the burden in his own way.

On the outside people, respected this man and thought he was brilliant and incredible. An educated and caring man healing the sick. As a family, we had money and social standing. Behind closed doors, our family dynamic was a mess. It is safe to say that I, on the other hand, was breaking. It was the 90s. There were few mobile phones, no real public awareness about mental health, and I had no relatives I could lean on.

Early on, I knew in my heart no one could endure this and not be forever changed and that a time would come when I would have to undo the damage being done to me. I made a promise to myself that I would do whatever it takes to heal. I had no idea the gravity of what that would involve, but I knew that it was my path and my commitment to myself. One day he would no longer control me like this, and I could be free.

Believe me, during these years I tried desperately to figure out how to make the abuse stop. I lost weight (my relationship with food is a whole other story!), I tried to save money, I studied hard, and tried to be who he wanted me to be. I was desperate for his approval. Whenever I thought I had found the magic formula and could stop running, like a classic abuser, he would shift the goalposts and leave me running again towards a horizon I could never reach. It would take me many, many more years to really see on a deep level that I would *never* be who he wanted me to be—it was an illusion—and to stop trying.

The unacceptable abuse and my desire to escape and heal from it went on from 13-23 while I studied—first at high school and then six years of law school. In that time, I exhibited classic over-achiever behaviour. I tried to be who he wanted. I tried to find validation in my external success. I graduated high school as Valedictorian, was accepted into law school, passed law school, and graduated with a coveted job. As a young, accomplished woman, with her soul destroyed, I still felt like I fluked. I felt no sense of pride, accomplishment, or achievement. Desperate to get away, I moved to a city on the other side of the country and began life as a graduate lawyer with a global professional services firm. I hoped that getting away from my dad would give me the freedom I was after, but of course, I soon realized that this was not enough.

As children, we start out accepting our family circumstances as "normal." It is all we know and our main lens with which we experience the world. It is not until we are older (or things get truly crazy) that we realise that our "normal" is not the same as everyone else. Then begins the work of unravelling the false self we have created to survive or cope with life and finding our true strong and intuitive self underneath so we can be free to embody that.

By 25, I was a corporate lawyer in a top firm. I had my external independence. I was also broken and miserable. Overweight. On Prozac. Unapproachable, anxious, and stressed. I tried to numb and distract by partying and keeping myself very busy so I was never alone with my thoughts.

I spent my teenage and early adult years so busy defending myself from attack and feeling worthless from all of the abuse that there wasn't space for discovering who I was and creating my own identity. All of my energy and attention went to bracing myself for the attacks, surviving them in the moment, and then battling with the aftermath.

It all came to a head when my partying ways led me to a deserted beach in the middle of absolutely nowhere with two guys I did not know: no phone reception, no car, and no one around for miles. Although nothing happened, it was a deep shock and wake-up call that I could put myself in an undeniably dangerous situation. I had been dabbling around the edges of deep psychotherapy and emotional release work for a bit, but I immediately committed to it in earnest. It was the shock I needed.

After a year of retreats and sessions, I registered to train as a psychotherapist for over four years with the same Institute. Separately, I also completed a life coaching certification to help me with my corporate career. The journey of breaking free from my past had begun.

Step by step through dedication, things shifted. The psychotherapy was energy psychotherapy – chakra system and western psychology balancing the spiritual with the practical, and I loved it. I loved that it validated what I knew in my soul – that the body holds the memory and imprint of everything we go through. That what we cannot release and process is stored and held until we can – but we need to make time for that.

As spiritual beings, we seek a life that aligns with the truth of who we are. Trauma ruptures this and so, to create the harmony, great relationships, peace and meaning we crave, we need to first heal the trauma. However, as adults, we generally see and experience the world not as it is but as we are deep inside. The more damaged and hurt we have been, the more distorted our reality. Once you clear up the hurt and the beliefs and stories that accompany that you will get a clearer and clearer view of yourself and the world around you. It will never be completely "true," but every time you clear up a past hurt and release the energy stuck in that event, your intuition strengthens, and your connection with your higher self does, too. You step further out of the grip of the ego and its hurts and distortions and further towards a balanced and fulfilling life.

During these years, I began to have mystical experiences that I had not had since I was a child. These included visions during profound meditations where I saw past lives and even planning for this life. I saw how I had chosen my parents and the key events that would shape my life. These past life and pre-life visions were transformative as they showed me how much, much bigger I was than this life and these experiences. *I was not a victim of this life; I was a wise and deep soul who chose to come here and live this life.*

There was no instant enlightenment. The return of my intuition and self-love was built on consistency and commitment. All of my spare time and money went to my transformation, and it was hard work. But I had lived in a dark place for a long time, and I had hit rock bottom. It was time to make good on my promise to myself all those years ago and unravel the early trauma. I shifted years of stuck habits – poor boundaries, not being able to speak up for myself, shame, self-worth, and people-pleasing, to name a few.

I began to reclaim that awareness of my power, worth and potential. That my life is MY life and not to be lived for others. That I was loved beyond measure and that we are all interconnected and supported and guided beyond our wildest expectations.

Your life is the universe's gift to you. It is not meant to be lived keeping other people happy or doing what they want or expect. It is yours alone to explore, discover who you are, what makes you happy, and your unique contribution to humanity and bring that into reality.

During this time, after not finding success with relationships. I had spent almost three years choosing not to date so I could sort out my relationship patterns. It was hard being solo, and many times, I wondered if love would ever find me. I held onto the belief that someone special would come my way one day. And, as cliched as it sounds, the universe knew what it was doing and sent me the most magnificent man at the perfect time. He is intuitive, kind, intelligent, and supportive of my spiritual journey. We met in Australia and then lived in the UK for a while. Today, we are happily married (since 2006), and he is my best friend, my true companion and rock.

In love, there are two truths. What's meant for you will not pass you by, but t o experience a love and relationship that is not burdened by your upbringing, poor sense of self or early love experiences, there is much to be done to align you and resolve unmet needs, past hurts and fears so you can create the love you are longing for and know you deserve in your heart.

The one constant throughout this time was my investment and investigation in my healing path. I undertook deep psychotherapy sessions and retreats all grounded in spirituality. I spent a decade clearing up my hurts, and I was no longer in survival mode. I realized that I had not gone through all of these experiences for no reason. It was for my soul's evolution and so that I might help others, too. I felt the call to develop my skills. I started learning various healing modalities – Reiki, Theta Healing, Regeneration Healing, and Now Healing, to name a few. I invested a lot of time and money, particularly in Theta Healing—which I studied for many years and became a teacher. I wanted to make sure that by the time I worked with people, my own channel was clear and I had the tools I needed.

Again, new levels of healing happened—shifting and clearing my traumas, beliefs, habits and

generational patterns preparing me for the healer I was becoming. I began to see and sense

energy very clearly. I started to hear and know things about people. I had always known that th

my mum was psychic, but I learnt I was actually from a line of psychics (4 generation). I would see people's emotional and life blocks, karmic relationships, traumas, see their past lives, see and hear unhelpful beliefs, get messages from their guides and ancestors. In essence, I would be shown everything that keeps a person stuck, what they had come here to learn and who they are in their Divine magnificence.

We are a ll intuitive and have psychic abilities. These gifts are bestowed on All of us and are part of who we are. Sometimes we have experiences in this life and other lifetimes that have made us shut down our abilities and deny our intuitive knowing. The truth is we need our gifts, and the world needs women who are connected to their intuitive knowing, and we can reclaim them.

We all have pain. It is what we do with it that counts. We are not meant to carry it and let it make us small, distorted, and bitter. We are meant to feel it, heal it and learn the lessons and gain the wisdom. We are meant to move through it stronger and wiser, reclaiming our intuition in the process.

Now I work as an intuitive healer and coach. I help women around the world clear trauma from their past making way for their truth—for who they are meant to be and do the work their soul is calling them to do. While it is not conventional success, it is the most rewarding work I can imagine. I am deeply satisfied and successful in the ways my Soul planned for me to be, and I am a world away from the miserable corporate lawyer of 20 years ago.

My father and I have a close relationship. It is not perfect, but I honour him for who he is. He is more than just someone who verbally abused me. We have spoken at length across the years about what happened, and he has apologized many times. My father is a highly intelligent and very decent man who carried deep trauma from his own childhood. We pass on what we do not heal. He has taught me the value of education, independence, a strong work ethic, speaking up for myself, being generous, and having high integrity. He was instrumental in setting me on my path of growth. I love him and appreciate his role in my journey towards wholeness and healing generational dysfunction.

Healing and making peace with your past, working to release unhelpful emotions and beliefs from your younger years does not mean that life stops throwing challenges your way. Indeed, many healers and spiritually minded people experience more challenges and twists and turns than most people. What it does give you is a stronger foundation – a greater sense of who you are, of boundaries, of self-worth, and overall resourcefulness to deal with what comes your way. When you have the tools, and life knocks you off your centre (as it inevitably does), you can come back more and more quickly to your truth and balance.

In my life, I have many things that are going well. I also have and am living through kidney failure (I am waiting for an organ transplant). I have two children with additional and complex learning needs and challenges (including one on the autism spectrum). I have navigated through an unhealthy relationship with money and poor financial decisions to a place of financial stability and abundance. I have transformed my once complex and dysfunctional relationship with food to one that is normal. Lastly, I have left behind drama-filled female friendships filling my life with a group of strong, balanced and inspiring women who care deeply and are living passionately and purposefully.

Through all this, I know that change is possible and trauma can be transformed. Who I am today is a result of the work I have done (and continue to do) to transform and reclaim my true self and inner knowing. And that this path is open to every one of us.

MY WISH FOR YOU

Our paths are ours to walk, and there will be trying times for each one of us. My wish for you is that you do not walk alone, that you have the courage, humility to show up for yourself. That you value yourself enough to prioritise your growth and healing so you can release whatever holds you back from being the strong, confident, intuitive and loving woman you are. So you can feel good about who you are and what you have experienced and, if you are inclined, you can share your wisdom and help others.

REMEMBER:

You are worth fighting for!

You cannot find your life purpose when your energy is stuck on seeking approval or afraid of what others might think of you. Be willing to release what no longer serves you so you can be who you are meant to be.

You are an incredible being!

Learn to know yourself and accept and love that person = cherish her, stand up for her is part of this. Learn to have clear boundaries. It is a gift of self-love, and only those who are benefitting from your weak boundaries will resist you stepping into them.

You are a powerful creator and manifestor!

Learn what that feels like to be in your energy and how to recognize when people take or pollute your energy. Then you can direct it towards

Most of all, you are INTUITIVE!

Trust in your intuitive knowing at all times. Knowing you are always loved, guided, and protected and there are no limits you cannot overcome.

ABOUT THE AUTHOR

Justine Peacock is an executive coach, psychotherapist, and energy healer working with female entrepreneurs and professionals who want to reclaim their authentic selves realigned with their purpose.

Born in Canada and raised in Australia, her early years seemed stable but were later categorised by abuse and trauma, lack of confidence, and self-neglect. These events inspired a deep journey of unravelling who others told her she was, to reveal the eternal truth underneath.

This remarkable journey united her with her intuitive gifts and revealed a profound truth—that we are much more significant than our roots and people's impression of us and that our journey is ours to control.

After a successful corporate career and law and HR/Leadership Development, Justine walks in two worlds as an Executive Coach in a global company and as a healer and intuitive helping women see and embrace their potential and live for themselves and on their terms.

She is passionate about helping women transform how they see themselves, speak up and create boundaries and a clear vision for their life.

Justine works with her Spirit Team to clear karma, contracts, residual energies, and beliefs and channel insights important to her clients' healing journey.

Through powerful and transformative intuitive healing sessions and coaching programs, she has created profound and seismic shifts in many women's lives.

She lives in Sydney, Australia, with her two ids and husband.

Email: *Justine@justinepeacock.com.au*
Website: *www.justinepeacock.com.au*

KATIE CAREY

My parents met on Friday 13th May in 1966 and married on the same date in 1967. On 21st September 1967, they lost their first baby to stillbirth. I cannot imagine how they got through that tragedy. A few months later, my Mum was pregnant with me.

I have known about this story for as long as I remember. My birth was quick. Dad was away, and Mum was staying with his parents. Mum had a show at 5:30 am, and I was born (delivered by my nan) at 5:50 am. A 20-minute labour. I was keen to get here. Sadly, in 1970 when Mum was pregnant again, she had a miscarriage seven months into her pregnancy. The following year, by baby brother was born.

I grew up in a strict household—never allowed to play with other children or stay at friend's houses. A couple of friends came to stay, but never came again. Dad had dyslexia and taught me to read as a toddler. He made huge black bags of cardboard flashcards. I was terrified when I couldn't remember a word. When Dad went for a nap, I knew I had to remember it when he woke up. I remembered. The word was *silver*. I could read when I started school. I daydreamed a lot, learned songs in my head, and read books. I loved reading, learning, singing, and dancing.

When I was 5, Dad became ill. He had surgery and was out of work for six years. We were poor. He was in hospital often, and Mum got really upset. We didn't have much, but I had an old suitcase under my bed, filled with Mum's old books she read as a teenager. By the time I got to the end of infant school, I had read every book in my school, infant and junior. By Age 9, my reading test said that I had the reading age of a 16-year-old.

We were often punished at home—straight to bed after school with no dinner for a week, beatings with the buckle end of the belt, cold showers, and his slipper across our backside, multiple times. We had boxing gloves that he made us put on if we argued, and we had to fight it out. Mum was often beaten too. I have some memories of good times also. We sang together. There were times when we would sit and look at the stars and the moon, and he would tell me what they were. I remember waiting at the front door to run to him coming up the street on his way home from work. When I was small. Before he lost his job. When he was happy.

I spent a lot of time in my bedroom. I read books, wrote stories, and made up songs. Dad had a tape recorder and let me use it. He loved to record the top 20 on Radio One on a Sunday. We would all listen to it, and I would choose songs to write lyrics and learn them. I have sung for as long as I can remember. At age 5, I would sing for the dinner ladies in the school playground. I always had an audience clapping and cheering me on, I loved that.

Mum's parents visited us twice a week, usually 15-minute visits. They always brought us chocolate bars and big hugs and kisses. I loved them, and I did get to stay with Nan sometimes. Just me and her. She had twin beds in her room, and we slept next to each other and would chat for ages in bed. The next morning Grandad brought us tea.

1977 Age 9 – my other Nan fell sick and suddenly died of kidney failure. Dad was devastated. He disappeared for days, and when he returned, we tried not to show how upset we were. We went to her funeral, and I screamed and tried to jump into the pit to be with her. I sobbed myself to sleep every night for a while and then I prayed that I could spend one more night with her...and I did. I woke up, having dreamt that I was with her all night. I knew then that she had not gone at all. I felt her with me. That made me feel happier until my dog was hit on the head by some-one, went blind, and was put to sleep, Elvis Presley died, and then my new dog acci-dentally killed my rabbit while playing. These things were upsetting, but I quickly reminded myself that if Nan was still here, so were they.

After Nan died, my parents took us out of the Catholic school and sent us to a Church of England school next to our house. I got the chance to act in a school play and loved it. I learned gymnastics in my year-and-a-half stay there. Then it was secondary school. I loved the drama and music departments. I loved singing and wanted to be a Hollywood star. I especially loved musicals. I knew that money was a bad word in our house. They often argued about it, and we would have to hide from the rent man and insurance man. Like all the other kids, we never had pocket money, and our clothes mostly came from Dad's cousins. I joined a gymnastics class. I was great at that.

My first big show was the Wizard of Oz, where I played a Munchkin. I went on my first trip abroad to Germany—we only had one family holiday in Great Yarmouth. The teachers noticed my voice, and I sang in a play. Then I was chosen to play a solo in the next school pantomime, A Christmas Carol. It was scary, but I could always ask Nan for help. I never told anyone else that. I had learned a song in the church choir called Queen of the May with the lyrics: "Oh, Mary, we crown thee with blossoms today, Queen of the Angels and Queen of the May." My Nan was called Mary, and she died on the 4th of May, so I sang this song to her. It made me feel joyful and good things seemed to happen.

In 1981 Age 12, a traumatising event happened to my family. Some residents of our council estate broke into our house one night. They smashed the windows and doors. I jumped out of bed, picked up a pair of shoes to defend myself with, ran downstairs, and hit the man coming up with them, but he laughed at me. When I got to the bottom of the stairs, I saw Dad lying on the floor, three men kicking him. I climbed on top of him, but they carried on kicking him underneath me and laughing, while someone else smashed my mum's huge ornamental dog across the top of her head. No one called the police or an ambulance. My mum's head bled severely as we tried to get to the nearest phone box. We left Dad lying there. The police and ambulance came and took us to the hospital. Dad was black and blue from head to toe when they examined him. We thought he was going to die. I had to testify in court, but the case was dropped. It led to something great, though. We moved house to the same street as Grandad and my aunties. I loved that and spent lots of time with my grandad, listening to his funny stories.

1982, the BBC came to school to do a play for today. They had been trying to sell a pilot of a movie called "The Little Matchgirl" for years. My teacher asked for the script, and they let us use it for our Christmas show. I auditioned and got the part. It felt like that show was about me. My dad was often drunk, we were poor, and I asked my dead Nan for help. I asked my Nan to come with me on stage. Aged 14, I got on stage at the Irish Club and sang. I learned that Nan used to sing on that stage. We were taking the show to Russia. Some of our cast sang in clubs to raise funds. My living Nan donated a beautiful Swan to Raffle to raise funds, as my parents had no money. I was so lucky. I had a fantastic Nan in life and one in spirit looking after me too.

1984, I was invited to audition for a BBC period drama, Anna of the Five Towns. I got the part. We did a read through in a huge conference room. Then, I spotted him across the table. It was *Doctor Who*! I was starstruck and scared to read my part. I asked Nan for help, and It went well. I met my chaperone, Christine. I soon got to know everyone, and they were the loveliest people. We laughed a lot. Those six months filled me with joy. I wanted to do this forever. Whilst working on the drama, I was invited to audition for a radio play with some cast members of The Archers. The play was Winnie Holden's Angel, and I played Winnie Holden. I debuted my TV series and radio drama the same week. My life was a dream come true until I had to return home to my reality. I was upset when it ended. After loving working in TV, Radio, theatre, and the Edinburgh Festival, I was suddenly an adult, and acting opportunities stopped. Getting an equity card was difficult, and I didn't have the money to keep going to auditions. I had to get a job and decided to save for drama school.

1987, I fell in love. It wasn't plain sailing, though. I really loved his Mum, and she got cancer and died in 1988 before we married in 1989. He had already lost his dad when he was 16. He was a soldier. I was 20. He was in the same battalion my dad had been in. We moved 200 miles away. He went away for four months to Norway, leaving me alone and depressed, though I didn't understand what depression was back then. I was always crying. I found a job in an Officers Mess as a silver service waitress and made some friends. I was not fond of it much, but it wasn't long before a role at BT in Salisbury as an Operator appeared. I had worked for BT in Coventry and enjoyed that.

In October 1990, Grandad (Dad's dad) was ill with arthritis in hospital. He had been in a couple of weeks. I was told he was ok. It was an hour's journey on the bus to work. I started at 7.15 am. While on the bus, I felt consumed, and I needed to go home to Coventry...now. When I got to work, I cried, telling them I needed to go home because my grandad was dying. They took me into the office, checked for the next train to Coventry, and I got on the train. When I arrived, I got a taxi to the hospital but told no one I was doing that. I found Grandad, and he was happy to see me. He held my hand, and within 10 minutes, he died. I was devastated. I didn't understand what had just happened. How did I know that?

In 1991, I was made redundant. I bought an Amstrad computer and enrolled in an Adult Education course in Word Processing. I knew I wanted to work from home with a computer when I had children. Computers were Mos Dos floppy disc things. I must have known what was coming. We moved to Northern Ireland. I fell pregnant.

We were moving again when I was eight months pregnant. We spent the weekend with my parents before we were moving into our new home, on the Monday and Dad was looking ill and was drinking all night long. We decided, when our baby was born, we couldn't stay there again. I was so stressed when we got to our new house. I had to see the midwife and was rushed into hospital with pre-eclampsia. They kept me there for the last month of my pregnancy. I was induced and went into labour for 36 hours. They gave me an epidural during the labour but I wasn't numb on one side. Later, I had to be taken for an emergency caesarean. They told me I needed to stay conscious as I could die otherwise, so I agreed to stay awake. Half-way through the C-section, I was screaming. They gave me general anaesthesia and I was unconscious. I have memories of things happening around me as though I was looking down at them. I saw my catheter fall out and there was blood and urine everywhere. The next memory was waking up and seeing my baby boy for the first time. I was overjoyed, despite still being in intensive care. I loved being a Mum.

Whenever we went home, we stayed with Mums parents and I visited mine. A year later, I was a bridesmaid for a friend, so I popped in to see them. Dad looked really ill now. His tummy was huge. I hugged him and told him I loved him, but hated him drinking. Nine days later, I had to get to Coventry from my home in Newcastle (we moved 11 times in 13 years) when my Mum called to say he had been rushed into hospital haemorrhaging.

21st June 1993. The longest day! It was the day after Father's Day. My dad was conscious when I arrived and I stroked his head and he stared into my eyes. My baby was 13 months old and he said, "*Gandad*" for the first time. It made Dad smile. They took Dad for surgery to try and save him. They came back around 11 pm to the waiting room and told us he was out of surgery and was doing ok. Then just before midnight, they returned to announce his death. That week, my baby boy kept us all sane. He made us laugh and I spent the week leading up to the funeral with Mum. There were several spiritual occurrences—things switched places, and we laughed about it. A few weeks later, there was a toy battery-powered radio in my bathroom. I had taken the batteries out but during the night, I woke hearing it playing. It was flashing with no batteries! I knew it was Dad.

August 1993, I was pregnant. I climbed onto the stool to get something from the kitchen cupboard and fell. I bled for seven days. The doctor said, I didn't need to go to hospital, it was a very early miscarriage. After the bleeding stopped, I felt symptoms of pregnancy and didn't have a period. I had a test and on my 25th Birthday, I was pregnant. I was told I was likely carrying twins. We were happy. This time, a caesarean was planned. Late in pregnancy, I was diagnosed with Placenta Previa and told that I couldn't travel more than five miles from the hospital.

4th May 1994, Grandad (Mum's dad), the same date as my nan (Dad's mum) died of a heart attack. I couldn't go home and missed his funeral. Mum had lost her husband and Dad within 11 months of each other. I had lost my dad and my grandad. However, I knew they weren't really gone.

My second son was born on Friday 13th May in Chester. It was my parents' first wedding anniversary after my dad died. This was great for Mum. She came to stay when I came out of hospital.

1995 - A woman who booked me to do Ann Summers parties told me she had an alcohol problem and agoraphobia. She invited me to a Clairvoyant party. (There was a theme around addicts being attracted to my life after Dad died. Friends, neighbours, bosses). A man who did card readings came. He brought Dad through. He sang a song Dad sang to me and more. My fascination in spirit really started. I evaluated that Nan in spirit must have taken me to Grandad, knowing he wanted to see me before he died. Today, following years of studying Psychic Development, Mediumship and so much more about spirit and consciousness, I now know... I am extremely intuitive.

Life continued. We lived in a block of flats in Germany. The neighbours had regular all night parties, and I was about to have my third baby. I was exceptionally stressed and stormed off to the Families Office to report them. Drama unfolded, giving us even more worries. My baby girl was born by planned section, this time I stayed awake with a spinal block. Bizarrely, one by one things happened to the neighbours that had caused the issues, and they no longer lived in our block and then we were posted to the UK.

I tried all sorts to contribute financially. Ann Summers, Avon, Tupperware, typing up CVs for people, I even had an Astrology CDROM and printed people's birth charts. I became a childminder too. I wasn't sleeping, as my baby was still waking through the night several times a night. That happened until she was 12. We moved a few more times and landed in Rutland. I loved Rutland and worked at a bike hire shop as an admin and website assistant. I cycled to and from work ten miles a day.

Summer 2002, we walked along Uppingham High Street and looked in the estate agents window. Suddenly, we were viewing houses and bought this one. Early October, I got a call from Mum to say Nan had to have a chest X-ray. She was diagnosed with Lung Cancer one Thursday and the following Thursday she died. I was heartbroken and shocked that she died before I got to see her. We moved in on 31st October 2002 and Nan's funeral was the next day, a Friday. I had my 4th driving test on the Monday and failed again. I had to leave my job. I couldn't cycle that far. We settled here and made friends through the children, and socialised with neighbours some weekends when my husband was home. The discussion always delved into our childhoods. I became upset every time I had a drink and started to feel resentful of Mum about my childhood. My husband was in Belfast and when he came home, he went out with the friends he made in the village. I was concerned he would develop a drinking problem. I became depressed. I knew something was wrong, but didn't know what. I found out and asked for a divorce.

I was selling on eBay now and got friendly with people on an online Forum. I had said some stuff on the forum, as I was upset, and was suddenly attracted to someone. We became friends online and he came here to visit. Husband number one came back a few times over the following months to try and change my mind. I knew I couldn't trust him. He went to Bosnia for six months, and we were divorced by the time he came back. I was engaged to husband number two, a few weeks after the divorce came through. I felt he was my soulmate. We connected in so many ways and had much in common. He had a difficult childhood and painful first marriage. He suffered with anxiety and agoraphobia. That didn't faze me as sometimes, I felt anxious too. I felt that my Spirit family had sent him to ease the pain of the end of my marriage. I didn't process the feelings from the end of my marriage and didn't give myself time or space to heal.

He built a new kitchen, paved my driveway, seeming to be great at everything—even cooking—and he loved me, and he was always here. He couldn't seem to hold down a job because of his anxiety. He began to get angry with himself. Even though I loved my eBay business, I got a job because I wanted to take over the mortgage and keep this house for my children. I wouldn't say I liked that job. My boss was a bully, and I cried when I got home every day. I would later find out that he was Mentally ill and an addict. I was made redundant after six months on a Friday and started a new job on a Monday. I stayed there for three years and began gigging to earn extra money and because I missed singing.

We married in Dec 2007, and while on honeymoon, he had been drinking a lot because we had an all-inclusive deal. We also caught Norovirus for three days of our six-day honeymoon. We made plans on the beach for all the things we were going to do when we got home, and we were gigging, but that wasn't great for his anxiety. He was just trying to please me. A few months in, I discovered the alcohol hamper I had won at a school PSA Raffle was disappearing. A lot of the spirits were almost empty. I was raging. We went to the doctor's to ask for help, and the doctor wasn't nice to him. He crossed his arms and said, only you can put the drink down. He was so embarrassed. It took a while for him to go back. He tried to stop but struggled to stay off it. He saw a locum doctor, who sent him to see the alcohol team. He went into hospital in June 2008 for his first detox.

For the next 13 years, we would go through cycles of him drinking, getting sober, and relapsing over and over. He had many detoxes. I was working hard, trying to take care of my family. My eldest son left home at 18, and my second son went off to University at 19. I became ill with Labyrinthitis for seven weeks. David Knight, a spiritual author in my village, did some work in my garden. I asked about his books. Then, I read his books and discovered Abraham Hicks and The Law of Attraction, which explained many events of my life that had been previously unexplainable. I left my job, I enjoyed it, but I felt I needed more. In 2010, I worked as a PA at the hospital. In my first week, a colleague took me to a meditation session. I loved it and went every week. It was needed because some dramas happened at work, and I began to hate going. I discovered months in that my predecessor (as my boss always referred to her) had committed suicide. That felt awful. I wouldn't have had that job if she hadn't done that. dramas unfolded, at work and home. I felt a black cloud every time I walked into my office and when I got home. Thankfully, I found holistic therapies and Reiki, and that helped a lot. Things felt calmer. My husband was offered a course at the Mental Health clinic, and a lady wanted to know about my reflexology but said she couldn't afford my lowest price of £15. A thought popped into my head. Wouldn't it be nice to run a charity? The next day, a friend asked me to be a director for her non-profit project and asked me why I didn't do something like that with my therapies. So I did. By this time, I was studying for an Open University Open Degree. I needed to earn more and keep my family in our home, and the modules that came up always seemed to fit perfectly around the charity. Psychology, the Science of the

Mind, Counselling, Psychotherapy, Challenging Ideas in Mental Health, and several Management modules and three years into my meditation practice, I got a new teacher. We became friends. We chatted about my issues at work and home, and she was compassionate and understanding. The charity was going well at first but then drama after drama. Every time people came in to help, they were gone again, and I was left feeling disappointed and unsupported and with the weight of the world on my shoulders. All I wanted to do was help people. Why were people so horrible to me? I had trained in Reiki to train the volunteers myself, and I qualified in Mindfulness. My relationship with Mum got better because Mindfulness helped me to let go of my past.

My marriage got worse after each relapse, and everyone else in the charity was aware of our problems, which made things more difficult. I had to have long periods off work, during and after shoulder surgery, and had only been back to work a few months before kidney stones crippled me, literally. I was off work for six months, still trying to continue the charity and my degree. I had a pain injection in my back, which helped me walk for a while, but gave me tons of side effects, and when it wore off, I had pain in my lower back that wasn't there before. I was given a Lumbar Puncture. They went into my back 13 times before they finally drew fluid. I was left unable to move for two weeks. As time went on, I had pain everywhere, and I was in bed most of the day and unable to sleep at night. I was diagnosed with Fibromyalgia and Multiple joint Osteoarthritis. I was ill-health retired in May 2017. A drama in August 2017 occurred, and I told my husband to leave.

Everything was going great for me. I came off my pain meds. I realised they were causing my memory and speech issues and Stomach Problems. I knew I would struggle with my exam if I didn't stop taking them. I finished my degree and passed it, graduating in October. I won the Educational Spirit of Corby Award for my charity work in September and became a grandmother in October too.

My boys were both planning their weddings. I continued to learn taking online coaching courses, and in August 2019, I found EFT and trained as a practitioner. I realised just how much trauma was sitting in my body, from my lifetime of traumas and triggers. I was dating my husband again. He was sober for 13 months, the longest ever, but just as I thought things could work out, he picked up the drink again, and after a few more dramas, in October 2019, I asked for a divorce. I still felt that I loved him, and then I realised my feelings about him were the feelings I had felt about my dad, and I saw the patterns I had been carrying my whole adult life and realised why relationships didn't work. I saw the people-pleasing and good girl wounds and discovered that I had an ACE score (Adverse Childhood Experiences) of eight out of ten. I was carrying around so much energetic crap subconscious programming in my body, and I know I am an Empath, the way I feel so deeply. I decided to close the charity. The struggle to get money in and lack of support was too much for me and made me feel resentful. I was trying to keep the roof over my head, and in 2020, I decided to go deeper with my own lack and poverty money patterns during the lockdown. I finally closed the door on my marriage and went ahead with the divorce. Things again started to change for me. My travel business had gone down the pan, and my eBay sales disappeared, and then out of nowhere came an amazing Spiritual Business Coach. I knew she was perfect for me, and another opportunity to create a Podcast landed in my lap. I learned how to connect with my intuition again and to understand it and recognised how I had been unconditionally loving to everyone around me, but not to myself. I began to focus on self-love. I became a grandmother again. I started to build my online EFT Business, joined a Million Dollar Experiment, and an opportunity to write this chapter came up, as well as my TV series reappearing on Britbox USA. My podcast has been in the iTunes Charts and has been globally ranked. I changed my name and seemed to have come full circle, doing things that I love again.

At 52, I understand Dad was mentally ill with PTSD. He experienced physical and emotional pain that he couldn't cope with. Sadly, he took it out on those he loved. Mum didn't have many choices back then. It was not easy for a woman to leave. She loved him and was scared to leave him. I understand that he couldn't stop drinking. My second marriage showed me the real struggles of addiction and co-dependency. It's difficult to leave someone you think you love. This is usually a trauma bond. I learned the difference between my mind and my intuition and trust my feelings above all else now. I know I will never attract these situations again. I can see the patterns and the hypervigilance. EFT and my spiritual coaching tools help me stay ahead in this game of life and follow my truth and my joy. I passionately share what I have learned, with my podcast and my work, so that others can break these patterns and stop generational trauma that causes misery and resentment (because living in those energies, suck our very life force and ruin relationships with those we love the most) passing to their children and grandchildren.

ABOUT THE AUTHOR

Katie Carey is a passionate, creative, intuitive mental health advocate. She helps empathic women heal, grow and understand how past trauma, ancestral patterns, and lack of boundaries hinder them in their relationships and careers. She shows them how to change that paradigm and pass on healthier patterns to others.

Katie has transcended similar patterns herself. She was extremely connected as a child and manifested amazing experiences, had psychic dreams, knew things no one around her understood and sought help from her late grandmother in spirit.

Katie achieved her dream of working in TV, radio, and theatre as a teenager and travelled to Germany and Russia in school shows despite financial difficulties. In adulthood, Katie lost her connection and encountered poverty, leading her to work in jobs that she didn't enjoy to survive and fund auditions, hoping to return to her dream in entertainment someday.

Katie is a Reiki Master, EFT practitioner, and Mindfulness and Law of Attraction coach. She studied Psychology, the Science of the Mind, Counselling and Psychotherapy, and Challenging ideas in mental health as part of her degree and graduated in 2017. She also studied Mediumship and Psychic Development and Angel Therapy.

Katie hosts a podcast, Soulfulvalley, where she speaks to people in various energy healing fields and teaches the numerous natural healing methods. She won the Educational Spirit of Corby Award in 2017 for her charity work.

Website: www.soulfulvalley.com

KATRINA HAHLING

GRASPING INWARDS

* Dates and stories may vary slightly to reality for emphasis and due to bad memory

2014, 28 YEARS OLD

I stare out the plane window, forehead pressed to the glass, as we turn over the blue ocean, and I begin a familiar routine: picking out all the spots I know, trying to locate my house and my workplace; except this time, there is no house and no workplace.

Tears well in my eyes as emotions flood through me: elation at being back on home soil, excitement to plant my feet into the white sand and wash off my heavier emotions in the saltwater, grief at leaving a beautiful man and a solid relationship on the other side of the world; questioning what might have been, comfort to be in a place I consider my soul home, and relief to be coming back to dear friends.

As the plane lands, I wipe my tears and compose myself with deep breaths. The harder I try to hold tears in, the more they well up, running down my cheeks.

Twenty minutes later, I have my bags and make it through customs into the Gold Coast's warmth in spring. A welcome warmth after the cool summer and fall of Helsinki, Finland, where I'd been for the past few months. In fact, where I'd been based mainly for the last three and a half years.

Outside the airport, in the passenger pickup sits my friend Jess. Her little blue

Getz is clean and tidy as always. She springs out of the driver's seat to give me a big squeeze and help me put my large suitcase into the back seat of the car.

Once we're safely in the car, Jess asks, "So, what would you like to do?"

Being here is surreal. Me and my entire life packed into that one suitcase. Me, my dreams, my regrets, my failures. All right here.

In some ways, I've been craving to be here for many, many months. Now that I am here, I feel unsteady.

What am I doing here?

What am I doing with my life?

"I don't know," I eventually shrug.

"There's a cute cafe I think you'd like. Would you like some food?" Jess asks.

I could definitely do with a coffee.

I wonder how much money is left in my account.

Shit. I need to sort out a job—or at least some Centrelink payments to see me through until I find a job.

I nod. "Yes, food would be great."

When we're settled in the café, I can't shake the feeling of this not being real. Partly jetlag, partly dissociation as I'd upended my life and moved to the other side of the world.

Everything is familiar. I'd been on these streets before. Everyone speaks my mother tongue. Everyone is warm and friendly. Yet, I feel like I don't belong.

That night, sitting on a blow-up mattress in my friend's mum's spare room, I put my face into my hands and cry.

How did my life end up here?

I'm broke.

I have no career.

This isn't how I imagined my life.

I was a straight-A student at school. I'd always have good friends, good grades and was involved in sports and extracurricular activities. I love life. I love being involved. I love travel, novelty, friendship, deep connection, creativity, music. I love being.

How DID I get to be 28 and sleeping on a blow-up mattress in a friend's mum's house?

1991, 5 YEARS OLD

Mum has just gotten mad at my brother because he keeps saying he's bored.

She's standing at the sink, swearing in her mother tongue. I don't understand the words, but the tone I can. I hate it when she's angry.

I don't want her to feel angry or upset.

I promise myself I'll always be good and always try to make her happy. The grasping outwards begins. I spend most of my time trying not to upset my brother (if he wants a toy I'm playing with, I give it to him) and being on my best behavior to not upset mum (although this doesn't always work).

Harmonising subconsciously becomes part of my role in the family. Along with grasping outwards to the praise of being the 'good girl.'

1992, 6 YEARS OLD

It's the end of a sweaty North Queensland school day. The bus pulls up at our stop, and I jump up, sweat rolling down the backs of my knees.

Mum's at home waiting for my brother and me, and I'm so excited I run most of the way from the bus stop, through our spare block, and into the house.

"Mum! Mum! Mum!" I'm shouting.

When I find her, she's in the kitchen making us an afternoon snack.

"What is it?" she asks.

"My poem is going to be published in the school newsletter!"

"Oh, really? That's wonderful!"

The next week, my poem about a frog was published in the school newsletter, along with an image my dad kindly drew to illustrate my poem.

My childhood pride swells. My passion for writing grows.

1995, 9 YEARS OLD

We're one month into the school holidays. I've set myself a project for the day—to complete a book. My best friend Katie and I are horse-obsessed. We go to riding lessons every Wednesday after school, buy horse magazines and obsess over our favourite colours and types of horses.

I've decided to make a horse reference book.

With A4 pages folder over and stapled into a book, I set about cutting our different types of horses and different saddlery types.

I slave over my project all day until my book is complete.

I'm happy with the outcome. One day, I imagine it will be a real book.

1997, 11 YEARS OLD

It's 3 pm, and I've just left my classroom, report card in hand. Two of the 'cool girls' I know from touch footy catch me as I'm walking to the big covered area to wait for my bus.

One snatches my report card out of my hand and begins to read it—her eyes squint, a puzzled look on her face.

"You got all VHA's." she looks up at me.

"Yeah," I shrug.

"Wait, you *always* get all VHA'S?"

"Yeah," I say.

This is the first time it dawns on me that not everyone gets straight A's at school. Grasping out towards good grades begins.

1998, 12 YEARS OLD

Our primary school is turning ten years old. To celebrate, the school is holding a special fete and burying a time capsule. Each class is contributing something to the capsule. Mr. Hardwick's year 7 class (my class) is filling out a questionnaire.

I get the paper and immediately treat it as a test. I go through and answer all the easy ones first.

Where would you like to travel? *Easy! Finland and Switzerland—where my parents come from.*

What's your favourite food? *Anything Mum makes.*

What do you want to be when you grow up? *Skip.*

Eventually, I'm left with one answered question. What do you want to be when you grow up?

I don't know. I don't know. I don't know!

Time's running out, and panic is rising in my chest.

I look over to my friend Nikki Caswel; she's written *Teacher.*

I elbow her gently. "Nikki. You put Teacher; how do you know?"

"I don't know. I just do."

I look over to my other good friend Kerri; she's written *Hairdresser.*

I don't want to be either of those! I huff.

Soon, one of the teacher aides is knocking on our classroom door. She has a bright green cube box in her hands. The same ones they use to collect and distribute tuckshop.

"Time's up," Mr. Hardwick's baritone resonates around the room.

My palms are sweating. The backs of my knees are sweating.

I wrack my brain.

What do I want to be when I grow up?

What do I want to be when I grow up?

What do I want to be when I grow up?

I don't know.

I don't know.

I don't know.

I don't know!

Slowly but surely, everyone in class gets up and places their questionnaire in the box.

I'm the last person, and I can't bear to leave the question unanswered, so I write 'I don't know.'

I place my paper in the box, but the question stays with me for decades. What DO I want to be when I grow up?

1999, 12 YEARS OLD

It's the night before my first day at high school. I can't sleep. Crocodile tears stream down my face in the darkness as my mind runs away with thoughts.

What if I'm not smart at highschool?

What if I'm the dumbest person in the class?

What if I get all the answers wrong?

The thoughts get faster and thicker, along with my tears and snot. Finally, I go out to see my parents for some consolation.

My sense of identity as the 'smart girl' is being threatened for the first time. Who am I if I'm not the smart girl?

2001, 15 YEARS OLD

I have my elective list in front of me for year 10. Years 8 and 9, we got to try everything. Now we're expected to narrow down our subject list to support our career.

I don't know is still my selected career of choice; hence I'm struggling to choose subjects objectively.

I thought I'd let my grades decide for me.

But I got A's in everything, so that didn't solve anything.

I guess I'll just go as broad as possible. That way, nothing will be entirely ruled out.

So I do a bit of everything. Maths B, Chemistry, French, drama, English, Business Principles, Touch Typing.

Grasping out towards a 'title' begins.

2003, 17 YEARS OLD

Mum and I are sitting on the patio. I've got six months left of school. I'm anxious as university applications will soon be open, and you know, I still 'don't know.'

"Mum, what should I do?"

"Didn't you always like English? You'd be a good researcher or writer."

"Ughh. I used to, but I don't like it anymore. It's so boring."

High school English had turned me off my obsession with books and writing.

"Plus, it's not like you can make good money as a writer."

I'm not sure where I picked that belief up, but any dream of becoming a writer had been dashed by this time.

2003, 17 YEARS OLD

The university handbook was released today. It tells you the cut-offs for each course. I leave school right and jump into my car.

I drive to the newsagency. I find the stack of books and head to the counter, and pay for it.

Mum's at work, and Janne's staying with dad. I'm home alone. Just me and the coursebook.

I still don't know what I want to be when I grow up, but someone who gets straight A's goes to university and has a glamorous and prestigious career.

At the back of the booklet is a career personality quiz.

I take a pen and paper, answering the questions.

It leads to me a page that says 'COMMUNICATIONS/PUBLIC RELATIONS.'

That doesn't mean anything!

What is that?

Who even does that!

I have to apply for something, so I apply for a double degree in Law/Arts three weeks later.

I have no idea what I want to be and vow to take a gap year to figure that out.

2004, SAID GAP YEAR, 18 YEARS OLD

I've been working full time at Target for 3-4 months. It was my part-time job throughout school, so I went full time to save for a trip around the world. Nothing like travel to broaden the horizons and help one find oneself, right?

My job is managing the layby counter. The days are long, and once I've paid rent and bills, the $500 a week I get paid doesn't go very far.

I also hate the horrible red shirt I have to wear and the obsessive customers that come in weekly to pay off, cancel and re-lay by weird items they don't even need.

My friend Kate is meeting me for lunch at Gloria Jean's.

I grab my bag from the storeroom and head out.

When I get there, Kate is on a sofa waiting for me. I plop down into one, exhausted.

"I can't do this, Kate," I say.

"Do what?" she asks.

"Work 40 hours a week doing something I don't love. I can't do this for the rest of my life." My shoulders sag.

Kate, ten years my senior, looks at me, and I'll never forget what she said.

'You just have to.'

I bit my tongue to shy to share my thoughts with Kate.

I made a personal vow that day to find work I loved.

So began my search for my one thing. Something I was passionate about. Something I loved. Something I was born to do.

2008, 22 YEARS OLD

I've been living on the Gold Coast for a little over a year. I love it here.

I thought the move would help me enjoy my studies. Turns out, wherever you go, there you are, and changing cities was not going to help me love my studies.

My mum is staying with me on her way back from a trip to see her mum in Finland. I'm in the middle of what I call my quarter-life crisis.

I've been seeing career counsellors, crying at the drop of a hat, trying to figure out what I need to be doing with my life (and it's not the law/business degree I'm now enrolled in).

I'd hoped the career counsellor would say, 'Be a journalist,' and I would say, 'Okay,' and live happily ever after.

Who am I here to be?

What am I to do with my one wild and precious life?

No one had those answers.

On Mum's last day, I drive her up to Brisbane. We chat about options and ideas in the car.

"I could be an air hostess for a bit."

"Yes, but then what?" Mum asked.

"I don't know," tears well in my eyes.

At the airport, I stand with her in the Jetstar line. Mum's the last person to board. I hug her and turn and walk away.

I can't look back because my face has broken into pieces, and I'm sobbing.

Grasping outwards at a job, a title, a career to give me a sense of self-worth, meaning and direction is in full flight.

2009, 23 YEARS OLD

We're in an auditorium on the Gold Coast. Graduating students, myself included, in our robes and hats. Parents, friends, and supporters in the stands opposite watching as we receive our degrees.

Not long after the crisis of 2008, I changed to a Bachelor of Communications majoring in Journalism and Writing. Some intuitive part of myself conjuring up my long-lost love of writing, books and creativity.

As our group is called up, I get my crutches ready, and my friend helps me steady myself.

A week earlier, I snapped my ACL playing touch football and am now waiting for an operation in January.

I apply for a few cadet journalist jobs and even drive out to Chinchilla for a job interview. I didn't get the job.

Now I'm out of work, have no university and have a knee that's in a straight leg brace. I move back to Townsville until my knee heals.

I still don't know what I want to be when I grow up.

2010, 24 YEARS OLD

I'm in my hometown, Townsville. I have no job, no boyfriend, no commitments.

The time without work or study and an inability to drive has forced me to slow down.

I fold hundreds of paper cranes. I teach myself to play the guitar.

I play intuitive games on the internet and stumble upon a place called Glen Helen Resort. It's 140kms west of Alice Springs and becomes the base of travel.

It occurs to me that now is the time to travel.

I load my car and drive out alone into the red dust.

I work six days a week and spend my day off hiking parts of the trails. I save $10,000.

Next, I move to New Zealand and find a resort there to work in.

The travel continues to include South East Asia with girlfriends, a trip around Switzerland with my dad, and then to England, where I have a job setting up marquees for Glastonbury.

The space and time begin my journey of grasping inwards. Spending time with myself. Keeping a consistent journal.

2012, 26 YEARS OLD

I'm boarding a plane at Heathrow airport. I've spent four months in England, and many of my friends were doing gap years living in London. It was easy to be there.

I contemplated staying on. Getting a marketing job like the others were doing.

Then I reminded myself of my childhood dream. I wanted to live in Finland for a while, learn my mother's language and spend time with her family.

I found a job as an au pair and was to be picked up in 2 hours at the Helsinki airport by the dad of the child I would be caring for.

I cried at the airport. I cried throughout the flight.

What have I done?

What have I gotten myself into?

What if I hate it?

What if it isn't a real job?

What if he kidnaps me?

It is a real job. I am not kidnapped. I have a lovely time.

I spend ten months looking after Bea one week and traveling and hanging out the other week. I take Finnish lessons. I visit Santa in Lapland.

I meet a French man and fall instantly in love.

At the end of the ten months, I'm due to go back to Australia for a wedding. My original plan included coming back to save money and then perhaps go to Canada or South America.

Love changed my mind, and instead, I went back to give a proper life in Finland a go.

2014, 28 YEARS OLD

After a few years of back and forth trying to make my life work in Finland with my beautiful French boyfriend and his young son, I find myself in the fall without a job, without any money and struggling mentally.

Our home life is beautiful.

I love our apartment.

I love our relationship.

I love our Friday night sauna and movie ritual.

I love our food, our conversations.

I love his son.

I don't love Finland.

I don't love the cold.

I don't leave the house because I don't want to spend the money I don't have.

I'm uninspired to find work.

In the evenings, when he has fallen asleep, I crawl into the bathroom and watch my tears mix with the water in the grout of the tiles.

In the mornings, I sleep in.

What's there to get up for?

I wake and make a pot of coffee, alone in the apartment.

I look at a few job ads. Uninspired to apply.

I won't get it anyway.

Then I put on a tv show and eat some toast.

Just waiting for him to come home and spend an enjoyable evening again.

Only to cry at night.

I know something needs to change, and I know it means leaving this love behind because what I need is the sun and the surf. What I need is a place I can find work and make money while I figure out what I want to be when I grow up.

That's how I wound up back in Australia. Single, broke, homeless, jobless at the age of 28.

Now, how did I learn to grasp inwards and rebuild my sense of self and my life?

2014, 28 YEARS OLD

Feeling lost and unanchored, I make a silent promise to myself.

It feels like you have nothing right now, and that's really hard.

So let's commit to writing every day. No matter what, write in your journal. Make that your anchor.

So I write every day.

Pages and pages. I set timers and brain spill. I sketch and write down lines from books. I ruminate on love, loss, grief, becoming, arrival, shedding layers.

I write about everything and everyone.

What do I think?

What do I feel?

What do I need?

What do I want?

My anchor in journaling also becomes the first step in learning to grasp inwards.

I never share my journaling with everyone.

Maybe I should write something I can share with people.

I commit to writing one poem every day as well as my journaling.

My daily routine now includes waking up early, making coffee, going to the beach and journaling, heading to a café, and applying for jobs.

You need to find a career worthy job. Something that pays well and has direction. You need to do something prestigious. Something 'they' would approve of.

I scroll through the marketing communications roles that I am qualified for:

Digital Marketing Assistant;

Marketing and events assistant;

Marketing coordinator.

The pay sounds nice. I could do the work, but as I write the cover letters and amend my resume for each job, my heart pools onto the floor.

I'll never get a job like that.

I don't have enough experience; I'm not smart enough.

Plus, it sounds terrible, sitting in an office all day. I'll have to wear office clothes. Work a nine to five.

If this is what I want, why does it feel so icky?

On one such day, I was sitting at a cafe, feeling down and out about my career opportunities, when Bob Marley came on the playlist telling me to 'lively up myself.' I listened to Bob. I listened to my intuition.

I closed the laptop, pulled out my journal and started writing poetry.

Twenty minutes later, three young men arrive at the cafe. They were reciting poems to one and another and before long asked me what I was writing.

The next week I was standing behind a microphone at a spoken word poetry event that the young men I'd met had organised.

At this particular event, I met someone who would introduce me to Sarah Truman.

This was the first time the magic of synchronicity showed itself to me (or I was open enough to see it). Had I not turned off my job search and leaned into my desire to write, the guys wouldn't have started speaking with me. Grasping inwards led to a touch of magic.

2015, 29 YEARS OLD

Sarah and I are sitting in the coworking space she has created. At the time, Sarah had recently completed a life and business coaching course, and we'd had a few sessions already. All around my struggle to find my purpose, my one thing, the thing I was going to be when I grew up.

"Hey, listen to this poem I wrote this morning." I picked up my journal, proud of what I'd turned out.

Sarah looked up at me and listened attentively, her blue eyes beginning to glisten and sparkle.

When I was done, she said, "That's your thing!"

Confused, I tilted my head and asked, "What is?"

"That!"

"What?"

"Journaling!"

My head is working overtime.

Journaling? Journaling is not a thing.

You can't sell journaling.

You can't make money from journaling.

It's not really solving anyone's problems.

"Do you know how many times I've been told to journal? To write?" Sarah looks at me intently.

"No." I shake my head.

"Thousands of times. Coaches, teachers, psychologists, and even books tell me to journal, and here's what I manage."

Sarah walks over to a stack of books and pulls out a journal.

"I buy beautiful journals like this." She flicks through the pages, all blank. "Only to write for two days and then quit."

'Teach me how to journal,' she looks at me. 'Make me a workshop. Teach me how you do it.'

I look at her, mind racing.

'But, I don't really know how I do it. I just do it.'

'Well, break it down.'

Sarah forced me to do something uncomfortable that day. Together we set a date and created a workshop.

One month later, I held my first of many journaling workshops and sessions. The beginning of sharing how to grasp inward began.

2015, 29 YEARS OLD

Staring in the mirror.

Ugh, my skin is so bad. I hate this adult acne.

I complain to my best friend.

'Surely there's something I can do, right?'

'Of course,' Lani nodded.

She gave me her beauty therapist's number.

I committed to myself that I would have clear, beautiful skin.

I found some products and started the daily ritual of washing my face every morning and night.

My skin cleared up in months. I was so happy I could proudly show my face to the world.

Little did I know this was another small form of grasping inwards.

2016, 30 YEARS OLD

Living with my friends, and they're in a bit of a health kick. They wake up in the morning, drink lemon water, have a coffee then go for a run.

They eat fruits and vegetables.

They look great.

I look at myself in the mirror.

I used to be thin, fit and healthy.

Europe changed that. Cooler weather, the cheese (Oh! The cheese), the wine, the bread.

I decide my self worth is going to be boosted if I feel better in my skin.

I commit to getting thin, fit and healthy again.

I start an at-home yoga practice.

Yoga takes the weight off and tones my body.

My mornings now consist of yoga, meditation, journaling and a coffee at the beach.

A bonus I wasn't aware of, yoga is another way of learning how to grasp inwards.

2017, 31 YEARS OLD

I'm sitting in my car driving back from a successful journaling class, thinking.
I'm going to have to find a new venue.
I hate finding venues.
Driving out to them.
Maybe I should put it online.
Maybe I could do journaling workshops online?
I pulled over to a park and filmed my first ever video. I shared a favourite journaling technique.

So began my online journey.

Before long, I was solely focused on bringing my work online, saving time and money for everyone. We could all be in the comfort of our own homes and still get the results we received in a class.

Feeling lost and ill-at-ease, I took an online business course.

While studying one day, I had an *aha* moment answering the question—what results do people get from working with you?

People who attended my classes found work they enjoyed, they saved up and bought their dream van to travel Australia. Another person recovered quickly from a workplace trauma and went back to work.
Journaling is simply the tool I use!
What I actually do is help people!
My life's work begins to take place. Helping other people to grasp inwards.

2021 (TODAY), 34 YEARS OLD

As my online presence grew, so did the formulation of my coaching framework. As I began to share how I got results in my own life (losing weight, clearing up my skin, creating work I love), I began to see a structure and formula taking place.

This formula is the premise of my first solo book, due to be released later this year. I'm writing this chapter you read. I've created a podcast I adore. I know what I want to be when I grow up!

On top of creating the life's work I'd been craving and searching for, learning to grasp inwards and create a life that's based on my values, my intuition, my passion, and my own vision I've created a life I adore. I have the healthiest and most solid relationship I've ever been in, my adult acne has disappeared, and my weight remains quite constant. My finances are the best they've ever been.

Who'd have thought it all begins from the inside?

I hope you leave this chapter knowing to;

- Make time and space for yourself, time alone so you can get to know yourself—who you are, what you like, what's important to you and what you value
- Follow the little inklings and nudges. The more you follow them, the more you receive. That's how intuition works
- Spend time doing what you like/love, whether it's work-related or not—when you're happy, you're more aligned and meet people and opportunities that won't present themselves otherwise. This is where you walk your way to purpose and meaning
- Sometimes you need help—seek out coaching, mentoring and guidance when you need to learn something, when you need a sounding board, when you need a little something to get to the next level. Continue to grasp inwards throughout this process and listen to yourself

ABOUT THE AUTHOR

At six years old, Katrina Hahling dreamt to be a writer and hold her own books someday. Somewhere between pleasing everyone else, receiving accolades for good grades, and the end of high school, that dream was all but gone. She found herself in l aw school, struggling to find her purpose, or a career she was passionate about.

She changed degrees, travelled the world and tried different jobs before returning to Australia at 28—single, broke, career-less and sleeping on a blow-up mattress in her friend's mum's house. Here, Katrina reconnected with writing, which in turn reconnected her with herself. She rebuilt her life from the ground up—new boyfriend, new home, more money and finally, her purpose-driven work.

She is the rebel researcher of Emotional Intelligence, creator of The Rebelle Podcast, co-author of Intuitive; Knowing Her Truth, and author of the book The Desire Manifesto; Creating with Emotional Intelligence.

Katrina is passionate about helping women spend less time feeling lost to themselves and avoiding their creative work. Through online courses and 1:1 mentoring, Katrina saves the creative ones years and thousands of dollars by guiding them to align with their soul, pursue their deepest desires while shedding layers of fear, doubt, guilt, shame and old stories. By creating online businesses and sharing themselves and their work with the world, her clients become who they came here to be.

Katrina believes we're all here for a reason and our desires are walking us home. When we pursue our desires, we unravel childhood programming and become the people we came here to be. Which is the greatest gift of all.

Website: www.katrinahahling.com
Podcast: www.anchor.fm/katrinahahling

KELLY PAARDEKOOPER

I recently read Dr. Rangan Chatterjee say: "authors write the books they need to read themselves."
These words echo the spirituality teachings I've heard countless times that we are our own medicine. The work we do is the work we need for ourselves.

But seriously, to write the book I need to read means revisiting my old emotional baggage, my messed up little world, hidden behind the scenes. Don't people want to be inspired and entertained? Or maybe that little voyeur inside us all loves to discover how screwed up others are on the inside? And perhaps also, reading the real truth behind closed doors gives us permission to accept and forgive our imperfections, to see how this is all part of the beautiful roller coaster experience of being human.

To share my story thus far and to read the words I need to read means being more vulnerable and risk being more exposed than I have ever been in my life. Showing my genuine emotions isn't something that comes easily. It is one of the hardest things for me to do.

In hindsight, it's this reluctance to be vulnerable and let people in that pushed me to my breaking point. It is that breaking point that cracked me wide open and allowed my intuition to shine through. My intuition led me to embrace being vulnerable.

Often, the control monster rears her ugly head and tries to push others away. She is always threatening to close the door to herself to hide the building chaos inside. So, I write this as my own medicine. To throw the door wide open and be vulnerable. To remind me of how far I've come and how necessary the journey has been. I write this too for those who might feel a similar inner pain and encourage them to embrace their unique balance of royally screwed up and divinely perfect. Where-ever you are right now is precisely where you need to be; your story is unfolding as it needs to, just as mine did.

THE PAIN

"Mary Poppins, that's what you are." My best friend in high school called me this one day during a heated exchange. It took me a little while to understand the cruel taunt, but once I understood it, the more it fueled my inner demons.

"Mary Poppins, practically perfect in every way." This is how my friend saw me. Is this how my other friends saw me? Is this how the outside world saw me? Did this mean they didn't like me? I can see now how irritating I must've been at times, trying to be perfect, always seeking praise. If only my friend could've seen the tormented teenager hiding behind the projection of perfection. But I didn't let her know, didn't let anyone know the truth. To some extent, my parents did, as parents often do, but even from them, I became masterful at hiding the truth. I believed striving for perfection also meant never disappointing anyone. Trying to avoid disappointing my parents was a huge motivation to keep up the appearance of being perfect.

The truth is I felt anything but perfect on the inside. By the time of the Mary Poppins incident, I'd already had years of insomnia, worrying about the mounting pressure of trying to be perfect. I'd also started to worry about my weight, trying to secretly control the food I was eating to manage how I looked. The pressure I'd begun to place on myself was so crippling and all-consuming. I was a young girl with no true self-confidence, a girl who measured self-worth by what others thought and the praise she received, a girl who never felt good enough unless everything was perfect.

My cousins called me "The Chosen One." The perfect child who everyone loved. If only they knew the pain I'd experienced that led me to strive for perfection. The first five years of my life were far from perfect; grief over the death of a sibling, loss of family unit after my parent's separation, change when my mother remarried, and then extreme bullying in my first year of school, leading me to require medical intervention. Thank goodness I had such loving parents and grandparents to guide me through those years (even amid their own pain). Somehow as a child, I joined the dots to create a story in my head that if I could control everything and keep it perfect, I would never have to experience that kind of pain again. I would also be able to save my family from any further pain.

As the years continued, I settled into a distinct rhythm, trying to be perfect, only letting the world see the very best outside whilst masking the torment on the inside. As life became more complicated, the older I got, the internal pressure to be perfect intensified. I found respite from this torture in food. When I was eating, I could surrender to the joy in the taste of the food. Emotional eating became my most prominent coping strategy. Yet, as anyone who eats to suppress emotions will be able to tell you, you become your own worst enemy every time you step on the scales. The inner pain becomes visible on the outside as unhealthy weight gain, cascading into fear of external judgment and disappointment.

Here re-entered the inner control freak, trying to maintain the appearance of perfection. Crazy fad diets and obsessive exercise became part of the vicious cycle of emotional eating. I now know in hindsight that this is considered disordered eating. I've also realised that my success in exercising control and losing the unwanted weight each time was because I cultivated self-hatred. Looking in the mirror each day and saying awful things to myself, genuinely hating myself, gave me the willpower to be strong and stick to whatever crazy fad I was following. Given my lack of self-worth and confidence were the core reasons I strove for perfectionism, this deliberate self-hatred was catastrophically detrimental.

Life had become a roller coaster of emotional eating to suppress the feeling of not being good enough and then hating myself to strive to achieve a weight goal. Once again, the feeling of not being good enough would become all-consuming, and the emotional eating would start all over again. Then back to weight gain, and again, back to hating myself... All this continued as a program, operating in the background whilst trying to keep up a Little Miss Perfect facade to the outside world.

For the most part, I was successful in this role. After completing my Bachelor of Pharmacy at university, I was nominated for a prestigious award in my first year in the workforce. The following year I was headhunted several times to manage different pharmacies. The year after that, I was invited to become a 50% partner of the pharmacy I had been managing. "Mary Poppins" was well and truly back. Everything was going great. My career was going from strength to strength. I had also just started an exciting new relationship, and my dreaded nemesis, my weight, was at an all-time low as I was too busy living the perfect little life to fall back into emotional eating.

My exciting new relationship blossomed, and we eventually became engaged. But by this time, the cracks had started to appear. My business partner and I had started to disagree more and more, and my control freak perfectionist had started to re-emerge in the process of planning the wedding and wanting to look perfect on my wedding day.

The first year of marriage was tough! I've heard it can be a challenging year for most newlyweds. Two grown adults, accustomed to living their individual lives their own way, coming together, trying to find balance as a couple. To make matters worse, we hadn't lived together until just before the wedding. I had never allowed him to be around me 24/7, to see the true depths of who I was. Despite falling in love and planning to marry, I had never completely let him in. I wonder if I had ever truly let anyone in. He fell in love with the Mary Poppins I had projected to the outside world, not the messed up crazy lady hiding within. To his absolute credit, he stood by me, and we are about to celebrate our 12th wedding anniversary.

It was touch and go there for a while, though. At one stage, I truly reached rock bottom, and a lesser man would've walked away. After our first child's birth, I hit an all-time high with my weight (it turns out giving birth doesn't mean the 30-40 kilos of weight gain doesn't magically disappear). Anxiety after a health scare early in the pregnancy saw me emotionally eat my way during the remainder of the pregnancy. I was sensible enough to know that my previous drastic measures to lose weight would be dangerous to the baby, but I felt helpless to control the constant food party, so the weight piled on (needless to say, I hadn't realised that extreme weight gain wasn't necessarily healthy for the baby either). As well as my increased size, I struggled to adapt to being a new mother; an unsettled baby and a control freak mother are a terrible combination. Being self-employed meant there was no maternity leave for me, especially with things going even further downhill between myself and my business partner. Overall, the perfect little world I'd created had come crashing down around me. I couldn't, and wouldn't let my husband in to support me, and to be honest, I don't think he was capable of supporting me at the time. He was still coming to terms with living with the complete antithesis of the woman he thought he married, a child he wasn't ready for, whilst dealing with his own immense grief at having recently lost his father.

I couldn't and wouldn't let anyone in to support me. To me, that meant letting other people see that I was a failure. It meant letting people see that I was anything less than perfect. I was scared I was at risk of letting the wall fall from around my heart that would allow people to see the real me inside, and it felt like once that wall was down, I wouldn't be able to build it back up again. So I reached out to the only place no-one would judge: God. I remember sitting in my car, after driving around for an hour to get my screaming baby to sleep, feeling at the very end of my coping skills. With tears streaming down my face, I cried out: "God, Buddha, whoever. I don't even know if you are real, but I need help. Please help. I can't do this anymore. PLEASE HELP!"

Here's the part of the story where I imagine you're expecting me to have heard some ethereal voice, to have been divinely guided to drag myself out of the depths of despair. It never came. There was absolutely nothing. Just the silence of a baby finally sleeping. To this day, I have never heard a voice or seen any sign of anything outside of myself.

What I did start to discover from that moment on was an inner strength. Until then, I had only been able to see one option to end the pain and suffering. I could now understand what drove people to do the unthinkable. I never truly reached the point myself, but it certainly crossed my mind more than once that all it would take was to hit the accelerator at the wrong time, going around a corner and over the edge of the cliff. I now knew the meaning of the phrase being pushed over the edge. But this would have gone against everything I'd ever known, it would let people see my pain, and it would also cause others immeasurable pain. No matter how much I was hurting, I could never willingly cause that pain on another human being, especially my family.

At that pivotal moment, I decided to wipe away my tears, take some deep breaths and find a way to keep going. Right then and there, something primal awoke within, a strength deep within my core, somewhere between my stomach and heart (something I've now come to learn is my Manipura, my Solar Plexus Chakra, the centre of self-confidence and inner fire). This inner strength kept me going.

The more I tapped into this deep strength, the more evident it became. Like a muscle growing stronger with use, so too did my inner strength. Over time, this inner strength became more like an internal compass, directing my choices and decisions, even my feelings.

Whenever I felt myself starting to dip back towards hopelessness, I knew there was something inside me—something stronger than anything the outside world could throw at me. Every day, I got stronger and stronger and was able to rebuild my relationship, my ability to be a parent, my career, and my overall health and wellbeing.

By the time my second child entered the world, I was hungry to learn more. I wasn't just content being a mum, a wife and a pharmacist. The inner fire that had awoken a few years earlier had been simmering away and pushing me to explore further.

INTUITIVE WISDOM

As a child, my mum used to get up early to do the family's ironing before the Queensland heat of the day set in. I used to love to get up early and sit with mum watching reruns of the tv program, Bewitched, whilst she diligently ironed. I believed this show was based on my family; in some parallel universe, this was us. My mum was Samantha, a modern-day witch, keeping her powers hidden from the conservative mortal world. It helped that my mum had a striking resemblance to Elizabeth Montgomery and my grandmother, the same sharp, dry wit as Endora. The missing piece of the puzzle was Tabatha. I looked nothing like her and I certainly didn't have any awakening magical powers of my own. No matter how much I wiggled my nose and wished from the depths of my heart, nothing appeared.

On the other hand, my mother had some kind of magic, some hidden skill she tapped into now and again. She had this uncanny ability to know things about people. Mum never spoke about it, she never flaunted it, but it was always something I knew existed. As I grew older, I associated it less with the witchcraft world of "Bewitched" and more of some gypsy ancestry that still lingered in my Mother's blood.

I still longed to be like her, yearned to have some special skill. To this day, I don't know if the desire to be special was a way of making up for my deep lack of self-love and confidence. Or perhaps it was that if I had some special skill, then I'd have more control over the world around me. There is also a possibility that I was experiencing an innate yearning to reconnect with my deepest self, my intuition.

Many say that we're all born intuitive, but as children, we're conditioned to switch it off and forget as we grow up and conform to society. In hindsight, I can see that I didn't switch off my intuition as a child; I just didn't understand what it was. My primary intuitive strength was that I was what many would call an empath, I had (and still have) the ability to feel and know other people's feelings and emotions. I could feel what was wrong with people. But I didn't realise that others couldn't, what I felt was my own normal, it was all I'd ever known. I also didn't realise that the over-whelming flood of emotions and pain I felt every day weren't mine alone. This sensi-tivity and awareness fuelled my pain and made me appear oversensitive when, in fact, this was, and still is, my intuitive superpower.

I had yearned for, longed, ached, to be psychic, magical, to have some supernat-ural power. If only I had known that that very thing that amplified my internal torture was the foundation of the exact thing I desired. This strength of feeling, seeing and truly understanding others, especially at the level of their health, was always there.

I can now also see that this led me towards the path of becoming a pharmacist. Unfortunately, that path was also the major roadblock that saw me totally and completely disconnect from my intuition. The demands of studying, my internal battle with control and perfection, pushed me further and further into my analytical brain and out of my heart space (the home of our intuitive wisdom). The more I studied and pushed myself down the path I thought would best help people, the further I strayed from my true strength that would help transform the lives of others.

Thank goodness for that rock bottom moment, sitting in my car with tears streaming down my face, and my son sleeping in his car seat in the back. Thank goodness I was pushed to the point that my analytical brain was ready to give up, making space for my heart's intuitive wisdom to break through.

Admittedly, it wasn't all rainbows and unicorns from that point on. Having immersed myself in the world of science and medicine, I felt like I had to have a foot in each world to move forward. One in the analytical world of facts and figures, and the other in a world I perceived as alternate, "out there" and something I kept as a hidden secret. It was only upon discovering the vast body of work behind the science of intuition and specifically quantum physics that I finally felt safe to allow the world to see the real me, as a woman, wife, mother, daughter and even a pharmacist, guided by intuition at every step. My intuitive wisdom guides everything I do. Even when dealing in the world of science and evidence-based medicine, I still always check in with my intuition. There is always something deeper and intuitive wisdom guides the way.

The single biggest lesson I've learnt is that everything happens for a reason. As cliche as it may sound, for me, this is the single defining truth around which everything is based. I am grateful for the painful times of desperate control, I am grateful for the years of study that numbed my intuition, and I'm so deeply grateful to have experienced my darkest moment. Every single second was instrumental in bringing me to today. Each step along the path was necessary to equip me with my unique combination of being an experienced healthcare professional and having extreme love, compassion and understanding for others through feeling their deepest truth as an empath. I now bring to the mix a pearl of intuitive wisdom that not only sees, feels and knows the truth, but also understands the ultimate truth of why things happen to people. I see how everything serves the greater good, just as my own pain and suffering served me.

All of my past experience has helped me become a medical intuitive, to fuse my medical background with the intuitive lens through which I now see the world. I help people to understand the wisdom within their own body, to learn to listen, and acknowledge the cues, and to understand the message hidden within. Sometimes these are subtle, like nagging thoughts in the back of the mind, or random symptoms that appear occasionally. Other times, it's a significant diagnosis, a monumental call to action, after years of ignored/misunderstood/un-noticed messages.

When I started actively nurturing and strengthening my intuition, I had grand delusions of healing the masses. I had hoped that I could unlock the single magic formula to healing. But the more I've learnt, the more I've realised that this is not my place, this is not my purpose. I have no right to cure someone. To do so would take the power away from another and rob them of the importance of their journey. Everything happens for a reason, and the journey of illness is not without its reasons.

My role is to support and guide, help translate the messages of our bodies wisdom, make the journey a great deal less bumpy, and help learn the lessons of ill health, a great deal faster than people otherwise would on their own. With me by their side, people no longer feel unafraid of their health, illness and the path ahead.

I speak the language of the body.

I translate the messages hidden within illness.

I help you see the reason this is happening. I help you see this as the catalyst for change to take you to bigger and better things. I hold your hand so you may walk the journey unafraid.

Every symptom is a message, a prompt to go within.

Every illness is a catalyst for change when subtle messages have been missed.

Learning to tune into the intuitive wisdom within each of us is the single most important step we can take to look after our health.

I have recently added End of Life Doula to my toolkit as the journey of health and healing doesn't always translate as physical healing. The greatest lessons and healing occur at a spiritual level. More often than not, this is reflected in physical healing, but sometimes, it's not. Coming to the end of life through illness does not mean the person has failed to heal. Caroline Myss said it best when she said: "healing is when the illness has no control over us anymore." We will all eventually come to the end of our life. When and how is just as much a part of the journey as the time spent living.

Our time on Earth is our story. Every plot twist, every roadblock, every paragraph of every chapter is just as significant as the next. Each one sets the scene to build into the following. They all help fill the pages of our book of life. No matter how short or long, painful or triumphant, your story is yours alone and it is unfolding exactly as it should.

ABOUT THE AUTHOR

Since childhood, Kelly Paardekooper dreamed of studying every modality possible to learn and understand health and healing from all perspectives, and then find its most profound truth.

Her dreams led her to study a Bachelor of Pharmacy, believing a pharmacist to be the most easily accessible health practitioner in the community, and be best placed to share her broader health perspective.

Her diligence at university and then focus on establishing a career, and then owning her own business, saw her dream of becoming a truly holistic expert, encompassing all modalities of health, fall away in the distance.

After having her first child and struggling to hold her perfectly constructed little world together, Kelly was forced inward to cope. Here she connected to her deepest truth, her intuition.

Since embracing her intuition as her guiding light, Kelly has come home to her original goal of viewing health and healing from a deeper perspective. Yet the need to study multiple modalities is no longer necessary as she now sees the truth is within us all.

Kelly now supports clients along their illness/wellness journey. As an intuitive health guide, using her unique combination of medical intuition and health transition doula, she guides clients to see that our bodies are always working in our favour. The pain and suffering we experience, occur when we reject or ignore the messages within.

Website: www.kellypaardekooper.com
Facebook: www.facebook.com/kellypaardekooperintuitive
Instagram: www.instagram.com/kellypaardekooperintuitive

KIT CAT

Welcome to your Camp Covid staycation, which has been extended indefinitely.

I t's 9 pm on the deserted island paradise of your dreams. My dog Charlie (Bali) is curled up on the couch next to me. Outside roads are turning into rivers as the rain pours. All-night torrential rain makes the scooter ride to the coffee shop in the morning an interesting adventure; with soggy shoes, as you *jalan jalan* through the pop-up rivers.

I asked myself a question yesterday: "Is 2021 starting out the way I had anticipated?" My immediate answer was HELL NO ... it's way better!

It wasn't always like this.

Eight years ago, I was depressed, anxiety-ridden, fighting in family law court, bankrupt, medicated, in therapy, struggling to get out of bed most days, and a single parent loathing her 8-6 job—which I felt was forced on me because being a working girl was not socially acceptable enough.

During this time, I had been searching for answers in all the wrong places, completely disconnected from the self and most definitely not connected to my intuition in any way. I was waging my one-woman war with the world, when really, what I would eventually uncover was that I was at war with myself. That war escalated; its peak was almost two years. It was horrible; I was horrible. My life then felt like being stuck on a horrendously nauseating ride at a fun park that I couldn't get off. My poor mum, my poor sisters, my daughter witnessed it. I don't need to mention friends because there were none. They ran like a "Flock of Seagulls" so far away.

Barrell of Monkeys, the game where you use a plastic monkey to link arms to pull another monkey out of the barrel, helped me talk myself off the ledge many times. When I struggled to see the light at the end of the tunnel—and there were times where there were no tunnels, just a maze of sadness—waterfalls of tears and unruly destructive behaviour. Barrell of Monkeys, the keyring edition (which I still have), gave me a mini project to focus on. Getting those 13 tiny monkeys out of that barrel helped stop the ruminations of the downward thought spirals. It allowed me space to remember that somewhere, somehow, there was a tiny seed repressed, this seed knew if it could just get out of *keeping up with the Jones-ville*, I might just be in with a chance, that there was a possibility that I could create something new, heal, rebuild and see something thrive. I had no idea what that was, and I had been searching for some 40 years. I had given it a crack a few times, but perceived failures meant giving up and returning to conformity and ultimate unhappiness.

Moving from Sydney to Perth cost me everything, at the same time, it saved me. That seed that I doubted and warred against stayed buried beneath all my layers of self-loathing. That seed dug deep and survived, knowing I had to go there where the sun sets over the ocean. For me, the joy of watching the sun sink beneath the horizon across the ocean that links us to distant lands is a reminder of joy-filled days spent in the sun, holidays. The beach is the country's outline standing as a reminder that the world is out there awaiting *adventure kitty*. I wanted to live my life like I was permanently on holiday. I mean, who doesn't?

It wasn't an overnight express bus to this dark period of my life; it was more like the preparation of puff pastry where events were layered one on top of the other, then pressed together, eventually forming a firm but buttery crust. I first remember a feeling of not belonging or being good enough when I was about 11. That feeling took a grip on my life, and unbeknownst to me, became the driver behind most of my decisions.

This belief was continuously fortified so that eventually I kept people at arm's length. Although it made me sad and angry and alone, I felt like a loaner. I kept it that way. I compartmentalised parts of me and denied people access. We all have secrets;

we all have walls. Aspects of my life, I have felt needed to remain clandestine to be "socially acceptable" to fit in. There are stories, chapters, a book's worth of Kit Cat's excellent miss adventures in an attempt to find the version of me that would stick. If I could talk to that girl now, I would hug her and let her know that this version of her she is trying on is not on the outside; it is a journey on the inside. I doubt that girl would have listened!

It is pretty hard to love yourself when your experience of self-discovery is thwarted by influential adults that want to mould you into socially acceptable mini them so that they feel better about themselves, instead of allowing and encouraging self-expression. In high school in the '80s, we would have the hems of our kilts measured to ensure we conformed to documented uniform standards. Nuns watched our every move. My act of rebellion in the uniform department was to wear my dad's Westpac work sweater, which was a delightfully wrong shade of navy blue with a fabulously prominent red stripe at the neckline. I am not sure how I got away with this for six years, and dad didn't notice that I had absconded with his sweater and demand it back.

We would then go from the discipline of one room where fear was the management tool to art class where we would be asked to be creative. Fear and creativity do not cohabitate well. Fear will scare off creativity and self-expression. Connection to your creative self requires self-love, confidence, knowing that you are safe and indeed welcome to express your inner creative genius. This connection effectively gets taught out of us at school. We aren't encouraged to become entrepreneurs or think freely; we are taught to conform and answer correctly. This frustrated me beyond belief. I regularly rebelled in very subtle ways like dying my hair, altering my school uniform, and spending more time at the gym and ballet class. I was a regular in the principal's office for fun misdemeanours. In my 5th year in high school, I told a bunch of teachers to fuck off in front of the entire school when they tried to discipline me for something that I was not involved in.

My frustration levels were so high I asked the school principal to make arrangements for me to attend a more creative school. My dad overruled my request, and I was stuck there for another two years.

I was not a bad kid. I was the *but why kid* that certainly didn't fit the private school girl mould. Just so you know, the entire school cheered for this outburst and the teachers let it go. My ripped-up disciplinary notes remained in the school file handed to my father when I graduated—which was thankfully not on the last day of school, because that day, I was suspended. That is another hilarious story. My rebellious moments make for excellent laughter-inducing memories. They also made me think on my feet and honed my abilities creatively problem solve in the blink of an eye. I still swear but am more considered when I do.

These experiences were not new to me. When I was in primary school, I had my first business, heavily influenced by the stylish, timeless beauty of Olivia Newton-John in Xanadu. I started making feathery hair combs. They were super cool with leather and glitter beads that hung the feathers down into hair (it's easy to find the clip version of these today in the unicorn section of the kids' department). This business was promptly shut down by the school principal as she uncovered my order taking process for my bespoke designs, that my friends were requesting and happily paying for with their lunch and pocket money, in the playground at recess.

Challenges continue to arise when you feel like you just don't fit in. Your sense of belonging is challenged, and your experience of growing up includes being berated by your peers for being up yourself at the faintest sign of self-love or self-care. Perhaps you were caught looking at yourself in the mirror for a second too long. That always got a group laugh when someone would yell, "You are never going to be beautiful enough anyway, so just give up." Or occasions when you put on your favourite Faberge jeans,your were told not to because you are going to get raped. God, how I loved those jeans, but they actually were called my rape jeans. The thought of rape terrified me as I wriggled into those suckers. Maybe it's that time you were told your body shape was just all wrong for a ballet dancer, so you didn't belong and your hair colour was blonde (apparently there was a 'no blonde ballerina phase'). Your parents separate, and you start to question where it is you do belong. Bold confidence developed as a mask to hide all the stuff I couldn't share, and the compartmentalising began.

I was super fit. My outward confidence improved like a turtle growing into its shell, but my *look you in the eye* brilliance took a dive. I was already prepared for harsh judgement, so I retreated before anyone had a chance to come close. This method of operation stayed in play until I started working on my inner journey in earnest—a journey I didn't know I would go on until much later in my adult life, thanks to making weird shapes on a rubber rectangle while trying to breathe and not vomit in a *Bikrim* hot room.

My life has taken so many random adventures. I always approached everything that I did with a can-do attitude—even when I had no idea, I would just learn on the way, using those early developed problem-solving skills. This has enabled me to go on many career adventures. I realised early on that I was project orientated, but I would NEVER admit this to an employer as it would be a clear indicator that my tenure would be short. Personality and psych profiles always revealed an independent free thinker, problem solver, and non-conformist, most likely to do my own thing. Not exactly your dream team member. If I could get in and creatively problem-solve like a "Ms fix it," it was all good. It also meant that I would get bored or ambitious after this phase, so I would look for my next adventure.

There was a longing to succeed for myself. I just lacked the courage because I was supposed to have all this other stuff and working for yourself meant risking not having all that. I was a regular recipient of the "most businesses fail in the first two years" lecture and the "buy a house, get yourself financially set up then do what you want" lecture. I hated the second lecture; buying a home meant that I would be married to a bank for potentially 30 years, and I just couldn't. Then there was all the other right stuff—the car, the holidays, kids in the right school, the right shoes, hand-bags and outfits, and husband.

So I kept going, trying on one job then the next, knowing they might be fun but never a forever gig. Because were we not told we needed a career? I wasn't sure when I would get one of those. I just wanted work to be fun! One time I was a Project Manager in a telecommunication's startup. An ex-boss who understood my skillset (which is why I managed to stay working for him for years) hired me. He knew me as a go-getter that solved problems and led and managed large teams. So I joined him to help solve some problems. When the project was delivered, the CEO asked me what I would like to do next. I said that I would love to join the marketing team. Her response was, "I don't mean to be rude but you don't have an MBA, so you can't join that team." I had just redesigned all their labelling and packaging, the drop ship services (this was the mid 90's) solidified their sales process, built relationships with suppliers to ensure our pricing remained competitive, so I was pretty certain I did fit. Impatient and offended, I resigned immediately and took a role at a competitor in their marketing team as a Brand/ Product Manager. When people tell me *no*, I find a way to make it possible. This is one example of a recurring theme.

Here is another from my hospitality career: not the hilarious story of the coke machine repair guy falling through the roof to a table of guests eating in the restaurant, or the one where I arm wrestle a fence jumper and give him a wedgie, or get a broken bottle held at my throat, or the story where I have a drugged up twit think he can fly off the roof of a venue; he survived. I am certain it was because he was high *AF*. A career in socially antisocial hospitality is the source of excellent dinner party stories that you never get to tell at a dinner party because you are always working when other people are eating out and having fun. I look back and ask if it was just another chance to hide from people behind a work mask so they never got to know the real me. If I keep you at a distance, then you won't have the chance to hate me as much as I hate me. Phew, I am safe.

I digress. This story occurs after being burned a few times by senior male executives in hospitality who think that they can work younger female managers to the bone and underpay them in the name of training. While our male equivalents get a posse together out the back dock, smoking during the dinner rush whilst being paid triple your salary. My last role in that overworked, underpaid period ended like this: I saw my job advertised in the paper for those Gen Y'ers. It was before the internet. Bold defiant connected Kitty orchestrated a meeting with restaurants owner (They had 12 restaurants).

Me: "I would like to apply for the job that was advertised in the paper."

Owner: (laughing)"You are already doing that job."

Me: "then I respectfully request a pay rise to match the advertised salary." I was earning $23K/year. The man's version of my job was being advertised at $55K/year.

Owner: "No."

Me: "Ok, I resign."

Owner: "I don't accept your resignation."

Me: (laughing) "Then pay me what I am worth!"

Owner: (with an arrogance that defied belief) "No!" Silently I slid my keys across the table to him. He slid my keys back

Owner: "You can't resign you are the best restaurant manager that we have."

Me: "Then pay me like I am!"

Owner "No, I can't"

I slid my keys across the table and walked out.

Unemployed, I ate Mexican spicy beans and potato; very different from my management perk of eat what every I wanted from the menu. When I landed a new job two weeks later, I heaved a sigh of relief and picked up my company car and petrol card. Most of the sales reps I had met previously always turned up to the restaurant at the most inopportune times and didn't seem to really want to listen So, I was pretty confident that I could better, and I did. I quickly became the top sales-person in our branch. I am quite good at making friends and having a chat. The boss saw the inner Kitty goodness, and took me to telco land.

Chameleon. Creative. Problem solver.

These 50 years' worth of stories are mine, I own them and now live happily with them. They have been good, bad occasionally, a little questionable with a dash of chaos, and more than usually a strong rebellious streak, with a dash of Louis Vuitton and Roberto Cavalli, for good measure. In spite of all my misadventures, my family and friends really love, support and know me. I once went on a work adventure that I took a long time to own and share as part of my story, fearful that I would be pushed further away from people that cared even with my compartmentalisation and puff pastry layers for protection. I share this story now.

One day I made a sales call to a massage parlour that used our services. To be honest, there were not many businesses that didn't need us. I was selling sanitary bins —women are everywhere, periods happen all the time. Periods have long been a normalised topic of discussion with me after ballet and aerobics gym locker rooms. When attending appointments with potential clients, the male owners would even-tually beg me not to say the "P-word" and ask me where they needed to sign. One day, my presence nearly caused a riot in a factory as women marched me to the office and demanded that the factory manager put sanitary bins in their toilets, to replace the built-in incinerators that often set off the fire alarm and caused much embarrass-ment when the fire brigade turned up. Nothing like a fire engine with all red lights flashing and sirens blaring arriving at workplace announcing that you are menstru-ating to the rest of your colleagues.

Any-who, back to this massage parlour: the bloke/ pimp/ guy in charge of girls— I am actually not sure what I would ever write on his job description, but it had a lot of ego involved. He told me I was hot and that I would make a lot of coin doing massage, and that I should give it ago. I was making a fair whack of coin so my ego let out an auto laugh and said thanks for the compliment, but no thanks. A week later I nervously knocked on the dirty "staff only" back door, curious and *curiouser*. What the fuck was a private-school-educated polygot who has been to college, lived over-seas and was by all accounts reasonably articulate and successful doing here? She was single curious, and loved the idea of extra cash. It would totally fit in with my cash saving travel plans.

Sexy-black-lace-lingerie-clad, I find myself doing a "trial massage." What the *eff* even is that? Where is Fairwork?? A not-so-naive Kitty would have hit him up for some cash, especially because they didn't tell me the bit about the mandatory provision of the happy ending, which was a surprise he waited to gift me at the end of the massage, almost like a dare. Ah, that's what the sanitary bins were for, as well; dual purpose *whoda thunked it*? Such responsible waste disposal in the sex industry.

Massage parlour pimps don't ask for references; they defiantly pay a higher hourly rate than any hospitality job. It certainly beats part time pulling beers for drunks who don't tip now three evenings a week. Instead of working at the pub, I worked at the massage parlour. I was definitely pulling tips, *ha-ha-ha*. I know you thought I was going write cocks ... but ladies and gents I remain classy.

The other girls were nice, some younger than me, another couple were older, read slightly more jaded, and had regular clients on regular days. It was their full-time job. I had determined it was never going be my full-time job. We got to wear sexy lingerie and talk a lot of girly stuff, which was quite fun after working in super male dominated hospitality industry and being out on the road by yourself in your company car. The conversation was educational and often just belly-laugh-roll-on-the-floor hilarious. One girl used the between-client time for studying. We snacked a lot through the boredom of waiting for clients, drank a bit of wine. No one was ever drunk, merry maybe but not drunk. Also there were no drugs present, that I witnessed. Seeing three clients a night was three hours work which gifted you $300, plus tips. I soon worked out that girls had regular clients because they performed extras. What's an extra you ask? Well, anything beyond a massage and a happy ending really... and it was up to the girls to make up their own prices. I am pretty certain some of the girls did full service (i.e. had sex) amongst other things, no judgement, but I did not.

Quickly, this became a familiar routine work: go to the gym, go massage for a few shifts a week equals *Kitty had some pretty good disposable cash money*. Enter pole dancing. Pole was just getting a leg up at about this time and the first Bobbies pole studio had opened in Sydney. I thought that would be fun diversion from my other fitness activities, whilst teaching me some sexy moves that might enhance my tip earning potential in the massage parlour. I would learn it was also about confidence, showmanship, self-love, self-empowerment, life lessons that I had learned but were compartmentalised and only available to some of the people some of the time.

Already the proud owner of *hooker shoes*, a mandatory masseuse wardrobe item.

Mine were hot pink Perspex with clear straps. I secretly loved them; they made you strut. You couldn't help but find your inner goddess. I also had a reasonable collection of aerobics gear that I could mix and match with my sexy lingerie, so no issues in the wardrobe department. The shoes and the outfits were a prerequisite for pole dancing. They got you in sexy mode. Perhaps I was being universally directed to the pole?

Pole dancing is not an easy game; its freaking hard work. Being an aerobics instructor and dancer, I loved the pole. It added all these other dimensions and relearning to hang upside down was childlike, like swinging on an adult monkey bar. Other lessons surfaced including; what it meant to be feminine, yet strong. It was empowering, with a spirited sense of *fuck you independence*. I super liked the rebellious aspect; you could feel the naughtiness in the air. The super woman body strength required is phenomenal, the bruises on your hips not to mention inner thigh markings are unpleasant and akin to getting a Chinese burn on your forearm when you were a kid. Pretty sure you are not allowed to call it that anymore. Anybody who knows, please comment with the PC term for inflicting this pain below. Being pretty fit and flexible, I took to that pole like dick to pussy. Bugger, I meant a duck to water.

The sexy stuff was harder for me to do. You see, I am not really an exhibitionist. I know that sounds contradictory based on the facts that I bounced around in barely their skin-tight lycra, bopping along with my Madonna headset teaching an aerobics class, and that I got naked three nights a week, giving massages for my travel fund. But there was something about trying to connect deeply to that inner feminine sexy power that ground me to a halt, like a deer in the headlights, a little inhibited. Mostly when I felt this way, I would mask it by cracking a joke and laughing it off.

Months into this routine, I was asked if I had considered dancing in a club. I was like, "ah, um, ah." Is massage like a gateway drug to further explorations of questionable habit holes? I think the answer might be *yes*. My first reaction, aka my intuition was, "I am not a stripper." I was definitely not a stripper, which seemed so at odds with the fact that I massaged naked for cash, one might think. The difference was public display, versus the intimacy of personal connection. There was a show on and I was invited to go and watch. It was an exhibition of pole dancing, an amazing display of professional dancers' skills and showmanship. They were super fit show girls. I was a little nervous about being seen in a gentleman's club. I checked my thoughts and laughed at myself considering my being up a pole and naked massaging accounted for four nights of my weekly schedule. Fascinated, I went.

The club was a daunting smoky underground cavern that looked glam at night, but no doubt looked haggard in the light of day, which thankfully it never saw. You could feel the pulse of Sydney after dark. Everyone in there had crossed some other line and detoured down this rabbit hole, sequestered on their own clandestine adventure. The performances were exceptional. These girls were in a league of their own; they were competitive, pole dancing champions. Pole was still pretty shady and certainly did not have the mainstream sports like acceptability that it has today. It was apparent these girls were athletes—scantily clad, super strong, confident, sexy athletes. They were stone cold sober, competing for titles and tips in their chosen sport where the competition just happened to be held in a strip club. Of course, this was not the average pole-girl story; these showgirls were the elite.

Though I am not an exhibitionist, I am a performer. There is a difference from being part of a group performance. Exhibitionists want your sole attention. As part of a dance troupe, you have a role to play, a responsibility to the collective., you are story telling together. Maybe I could give this a go. If these showgirls could treat it like a sport then perhaps so could I. But they were different. They embraced their feminine strength and gave zero fucks—where I was still building and occasionally attempting to dismantle the great puff pastry wall of Kit Cat. There was no way, first time round, that I would command the audience as they did. Did they start out small in shitty clubs to hone their skills? Yes. Yes, they did, so off I strutted in my high heels, after my massage shift into those shitty clubs, to ask if there was any work. so naïve, there is always work for new girls, aka: fresh meat.

The first time I ever went out on the pole in public was in Kings Cross, in Sydney's Eastern Suburbs. The Cross was the heart of club land and late nights before lock outs and curfews, and it was every bit as seedy as you would imagine—actually probably worse. I lived in Surry Hills, the suburb right next door. This den of iniquity/workplace even fitted in with my *don't live further than 5 minutes for work* rule (because, I knew that driving in traffic caused me maximum anxiety). I parked in the car park about two minutes from the club in a multi-story car park. My allocated shift time was between 11 pm and 6 am, and I was peeing my pants with nervous anticipation. That was until I walked up the stairwell and was quickly brought back to reality by a human shit in the corner of the stairs. OMG, was this what I was about to face? The shit in the stairwell crowd?

Down the stairs, into the den, double down den of extra iniquity, it was a house half full. I was nervous AF. During my shifts at the massage parlour, I had been playing with the art of fake eyelash application, alongside a glittery collection of eyeshadows that helped me create a semi disguise. This disguise would require applying this evening. Fingers crossed, it would be an opportunity to breathe and calm my nerves, hoping I didn't poke my eye out with the applicator. Also, bless the bartender, a shot of tequila was offered and I went for seconds. I should have got a wig; maybe I could have adopted an entirely different persona, not just a new faux stripper name. I don't remember the other girls. I think I was just too bloody nervous.

Unfortunately, I didn't poke my eye out, so backstage, shitting bricks, about get half naked and swing sexy style around the pole for cash. The financial *sitch* is this: you don't get an hourly rate or an appearance fee, you get stripper dollars that you exchange at the end of your shift for real dollars, which incidentally could actually be just dollars, not $100 dollar bills, as Fiddi Cent would have you believe. If you perform well on the stage and get some soggy stripper dollars, you could exchange them for some waterproof pineapples (Australian slang for our $50 note). Perhaps you catch the eye of a would-be suitor and you get booked for a private dance, which is where the money is. It's supposed to be 'no touching' but who really knows what goes on behind the shabby velvet curtains, where real pineapples might be in play? There is a rule in NSW: you can't flash your lady garden in full so that's good news, right?

It's well before midnight and I am, first time in public, up that pole attempting, I think unsuccessfully, to play the role of sexy stripper. I bust some moves, there is nothing comfortable about this. I am not comfortable in public up a pole. It feels like that scene in flash dance where Jeanie fails as an ice skater and becomes a stripper; I am Jeanie. Unfortunately, not my preferred character as played by Jennifer Beals, the amazing stripper/ professional dancer, Alex. I am so relieved when I am allowed off that pole. I have received a tip—this is good. I've been booked for a lap dance, so that's good. It's not an entire waste of time. I go back to the girls' locker room to look myself in my sexy stripper eyes and check my disguise. I don't get long to do my repaint as you are then required to work the crowd for extra Tina Turner Private Dancer moments, until it's my turn to get sexy up the pole again. This cycle repeats itself five times into the wee hours of the morning.

It's 6 am. I have exchanged my stripper dollars for $500 in cash afteer paying *a cut to the house. The sun is rising, and I am finally released from this alternate stripper universe. I am exhausted. I stink of sweat and cigarette smoke. The sweat is mine the cigarette stink is not This shift has taught me to bath with baby wipes. Just like in any hospitality gig smokers get those extra breaks because their nicotine addiction. It's some sort of license to wag and still get paid. I am reminded, as I head into the stairwell that I have to walk past human faeces. It was the moment that I realised I would be a way better working girl than a stripper.*

This was my first shift, there were a few more because I wanted to see if I this was first-time nerves or I'd develop the skills set. I didn't. The feeling of being so naked and so public was so very uncomfortable. Some girls relished it and were amazing; me, not so much. You would think that the natural course of action here would be to turn to drugs to get through the shift. Well, that was not my answer. I just didn't go back.

A few years later, I had just broken up again with my on-and-off boyfriend of five years, so as further punishment for him never being with me again, I was going to go work in a brothel. My logic was that if I am going to get used by him for sex, then I may as well make money "doing it." Also, I had danced half naked up a pole, surely this would be a cake walk. I went and looked at a few brothels. I picked one that wasn't a sad, stinky den of disarray and drugged-up girls. A sober, leggy blonde was an easy hire for a brothel, so it was a case of walk in and get the job. The challenge was the other girls; I was on their territory, and they knew most fresh meat didn't last so they took bets on how long I would last.

My first client was a Chinese taxi driver. I won't lie, I was nervous and shaky—the whole episode from shower to shag (if you could call it that), and back to shower lasted 6.3 minutes, I made $250. He also tipped me for being "New Girl."

I grew some lady balls on that day and started to take back control of my life. Working when I wanted to and doing things almost on my own terms. This was the beginning of finding my way back to me. It taught me so many lessons. I leaned in and learned things from the men I met, who shared stories about anything and every-thing. I called it the naked truth—the stories you get when there are no barriers sepa-rating you from one another. I finally felt a sense of belonging everywhere and nowhere at all doing my thing on my own. As a working girl, I had a persona and a name, but I attended those bookings as me, not lies and fictitious stories. There were plenty of adventures and there are so many amazing stories—too many to fit in these brief pages. I enjoyed my time as a working girl, I will never regret it, it was a choice that I made not one made under duress. I wanted to go on these adventures.

The end of my working girl career came about because Family Law Court. The court's employees and opposing council view working girls with dangerous sweeps of side eye and mistrust and a lot of *tsk tsking*—you know the noise that is supposed to make you swim in the shame pool. They protect themselves, with many of the facilitators playing in this arena not wanting to be caught out on their clandestine assignations. That and age-old social stigma that prostitutes' are workers on the dark side, from the wrong side of town, bad girls doing a sad job. Its all untrue. Like me, many of these girls were single mums who actually were there before and after school to pick up their kids. We didn't work 60 hours a week to make ends meet. We went to the school events. We loved our work! Some were girls studying, some just happy with their garden at home and a cat. Some religious beliefs share the message that the work is "wrong" there is a lingering belief that most working girls are drug or alcohol addicted. This is, in my experience at least, was not true. Never mind the reduction in rape statistics due to the provision of the service, layer on top of that, unwanted pregnancies and terminations improving the mental health of women and men. Look, this work is not for everyone, there are so many discussion points. Family Law Court literally demanded I walk away from the work of my choice, give up my freedoms and flexibility and return to the inner-city beehives so that I could appear *normal*, and there for a better, more acceptable, easier to measure member of society. I would NEVER fit that mould. What it made me was a depressed, anxiety ridden, financially bankrupt, medicated, in therapy, struggling to get out of bed most days, a single parent hating her 8-6 job, which I felt was forced on me because being a working girl was not socially acceptable enough. Therefore, I was not good enough.

When I was a kid, my dad used to drag my sisters and I to Amway meetings—big stadium sized meetings where 1000s of people were being told how they could rebuild their lives selling Amway branded product. I was the *but why* kid at school... So I was the *but why* kid here too. My internal dialogue was, "*sooooo*, you're telling me I can choose how I want to live my life, but you're telling me I have to live it this exact way... then that doesn't really work for me either." However, I saw some amazing speakers that said things that stayed with me. I was 17 when I first heard, "Get rid of what you don't want to make room for what you do." I was 47 when that statement showed up with meaning and gained momentum changing my life.

I learned about goal setting. My first and probably only goal that I ever wrote back then was, "I want to retire when I am 50, so that I can be where I want to be, when I want to be there." When I tuned 50, I realised I was doing exactly that. Mum always said, "Be careful what you wish for!"

These two small sentences, combined with a life in yoga amounted to massive life changes in my 48th year on the planet. I finally leaned into me, connected to my place of self-acceptance, self-love my place of joy and happiness.

That little seed was my intuition. It never went away; it was just buried. It took yoga, asana meditation, and self-study to allow it to find light, water, bust out, and bloom.

Your life is always an adventure that takes you on a journey to another adventure.

I think it's why self-love is such a big component of my coaching today... but fear not! I am far gentler than to force you up a pole or into a massage parlour!

Peas, love & mung beans
xxxkit

ABOUT THE AUTHOR

Kit Cat is a mother, daughter, sister, friend, lover of food & the ocean and fur mum to Charlie who often features in her yoga tutorials and posts. She currently lives in Bali the deserted tropical Island of your dreams and luckily her dreams too!! She recently opened @omiesbali vegetarian café by the beach in Seminyak.

From this yoga lover's paradise, she helps new to the rubber rectangle yogis develop a sustainable yoga practice one breath at a time. Helping them to find more joy & happiness

It wasn't always quite this idyllic. She was a kitty of chaos and her life was more like a series of excellent miss adventures layered over the ups & downs of anxiety and depression as she made her way.

In and amongst this list of career adventures kit went down a fascinating rabbit hole that found her massaging in a "after hours" parlour, pole dancing & stripping in gentlemen's club's which was not really her cup of tea. Eventually becoming an escort, a job that she loved and calls "The Naked Truth."

Today she is living her life by design having finally found more joy & happiness than she ever thought possible! This is why she coaches her clients to find the same through her teaching, online trainings and one on one coaching and mentoring program where you learn to get rid of limiting beliefs and create the life that you have always dreamed of. Give kit a call she makes learning about a life in yoga doable & fun!

Facebook: www.facebook.com/kitcatcahill
Instagram: www.instagram.com/perfectly_imperfectyogis
Website: www.perfectlyimperfectyogis.com

KRISTEN MCDONALD

I could see branches and leaves being thrown about in the violent wind. The sky had turned an eerie yellow-green. My family was frantically preparing for an oncoming tornado. At that time, we lived in a mobile home. The final and quick decision was for everyone to lay on top of each other in the most secure place. I was three years old and at the bottom of the people heap. It was thought I had the greatest chance of being swept away by this grey whirling beast coming our way.

My first memory was of a frightening and chaotic situation; a destructive force out of control. We were barely missed that day, but our neighbor's farm did not fare as well. All the horses that I gave sugar cubes to in the morning were gone in an instant. The entire landscape was torn and mangled. Little did I know this would become a reoccurring theme in my life. As a child, I did not have a choice. I had to survive the heartbreaking and at-times terrifying circumstances that intermittently plagued my family and me. As a child, I also experienced wonderment and joy beyond words. Hanging onto these moments kept me grounded and my internal world safe.

During these early days, I recall my mother sobbing as she drove myself and my two older sisters late in the night searching for her new husband, our stepfather. He would be missing for days. I can still hear the song Summer Breeze by Seals and Croft

143

playing on the car radio. He would be found at a local tavern. Eventually arriving home, he would physically tear through the backdoor. This would lead to all night arguments and the sound of fragile objects smashing. Along with them, any sense of security and safety in us, the children. We lived with my grandparents on and off in my earliest years. They were such a blessing, my rock when I small. I recall the smell of country air and homemade cooking. The feeling of peace, knowing someone who loved me and could keep me safe was there.

Initially, I would hide when my stepfather came home. Finally, salvation had come in the way of Alcoholics Anonymous. My stepfather completed the AA steps and started his own business which did very well. My mom did his bookkeeping and was a big part of running the business. We felt the comfort that comes from being a part of a community and local church family. Our family was doing well financially. We had numerous vehicles, travelled often, and had someone to clean our home and take care of the yard. It brought a superficial sense of contentment.

Gradually I learned to trust hiI would sit on his lap every Sunday morning. I recall the different flecks of green and yellow in his brown eyes that I would stare into as I would listen to his fantastic stories of times in the Navy and many other colorful tales. I enjoyed watching him shave. Where or who my biological father was, I was unsure. My mom did not refer to her first husband as my dad, though I logically assumed he was. My origins did not entirely make sense, but neither did many things in my childhood. Occasionally I would find my mom crying. She would tell me she was thinking of my dad. She always described her first husband as an abusive and cruel man. My mother's overwhelming feelings and emotional energy were admittedly too much for me, and I did not question her. I accepted my stepfather as my father during this time.

Some battles still woke us in the middle of the night throughout our childhood, but at least now there was not the drunkenness of my stepfather that brought things entirely out of control level. There would be talk of divorce, and my siblings and I wished it would finally happen to end the sleepless madness. My mom finally stopped pleading for the attention and interest of this detached man. She started sleeping more often and became quite irritable when awake. This would be followed by late nights of painting magnificent pictures which she would say my father inspired. She was an artist. These paintings would become the basis for income in later years when times became tight. To say my mother was overprotective is an understatement. We were incredibly restricted in all our activities. She had lost an infant daughter before I was born and the rawness of that grief never subsided, it turned into constant and disproportionate worry for the children still alive.

My mom was hospitalized for nearly a month when I was four years old. We were told she was diagnosed with Multiple Sclerosis. I stayed with strangers my parents had met in the AA family during this time. I missed my mom but enjoyed this family immensely. I stayed with them during the days my sisters were at school and sometimes into the evenings. This family enjoyed time and activities together. The children would delight in showing me treasures in their room and playing games. When they returned me to my home the final time, I became hysterical, grasping the upholstery and anything I could to prevent being pulled out of the car. Desperately sobbing and pleading, I of course lost in the end. It gave me a feeling of how life could and should b,e which I cherish to this day.

I was guided through my childhood with an intuitive sense and an inner voice that saved my life on more than one occasion. This sense was an accessible vessel of hope. I know without question there is an unconditionally loving presence always with me, with all of us. I can feel and sense it. For a profound moment, I saw it in the form of a beautiful angel gazing at me in my bed. To be honest, it made my heart beat out of my chest in fear. Without moving their lips, they said, "don't be afraid." I then felt instant peace. I revisit this sense of knowing when this world gets to be over-whelming. It is an anchor of peace when I need it most.

My mom had a strong spiritual side. She also had a contagious laugh and a robust sense of humor. She listened with great interest in my stories of wonderment. My mom also had a terrifying rage-based side. Her words could be cruel enough to pierce you more painfully than a knife. She often spoke of a corrupt and evil world that was always on the verge of ending. My experience in the world outside of my home did not feel as dangerous as my mother's out of control fears and occasional behaviors. I realized it felt good to be a part of the world I was warned all my life to fear.

My first-grade teacher, a young nun, took me under her wing. She would take me to the park, and I loved every moment with her. She kept in contact with me after moving away that year and begged me to continue writing. When I was in fifth grade, I stopped writing; I was too filled with shame and guilt. I had walled myself off from the world after my stepfather had molested me. I felt utterly alone. The most unfortunate part of being a victim is somehow you take on the guilt and shame of your perpetrator—especially one who vehemently and convincedly denies any wrongdoing.

It was terrifying when the positive energies I used to sense felt like intense darkness had taken them over. I had night terrors and finally was able to stop dreaming altogether, or at least stop remembering my dreams. I prayed and begged Jesus and God to protect me from these demons I could now feel around me. The negative vibrations of the emotional and sexual abuse taking place in our home caused this spiritual distress. One day I felt a calling to go outside. There was a beautiful rainbow directly over our house. I called my family to come see it with me. It felt like a miracle, a message God was still with us. What a delight to behold and give us hope.

My stepfather went to jail the month I began fifth grade. My mom soon started dating a man she had known before marrying her former husband. We were soon moving into a 100-year-old home in ill repair and infested with mice, ants, and squirrels. A drastic change from prior living conditions, we had lost everything. I changed to a public school after going to a catholic one previously and now received free lunch. There were so many changes. I remember the boxes of food, government bricks of cheese that did not quite look like cheese.

My mom became pregnant, and we were all in joyful anticipation. A year from the night my middle sister came forward with the horrors we had endured at the hands of my stepfather, we had a new brother. Less than 18 months later, we also had a new sister. The joy in our home was because of them, and I am so grateful for them both. It may in part have been post-partum depression in addition to a chronic mood and personality disorder that contributed to the years that followed. I have spent too much time intellectualizing to understand and get into my head as my heart was too painful.

During this time, I felt like I was now in the middle of that tornado that narrowly missed us years ago. I felt ganged up on. At one point, my older sisters thought it was funny to tackle me and duct tape me to a chair. I stayed that way until my mother came home later that evening. I was ten years old and had just experienced my body violated, and trust destroyed a month prior, this was devastating and terrifying. I was a traumatized mess, and no one had the patience or time for it. My mom made it clear I was too much for her and asked if I wanted to go to a foster home. I felt too ashamed and damaged to spend time with my grandparents. My soul felt as though it had been permanently scarred.

My mother took me to a counselor. I described to him the irrational and frightening rages my mother would have; how I felt defective. I described the disdain my sisters felt for me. I felt unwanted, unlovable and was in desperate pain. This man told me I was exaggerating about the severity of my mother's rages and home situation. She presented as very calm and put together at our appointments and nothing like what I described. It was like torture having to go see that man for the rest of the summer. I do not recall feeling any empathy or understanding. I did not believe it possible, but I felt worse.

I am grateful for a friend I made in school that year. Spending time, having fun the way normal sixth graders do reset my spirit. It was like when you can completely distract a sobbing infant and make them roar with laughter. I recall during these times making a mental note of how I wanted my life to feel. How once I was free, I would create a life and world that resembled that of the people and situations that brought me joy growing up. I felt like I was living a sentence until I was eighteen. The wonderful friends I made in school created a healthy temporary escape, as did the copious books I escaped into. I still have dreams I am back in my childhood bedroom, counting the days until I graduated and could start to really live.

Home life was crazy, unstable and chaotic. I never knew what my mom's mood would be. At times during my childhood, I felt complete adoration, understanding and love. She could have the most amazing, creative and intelligent perspectives. I tried to carefully behave in a way that would draw this side out of my mom. She was an extremely wounded and oversensitive person. I did not understand the extent until I was much older. Unfortunately, all her profound losses and traumas were not healed and came out in powerful and destructive ways. Sometimes without much forewarning.

During this time, there were five mysterious murders and disappearances in our county within seven years. A room in our home became filled with maps, frightening symbols and numerous newspaper clippings. Boxes of evidence my mom had become obsessed with formulating. She believed my former stepfather was involved in a satanic cult. She was intent on bringing justice. It was the most frightening time of my life. This became our world while I was in middle school and early high school. The babysitting jobs I relied on to buy clothes were cancelled as my mom was certain I would be killed. My mom believed most outside of our family unit were the enemy; at times, those in the family became the enemy.

My mother was a brilliant storyteller, and she believed her stories wholeheartedly making them so convincing and appealing. A private detective hired by one of the murder victim's family believed the possibility of some of my mom's stories. She was able to show cryptic codes she would find in the newspaper and Plat books. Letters and numbers had different meanings. Huge motion sensor lights were placed all over the yard to warn of intruders. At times, the adults would stay up at night with guns to protect our family from this cult coming to murder us. I recall having to have a bag packed in case we had to escape in the night. My mom bugged the phone, our conversations recorded on a cassette recorder connected and hidden under the basement steps. There were sensor mats placed under our carpeting throughout the house which would set off an alarm if stepped on in the night.

My mind was filled with terror, and it was difficult to be in the moment with friends. They had no idea what faced me at home, and it was nothing I could share and still be a normal teenager trying to fit in. I recall being teased about being "Spacey." My mind was on survival tactics, and the possibility people were out to kill my family and me. I had to have a physical for school around this time, and my blood pressure was dangerously high. A part of my mind realized I needed to detach for my own health and wellbeing. I became more a part of the world and less a part of my family. I finally realized my mom was delusional and out of control.

The story made the local nightly news. I recall the song Private Eyes by Hall and Oats playing in the background of the news clip. On the news and in the newspaper, the Sherriff stated this story's source needed to be considered, and this information should "be taken with a grain of salt." There was a slow shift after this. The maps and information on satanic cults came down. The room gradually transitioned into a typical office space. There was always an undercurrent of conspiracy theories of local corruption and supernatural darkness that would invade the conversations in later years, but the emphasis on the murderous satanic cult had passed.

In my junior year of high school, I was finally healing and focused on my life and my future. My history teacher had taken favor with me. He set up a day for me to go to the State University and tour with his friend, a meteorology program professor. Meteorology had become my interest and passion. I was gaining confidence and found my voice that had been silenced most of my childhood. I was having a blast with a great group of friends. I started dating a young man, and we spent every moment together. We enjoyed sharing meals, fishing, tromping through the woods.

A month after he graduated high school, I was pregnant, and I still had a year of high school left. We were so scared and overwhelmed. I had to tell my mom. I engaged her in an authentic conversation. During this conversation, she shared with me who my actual biological father was and that he had died when I was a little over a year old. She said they were deeply in love, but each in toxic marriages to someone else. He was the first man to tell her she was beautiful. He had aspired to become a meteorologist until circumstances forced him to take a different path. She said he was preparing to be with her and me when he suddenly died of a heart attack. I was now shocked and overwhelmed by not only my own sudden motherhood at seventeen but of my origins.

Despite my mother's advice to avoid embarrassment and get a GED, I was determined to graduate. I worked out a plan to graduate a semester early. I would have enough credits if I took art class instead of lunch. Being pregnant while in high school brought flooding back all those feelings of shame and guilt. I would redirect these thoughts to the beautiful melodic heart tone I had heard within me. I became engaged in an educational support group for teen parents given by our school nurse. I have had so many beautiful souls come into my life at the perfect and most needed time. Nurse Ann has been a guiding support and mentor to me since I was seventeen. Her non-judgmental way and grounded advice helped me recreate my life. I would not be a nurse or who I am today if not for her. It was through this group I also met my lifelong friend. She and I have been through so many trials and triumphs. She taught me to laugh at myself and the world. My grade school friend's mom also provided generous support as she had been a teenage mom herself. She instilled the confidence I would not have had otherwise.

On April 1st, I gave birth to a beautiful eleven-pound boy. Being April Fool's day, everyone thought we were joking when we called to make the grand announcement. As I held him in my arms, I felt a rush of unconditional love and warmth that I had never known. It was almost too much for my body to contain. I would give up my life for this child. I suddenly felt a greater sense of purpose. I needed to give all I had available within me. I was further blessed by my beautiful daughter nine years later and second son twenty years and twenty days after the birth of my first. Seeing my children's amazement and discovery of a brilliant and inviting world has helped me see and experience life in a whole new light. Life is good; life is magic. Each child came with unique and beautiful attributes that I continue to be in awe of and learn from. As Kahlil Gibran had written, "Your children are not your children. They are sons and daughters of Life's longing for itself. They come through you but not from you. And though they are with you, yet they belong not to you. For they have their own thoughts."

Life was busy, happening and fun despite the hard work and lack of sleep. I remained on the dean's list throughout nursing school. I became engaged to be married at the same time I graduated. So many things seemed to be going right in my life. I had stayed busy and distracted. I did not work through the dysfunction of the past. This led to making decisions from a warped perspective, I had silenced my inner voice. Without the tools I needed on an emotional level, I was still in a victim mindset. In my young adulthood, I continued to allow control and maltreatment from others. People with narcissistic and abusive traits still had a leading role in my life. I became addicted to the saturation of adorations, which were withdrawn in an instant and then reinstituted strategically to keep me hooked. There was domestic violence, crazymaking, threats to my life and wellbeing. I was too afraid of the repercussions to speak up when I should have. I had to learn what in me was attracting these situations and people into my life. I had yet to be introduced to healthy boundaries.

I was drawn into years of custody battles. I went financially and almost emotionally bankrupt. It felt like the other parties' need for control was greater than the affection for the children involved. My mother tried to become entangled in the first of these. I bravely told her to step back. Her ego was injured. She first went to the Guardian Ad Litem in the case and then to my home. She proudly shared that what she had done would effectively remove my children from my care and strip me of my nursing license. My mother already had a reputation in the county, and the story she shared was taken with a grain of salt. My attorney said, "Like a deadly flu, you need to keep yourself and your children away from this woman."

It was then my partner and I decided to follow his dream and move to Alaska. All things fell into place, making what seemed impossible, possible. I left all I had ever known for this new adventure in the hopes of finding the joy filled life I deserved. By God's grace, I prevailed over all the custody battles that came and went over twelve years in different forms and venues. I am so grateful that part of my life has concluded. It drew every drop of strength and resilience. It prevented me from having the time and giving all the attention my children deserved. I also wasted too much of my energy ed on my codependent obsessions. An unevolved part of me grew up believing I needed to heal the wounds of someone as broken as myself to earn love. The custody entanglements helped me find my strength and confidence. I would need that to move forward and focus on my healing.

I did not talk to mom for years after this. I realized it was hurting my younger siblings and me more than anyone. I made peace with my mom, and peace came to my heart. She did eventually and sincerely apologize for what she saw as her part. I realized she could not be the mom I always hoped for, but I accepted her as she was.

She had taken to reading books that offered her a better way of being and thinking. There were still times when the old patterns popped up, but I accepted it now, I had boundaries. I was with her years later when she passed away. I held her as she transitioned from a coma into her next adventure. I asked her to please let me know from time to time she was still with me, and she miraculously squeezed my hand. I felt her fears lifted, and a transformation into her best form began. She was with my sister and my father now, and then my grandparents came to greet her soon after.

As Albert Einstein is quoted as saying, "The most important decision we make is whether we believe we live in a friendly or hostile universe."

I have been asked how I did not become addicted and, in most ways, appear unscathed from my past. I am not unscathed. I have been to the darkest of places and behaved out of insecurity and fear too often. I have fallen into people-pleasing, poor communication, destructive patterns and codependent habits which I will spend my lifetime fully resolving. When you are overwhelmed by your pain, you do not always realize the pain you are causing others. It took me many years to realize I was recreating my childhood's unresolved grief through relationships that were abusive and lacking emotional connection. I needed help to learn a healthy means of resolution. I started to find healing through the EMDR offered by a kind and empathetic therapist. She was there to hold space as all the emotions suppressed by too many decades came gushing out in tears. Going to a facility called "The Meadows" also helped me make internal shifts faster than I could have without the intensive focus offered. I continue to seek counsel and support readily. When I start slipping back into a suffering mindset, I find whatever is needed to get me back on track and seek the positive.

I started clearing my mind through meditation and healing my body by running. I ran two marathons during my forties, and it felt fantastic to put forth that dedication and push myself to the limit. It helped me trust myself and that I was genuinely invested in my own wellbeing as much as I had been in others. During this time, I had the opportunity to advocate for the American Cancer Society Cancer Action Network. I was able to be a part of Lights of Hope in Washington DC and speak with our Senators and Legislator regarding keeping the fight against cancer a priority. I travelled to our State Capitol to support this mission as well.

I now have more years behind me than ahead, but I am excited about what I continue to create. I desire to be a support to those going through dark times. To inspire finding the light that fills us with hope and purpose from within. I was blessed by so many beautiful people that showed up in a way that guided my path of growth and healing. It is time to be that for others. Another priority is to be present for my children and make them feel like the precious creations they are. They are the most important part of my life. I cannot make up for the times I was a weak and distracted parent, but I can build beautiful memories with my children in the present.

We cannot get it wrong in this life or mess up our opportunities. Our choices are different paths for our soul's lessons. When we miss the lesson's message, it will come up again in another form and situation. Have faith that what is meant for you will show up. Acknowledge disruption and chaos but do not let it become you. I believe this life is an opportunity for the evolution of our souls. We will clash and contrast with those meant to provide us with our most significant growth challenges. These kindred spirits help us level up.

There are subtle signs of loving support if we pay attention. Practice being mindful and tap into your intuition.

As I was walking a snow-packed trail in the middle of winter, I noticed a small wild rose in bloom. I remembered my mom painting wild roses on a plate she had made for me. I thanked my mom for letting me know she is still with me.

ABOUT THE AUTHOR

Kristen McDonald has been a registered nurse for 28 years. During those years, she has supported families while bringing new life into the world and comforted souls and their family as they transitioned to the next world.

Kristen is a certified case manager. She spent most of her years in nursing with those in need of additional support and a non-judgmental attitude to help them get through stressful situations.

Kristen has walked through many fires herself. She has gone from a comfortable life to losing everything both in her childhood and in adulthood. It has taught her never to take anything or anyone for granted. She has navigated through the traumas which come from loving those with unresolved addictions and untreated mental illness.

Kristen sometimes stumbled and had to recreate herself and her life. She realized these obstacles were a means of helping her evolve into the person she was meant to be. Kind and loving souls have shown up when she needs them most. She has thrived by having an awareness of a loving spiritual presence always supporting her and that we are much more than our earthly presence.

Kristen has learned an important lesson to go with the flow of life. Keep an open mind, and you will see a new world of possibilities. Kristen had planned to spend her days as a meteorologist in Arizona. She has now enjoyed living in Alaska for over 20 years, qualifying her for the proud title of "Sourdough."

Facebook: www.facebook.com/kristen.mcdonald3
Email: tokristenmcdonald@hotmail.com

KRISTIN FOLTS

HERE IS YOUR SIGN

The massive hot air balloon rising into the heavens in the distance was a beacon of hope, lifting me up from a soul-crushing morning.

I had just left my heart, my precious spirited toddler at the airport with her other parent to fly off on an adventure with her newly introduced potential step-family.

Part of my focus in this new chapter of co-parenting was to continue to heal the secret emotional wounds I endured while being married to a covertly abusive spouse.

I was having a hard time processing my deep emotions over leaving my little human to fly states away from me. In all truth, at this point in her young life, I didn't want this trip to happen for all the reasons a momma bear protects her young. My inner-voice kept telling me: "trust the process, she has her own path to walk," so I let her go despite my worries.

My internal struggle with this trip boiled down to my concern over the influence it would have on my daughter's little heart and emotions. Not fully trusting that she would be returned to me in the same emotional state in which I left her, dropping her off at the airport had me in knots of self-doubt and agony. I wondered if she would indeed come back to me without a change in everyday life, like the last time there was an extended unplanned adventure decided solely by the other parent.

Do I really have to do this right now?

I began agonizing over it again—it was unnerving to leave her at the airport to travel across the country in a pandemic, with a parent who consistently appeared to be indifferent towards our child's emotional distress. I questioned my intuition and myself because of the wounds I had also received from being in a marriage for years too long that broke my spirit and wounded my emotions and inner voice many times over.

Seeing that hot air balloon a few minutes later, a gorgeous symbol of freedom, crossing my path, reminded me to embrace the adventure to my destination, to have hope and enjoy the ride.

You see, one of the deep wounds I was still healing at that moment was trusting my intuition when it came to my daughter's journey with her other parent. This was mainly created because in the past, her emotional best interest appeared to be ignored while not in my care, which resulted in me being left with so many unanswered questions on more than one occasion. Answers that would have helped me, help her, process what she had experienced.

My daughter's other parent was publicly charming and fairly attentive to her as a co-parent, and played that role convincingly to the unknowing eye. The reality we lived was different behind closed doors. I had been silent about the true situation in our home for years, the anger, and living in fear that the threats against us would become a reality.

Unfortunately, many did come true and I had to dig deep in my faith to survive the unthinkable. The emotions of 10 months prior when I had no control over what was happening with my child was agonizing. I didn't know if she would even be returned to my safe embrace and the thought of losing her forever haunted me at night while I waited for her to be returned to me.

The emotions of this morning at the airport were the same emotions I felt from the last time my daughter took an unplanned adventure solely determined by the other parent as she left my arms. In many ways, I felt like she had been kidnapped back then and I was secretly reliving those memories from months prior in the airport.

I had a smile on my face, but my heart was hurting.

I will never forget choking back my tears—holding on to my smile as long as I could and wiping the tears quickly as she walked away from me, waving goodbye to me with excitement for her weekend adventure.

I wanted her to see this trip as fun and have good memories of her childhood. That is what was and still is most important to me as her mother.

156

As the protective momma bear that I am known to be, this was most definitely kicking up some emotional dust for me. My intuition and my trust in myself had some more healing to do, apparently. At the time, I didn't know I would be going on an adventure of my own that weekend.

"This is so hard," I thought to myself, as my daughter walked away from me. I heard it again. "Trust the process." I silently argued back as I choked down the tears again that had been building for days. I got a little salty with my inner voice: What does that even mean? Trust the process?

I heard the small voice request I use this time away from my daughter to heal some more layers of myself and do some deep self-reflection. Various cataclysmic stages of emotions from the past few years had been welling up, forming a perfect storm within. The gale-force winds had me stressing as I floated in my emotions. Trying to anchor myself to something solid and strong, I was focused on trans-forming my emotions and mindset from surviving to thriving.

At the same time, I was being beckoned to rest in the peace of the eye of the storm. Letting the winds blow around me while standing in my truth was giving my soul signature superpower permission to strengthen even more. I just needed a reminder encounter.

As I slammed back to my reality and drove away from the departure area, I began to piece my heart back together on a soul level, when I looked up and saw in the distance this gorgeous hot-air balloon not following the rest of the pack of balloons, and I knew it had a special message for me. It appeared just moments after I saw a billboard that said, "It's time to heal." Okay, I guess a gigantic billboard was a big enough sign for me to agree that I had a larger-than-life invitation to do some inner healing as I counted down the hours until my daughter's return to my arms.

"Fine!" I said aloud, as if my inner voice was riding in the front seat with me. I knew who was talking to me. My Creator. The small voice inside my head and heart inviting me to "trust the process." He had audibly ridden shotgun with me one other time when I was fearful of my future steps. He answered my plea with truth and strength that morning as well. I had to tap into my faith system even more as I was walking my healing journey to wholeness that day too. There had been many days where I had to heal the onion layers of life experiences that had wounded my intu-ition, but today was different; this morning would up-level my life forever.

My eyes lifted to the balloon pack as I was gaining ground on them in the distance. That one magnificent example of strength, fortitude, and sovereignty was speaking to my soul. My truth. My inner knowing and it was cheering me on in my moments of vulnerability as I begged to heal more layers of the wounds being triggered by this morning experience.

The hot-air balloon did not disappoint me as the mist of the early morning fog began to dissipate. Still, a few miles away from being up close to it, I felt a nudge to take a detour off the interstate to a tiny town that had been another one of those life-altering encounters for me 13 years prior. That tiny sleepy town had already changed the trajectory of my life twice in my life. Looking back, the third time would be the charm. I would find my authentic self that morning which would lead me on a journey to make a conscious choice to embrace my flaws, heal more layers of the wounds of not trusting my intuition from years past, and make a decision to trust the process. I needed to give myself permission to do deep vulnerability work on myself.

I pulled into the quiet park overlooking the large lake in that sleepy little town that morning. The grass was cut just the same as if 13 years hadn't even happened. It was cathartic in a way for me. I gave myself permission to walk down memory lane and change the direction of my healing journey, yet again, and to create more inner peace, self reflection and freedom to trust the process.

I felt like I was being led to meet someone there that morning. I leaned into trusting myself and listening to my divine support team guiding me to my divine appointment. I was here to meet my authentic self. I just didn't know her in my present healing yet still wounded state.

Everything seemingly important to me that morning would disappear from my grasp, and I would go on to do several rounds with the higher version of myself before finally embracing the whole idea of "trusting the process," while healing the secret layers of failure I felt in the depths of my soul. I was setting the stage to transform my wounds to wisdom, my chaos to calm and my trauma to trust. To trust my truth and saying *yes* to the next level of my divine life path.

Have you been where I was that day in your own healing journey?

At the crossroads perhaps, not sure which direction to turn, but knowing deep down you had to go somewhere because the spot you were currently at wasn't the best spot to take a break at?

She is finally home again!

In the end, my daughter did make it home but it was a very long four days.

I learned so much about myself while she was gone and I am grateful I trusted myself to let her go despite my fears of the unknown.

Just like with any transition, there were some challenges to work through, and we held each other close when we were reunited and we continue to hold each other when we have big feelings or feel triggered by the emotions of the past. I have more amazing tools to help support the healing journey and now the layers of emotions from the past are released for good, and are no longer a catalyst for tears and terror.

There are some days, even now as I write this, that we focus on making it through one more round of big emotions that are being healed by trusting the process, and leaning into the inner voice that says we will be okay.

"Keep holding space to heal," is what I keep hearing now and, "keep healing the layers," knowing eventually this time will end and total freedom is waiting on the other side.

Remember to trust yourself and the healing process as you turn your chaos to calm and your wounds into wisdom isn't always a glitz and glam experience. It takes heart and fortitude to face the darkness and then say, "enough is enough; I have to heal this because this trauma and dysfunction stops with me."

To heal the future sometimes you have to Duke it out with the past...so I once thought.

In my field of expertise as an Emotions coach and Energy Medicine practitioner, I walk in high vibrations when I am working with the healing journey alongside the Divine for others, and then there are moments where I feel the lows and deep dark secrets of a client without them telling me a word of their trauma story. This is partly my intuitive gifts coming into play with my life calling as an Energy Medicine practitioner, also known as an Energy Healer.

This allows me the freedom to be authentically who the Divine created me to be and to speak my truth without fear or judgement while guiding others on their own healing journey.

Being an Energy Medicine practitioner doesn't mean I have my life together all the time; it simply means that while I am actively working on my own healing journey, I am not letting my own story stand in the way of helping others start or strengthen their own healing pathways. Sometimes it's as simple as giving yourself permission to heal, honoring the journey, and then releasing it for a new belief around the memory/story to take its place with joy.

The past needs to stay in the past, but at times, it needs a voice so it can be at ease with what we experienced and that takes the emotional charges out of the equation. It works. I am a testament to energy medicine transformations and you can be too.

How do I trust myself after all I have gone through?

My awareness that I needed to heal my intuition did not start the moment I experienced that big life trauma I mentioned earlier in my chapter. My journey to healing/trusting my intuition started many years prior. At the time, I didn't know that the mistrust in myself would lead me down a road of deep struggle and grief before I would come full circle. Once I embraced my divine gifts as an Energy Healer, I found I could heal my intuition and therefore my future.

The beauty of my story, my truth, is that after much heartache, trauma, and agonizing for days/months/years of wrestling with myself, if I did the right things in the pivotal situations of my life, I fell in love with myself along the way. Had I only trusted my intuition, known and stood in my power, while honoring my still small voice, I can only imagine where I would be today. But I am so thankful for how far I have come despite my own worries of being judged for who I have been called to be and standing up against the darkness. My story matters and I pray my journey to wholeness helps you heal too.

I may have had to walk the journey that unfolded anyway but I would have done it with more grace, more ease, and not felt like I was going to die while still breathing.

Like anyone that has breath on this side of the veil/ heavens, there are moments in life that go down as pivotal moments when we *"should"* all over ourselves and make what seem to be decent decisions—or what appears to be the right decision at the time but they are laced with self-doubt, lack of authenticity, and don't honor what we know in the bottom of our heart to be what we should be doing. It's time to stop "shoulding" all over yourself!

As an Energy Medicine practitioner, there are times where I don't even believe what is being revealed behind the scenes in the subconscious minds and energy fields of those that have entrusted me with their energy, childhood traumas, and their belief systems. If they only knew what kind of conversations I have had with their inner child and their inner voice, they may not come back to me. However, they always do, because they feel the shifting in their inner chaos becoming aligned with their inner need for peace and begin aligning themselves with truth, and emotional strength. Ultimately, I help my clients find their inner JOY.

It is my personal and professional experience that, when you add in some energy work, release some residual childhood trauma memories, honor and release family/generational beliefs that no longer serve a positive purpose, you have the potential to have some significant energetic and emotional shifts to joy and peace, which raises you above the trauma layers so you can see a more healthy version of your life journey in a relatively short time. While I have only visited your past energetically, the things around you start shifting in amazing ways, you are now finding peace in your current life for yourself, and you are learning to release your emotional baggage on an energetic level, which aligns you to live a life of freedom and Joy.

Trusting myself and trusting my intuitive gifts have now created an avenue for you to taste emotional freedom and energetic joy by experiencing my energy medicine gifts. If I had not said yes to my own healing journey and began to trust my intuition again while continuing on my own self-discovery adventure, I know for certain you would not be reading my story now.

Saying yes to your own healing story starts in the small steps of life.

It's the small steps in life that make the biggest impacts.

The moment I crossed the path of the straying balloon, I crossed under him as if we were destined to meet on the road of different paths to intersect just for a moment in time to say, "I see and honor you doing the hard stuff on your healing journey and here is a little gift to brighten your day."

That experience reminded me that you don't have to follow the pack to make an impact in someone else's life. You can walk your own divine journey, and it doesn't have to be straight and narrow. It doesn't matter which way the wind blows because it is the life experiences you bring to the journey that matters to the adventure. The choice to trust the process is only your responsibility and no one else's choice.

What do you choose to do differently so you can trust your intuition and have soul-level Joy?

Do you answer the call to heal your intuition, or do you head for the hills and pretend your life experiences don't control your every move?

What is your personal truth, and do you embrace it from the depths of your soul?

Do you know yourself well and walk in your divine calling daily?

My current healing journey path looks bright and healthy.

In reflection of the past few years of my healing journey to say, "I trust my intuition," there have been deep layers that I have had to give myself permission to bring up because they were packed like sardines in the deep crevices of my soul.

I lightly refer to these layers and my healing journey in my TEDx Talk, *Give Your Inner Child Permission to Heal,* about having two options:

Option A: is to tuck away parts of your traumatized self further down into your wounded soul and pretend everything is okay with a smile on your face.

Out of shame, I did this for years to survive the secret horrors in my marriage. It didn't make it any easier during the moments of terror but along the way, I learned that there is freedom in surrendering to the unknown and standing in your truth and only then could I break free of the chains of trauma holding me back from walking my Divine calling and leave that situation for good.

Option B: is to invite the parts of yourself that make you feel vulnerable and fearful to be healed and release the layers of trauma holding you hostage to your past.

Which option do you choose?

Your future is asking you to make a decision to heal so you can live a life of Joy and freedom.

You will get to a point in your healing journey that the cost to your soul by living option A outweighs your fears of option B.

There is freedom and healing in choosing option B for yourself.

Imagine how freeing it would be to welcome in the new and improved version of your adult self, with less emotional baggage and more Joy.

Releasing the layers of your emotional wounds is the way to healing yourself fully. The journey looks different for each soul.

The whole TEDx experience was life-changing for me. It was a journey that brought me healing and more Joy. I physically stood in the darkness and shined my light.

Two years later I still receive testimonials of how my words spoken in faith have helped others heal and make peace with their past. It is an honor to hear their healing journey stories.

It had been on my vision board for a few years at that point and as I entered into the first few phases of releasing the toxic relationship holding me back from my divine calling and trusting my intuition, I knew it would be a lifeline to healing my voice, honoring my divine calling and standing in my God-given power and saying to the masses, "My story matters too."

My TEDx journey was life-changing and pivotal to saying yes to fully healing and learning to trust the process.

How can you trust the process and listen to your intuition at the same time?

Your next chapter in life has yet to be written. Embrace the messiness of your life and trust the healing journey to bring you more freedom and joy in your daily life.

Trust is about having the faith to walk your journey from chaos to calm and transform your wounds into wisdom without knowing the result.

Your intuition has a filter and a lens through which you see it as a help or a hindrance to your divine path in life.

Can you trust the process of your emotional transformation journey?

What do you need to release and heal so you can full-heartedly trust your intuition despite your life experiences and stand in your truth as a Divinely inspired human walking an earthly experience?

Trusting the process can be unnerving at times. I get your struggles with doubting yourself, feeling unworthy, identifying being blocked from abundance and joy, but what if you are being called to release those things and transform your emotions and thought patterns to a higher vibration so that when life experiences knock you down or make you question your divine calling in life or your intuition, it is more of a learning curve then a head-on collision?

Lean into your inner voice. Your intuition. Listen to what it is telling you to allow in your life that will bring you into the next phase of your transformation journey.

Will you answer the call?

* * *

How you can connect with Kristin:

If you feel like learning how to trust your intuition is something that I can help you embrace while guiding you on how to listen to your inner voice from a place of truth, please reach out to me by finding the links in my bio.

ABOUT THE AUTHOR

Kristin Folts is an Emotions Coach and Energy Medicine practitioner. Her passion is empowering moms while transforming their emotions from chaos to calm, creating a peaceful oasis with their kids, and bringing joy into their lives by releasing the energetic, emotional baggage holding them back from saying yes to their best life.

Kristin's calling is to guide and uplift moms and entrepreneurs to embrace their feminine magic, heal their inner child, abundance mindset, and self-sabotage through coaching and intuitive energy medicine work.

Kristin is a momma to a spirited special needs toddler, Energy Medicine Practitioner, Intuitive Emotions and Parent Coach, TBRI Practitioner, EFT Guide, Speaker, Trauma Trainer, Mompreneur, Former Child Welfare Worker, and a TEDx Speaker.

In her TEDx talk, "Giving Your Inner Child Permission to Heal," she inspires those impacted by trauma to use their voice to transform themselves and others by embracing their trauma healing story.

Kristin lives with her daughter in Florida and enjoys being an 1800's Living History Reenactor, gardening, yoga, essential oils, camping, and educating others on the benefits of living a whole-mind-body-soul lifestyle.

Group: *www.facebook.com/*
groups/TheEmotionalHealingCollective
Facebook: *www.facebook.com/KristinPitcockFolts*
Page: *www.facebook.com/HealingHomeCoaching*
Website: *www.healinghomecoaching.com*

MARION DREW

I have walked the winding road of never-ending twists and turns to self-improvement and found who I truly am along the way. I have ventured from people pleaser to soul pleaser. I have learnt to believe that I am good enough to achieve whatever I desire with my life without the limiting beliefs from myself or others.

My journey started out in a small rural primary school; a place that was supposed to be safe and secure. During year five, I had a teacher who used to hit and verbally abuse me and many others in our little classroom when we didn't get our work 100% correct. This happened every day and subsequently made me hate school for the rest of my schooling life. I was then afraid of learning and trusting people, which took away every bit of confidence that I had.

Looking back now, I believe that my strength and resilience got me through that ordeal in my early life. It was not until many years later that I realised, deep down, just how much it had destroyed my soul. I lost who I truly was. From then on, I tried so hard to keep everybody else happy as I tried to fit into a world that I felt wasn't for me. Keeping yourself happy was frowned upon, or so I thought.

I live on a beautiful property called 'Anunaka', meaning 'our home' in Aboriginal. It is a soldier settlers block situated between Cootamundra and Junee in NSW. I am a dedicated farmer's wife who runs a farming business specialising in fine wool Merinos, cropping, prime lambs and hay production. I achieved all of this whilst working alongside my best friend and husband, Pat and our two beautiful children, Christine and Tom.

The morning of New Year's Day in 2006 was very different from that of your average day. I woke up feeling that I should water the lawn and put things in place just in case a fire started today. From the very start, I just had a feeling that this day was going to be different. By 6 am, it was already sweltering outside and the wind had started to pick up.

At about 2 pm, Pat, being the local fire brigade's deputy captain, got a call explaining that a fire had started at the Jail Break Inn along the Junee/Temora road. Someone had thrown a cigarette out the window. Pat and our neighbour, Alan, jumped in the fire truck and went off to fight the fire. Pat gave me a few instructions on what to do before he left; it was imperative to have a plan. At this stage, the fire was not coming our way, but we had to be prepared just in case. I thought to myself, how can I do this with no self-confidence, believing that I have no skills whatsoever and whilst ensuring Tom and Christine's safety, only five and eight at the time.

In the end, I did not have a choice, the adrenaline kicked in, and I was right to go. I drove the ute down the paddock to move our breeding ewes off a stubble paddock. By this time, we were experiencing 45km/h winds and a temperature of 45 degrees. I sent the working dog, Possum, around the sheep as best as I could, considering I could not drive through the thick stubble for the risk of starting another fire.

But Possum decided she wasn't having a bar of moving those sheep in that heat. So, what do I do? I beeped the horn, and the ewes took notice and started walking up the fire break. It was as if they knew something was wrong. It was unbelievable to watch and know that they trusted me for their safety.

I had the gate open into our feedlot, as it was bare ground and had a reasonable fire break around it. They just walked straight in. The readers that know sheep will understand that this does not happen without a fuss.

The kids at this time were stressed and hot, so I knew it wasn't safe for them to stay any longer. I called my good friends, Kim and Julie, to come and take the kids to Cootamundra before things got too bad. Pat called me not long after to tell me the wind had changed to a north westerly, meaning it was heading straight for our home.

I had to speed up things, and rang a great friend from Lockhart, Peter West-blade, to see if he could help me. He and his beautiful wife, Di, drove out without hesitation. While I was waiting for Pete and Di to arrive, I went and got another mob of sheep in and put them in the sheep yards near the house. By this time, the smoke was thick and black, it really scared me, and all sorts of bad thoughts crossed my mind.

I kept in touch with my neighbour Julie, Alan's wife, as she was home alone as well. She brought her son's horses up to our yards to keep them safe. Even my horses just came to me and followed me into the yards.

I then drove the header out of the shed put it on bare ground and started protecting the house.

By this time, Pete and Di arrived and were very lucky to get through. Di helped me around the house whilst Pete went and saved our lambs. He managed to put them all on a dam bank while the fire went around him and the mob of sheep, a courageous thing to do. Not one lamb was lost. I did not know this had happened until weeks later.

While this was happening, Pat and Alan were on their way back to save their farms.

As it turned out, they had a close call with the fire changing direction and jumping the fire truck twice. They had to drive back through the fire front and onto the burnt ground for safety. The smoke was so thick, and breathing became so difficult that they wet their bandanas and used them to breathe through. The trucks that were used back then are not as good as the ones we have now. It was fortunate that they both escaped unharmed and made it home to help Julie and me.

The fire did end up going through our property. However, we did not lose any buildings or livestock. Unfortunately, we lost all of our pastures and the majority of our fences. One thing that really sticks in my mind was that night, where all you could hear was the crashing of trees as they fell along the road and then the dead silence that followed the next morning. It was very eery and confronting.

The next day we were totally exhausted, but the beautiful thing was that we had many phone calls and offers of help to clean up. We were lucky enough to have food and water delivered as we had no power due to a few of our power poles having burnt down. As our paddocks were now burnt and dry and pasture was scarce, our wonderful neighbours allowed us to put our sheep on their land after the fire. Their generosity was amazing.

Before the chaos of the fire, Pat and I had built a feedlot. As the numerous donations of hay made their way to our property, we were able to rebuild and move our sheep from our neighbour's paddocks and into our feedlot. The generous hay donations meant that we could start again and protect our land and topsoil from blowing away.

I felt fine and doing okay, but I wasn't okay for some reason, and I did not know it until nearly twelve months later.

During that time, I had a lady tell me that I was okay because we didn't lose much and that I should get over it and get on with my life. Those words stayed stuck in my head for a very long time. I didn't slow down or talk about what had happened; I felt I wasn't allowed to show emotion because I didn't lose my home or significant structures. I just couldn't comprehend why this lady had said this to me and why she had used such a mean tone. It was like my experience didn't matter.

My mindset started to become very negative, I hated who I was, and I became blinded by what other people thought of me. These feelings were fuelled by my experience and the fact that I was not confident, did not like whom I was, and was trying to keep everyone else happy.

These feelings continued to worsen after the fire, as we went into a ten-year drought. Our farm had no rain to help our property recover, and life became even more challenging as a result. I was young with two little children and had just started to grow our farming business with limited finances.

My friend Darlene asked me if I was okay and commented that I was not myself and that I might need to talk to someone. At the time I thought, 'Wow, what does she know. I am okay and have gotten on with fixing everything. This how I am: tough, I can get through anything without help.' Or so I thought. As a farmer, you have to endure everything that you are faced with without emotion, and that is hard to do all the time, especially when you the thought the way I did. What will people think if I cannot handle stressful situations?

On the outside, my husband Pat seemed to be handling the situation, but deep down, he wasn't either. So, he decided to start bike riding and running. I thought to myself, after a bit of time, maybe I can do this too. I had never run before and boy it showed! I started by trying to run 1 km, and my breathing and running style were shocking. While I was running, I thought about what Darlene had said. I decided she was right; I probably do need to talk about it to someone that understands. So, I did, all whilst hoping that no one finds out or they will think I'm crazy.

I booked an appointment and off I went. The lady I spoke to asked me a series of general questions and then asked what I was doing to help myself. I told her that I had started to run. She said, 'That is fantastic. Keep doing it.' Then she asked me about the fire, and I had to give her all the details that I hadn't talked about before. She informed me that I had a touch of Post-Traumatic Stress Disorder. I only had one more session with her, which was great, so I was on the road to recovery.

My healing started with running. I learnt that it was not a bad thing to ask for help. My intuition was telling me to start running so that I may begin to heal. I did not understand this at the time. I believe we are always guided in our lives if we have an open mind and don't dismiss the signs presented to you. This is hard to do when we live in a world telling you the exact opposite and that intuition and signs are just crazy stuff. Before becoming open to it, I was one of those people half of the time.

My running gradually got better, but I didn't know what I was doing in terms of training, so I developed quite a few injuries from not been strong enough. This became very frustrating. So, I decided to go to the physio and found one that could help me with my running style and understood what was going wrong as he did the sport of running and triathlon himself. I will be forever grateful to Marcus, who just wanted to help a runner to get better and enjoy the sport.

Initially, not looking like athletes who were long and lean caused me to have negative thoughts regarding the fact that because I didn't look that way, I wouldn't make it as a good runner. But this thinking was coming from other influences around me. But I still kept going as I knew it was healing 'old war wounds' as I call it and making myself healthier. As I became more confident, I started to join Pat in the sport of triathlon. I figured it would be a great thing to do together while we were going through the drought and the aftereffects of the fire.

Being in our situation, many people would turn to alcohol or drugs, but this was not me as it wasn't my thing, and it never agreed with my body. Not being a drinker also made it hard to fit in, so walking alone wasn't anything new to me. I never followed the crowd, so it was tough to find my tribe. Not finding my tribe was also attributed to me not thinking with my heart and soul. Sometimes my mind was my enemy.

During my training, I had plenty of backlash and was told I was obsessed and wearing my joints out. These sorts of comments hurt me, but I still didn't listen, this is what I had to do. When it came to triathlon, I realised I could not swim or ride either let alone run. I had no natural talent. What a battle this was going to be! But I was up for the challenge no matter how hard it was and with all the negative comments. I was hard enough on myself, let alone listening to other people.

One comment did stand out to me was when I was learning to swim. I had the swimming coach give me some lessons as I sank like a drowning rat. The comment they made was, 'are you trying to be Olympic champion?.' At that moment I thought, 'Wow, is that how I'm coming across? Should I keep going?.' Yes, and keep going, I did! Comments like that began to fuel my fire even though they hurt at the time. I have found that the more down on yourself you are, the more those people that love putting you down, show up and make it worse. I now know that they are there to teach you a lesson, but I didn't see it that way. Deep down, I hated who I was even more, and I found I could just hide it very well.

My running and triathlon became such a massive part of my healing from past events. I entered small races such as 5km runs and enticer triathlons. I loved it and the way it made me feel until I came to the open water swimming. I suffered anxiety attacks in the water, which was devasting for me, as it was such a big fear to be in the open water and a non-swimmer. It became just another battle for me to overcome. Mentally, I had to dig deep to overcome this, and it took about two years.

My running became better too, so I decided to do a half marathon, which I loved. I have now completed six others and two full marathons. Completing these distances was exciting, and I felt like I had achieved something I never thought I would.

My next challenge was to do a Half Ironman; 2km swim, 90km bike ride and 21km run. This was a huge step for me and the way I thought about my ability. I felt after four years of doing the smaller distances, I was ready to take the next step. Most people around me had done the longer ones, but I was not mentally prepared to take the next big step when they did. You have to be ready in your own time and not be pushed by others and their achievements. Life is not always a sprint; it is a marathon, so enjoy the journey; words I was constantly saying to myself.

The next step was to get a coach since I had no experience in the style or structure of training required. I found a beautiful coach named Katie Gray-Pedicini, who understood my needs as a woman training for this event. She understood my needs regarding my hormone issues, adrenaline fatigue from the post-traumatic stress and how run-down I was. Katie started me from scratch, built my fitness and endurance and changed my eating plan. I loved the training process of my first half ironman, but I still had a small element of feeling like I wasn't good enough or fast enough.

My husband Pat has achieved a full Ironman, and I can remember watching the athletes coming in at the back of the pack. They were everyday warriors fighting some sort of a battle, all in different shapes and sizes. I then realised I was one of those people, the triathlon world's warriors, everyday heroes that stay under the radar. The light bulb moment hit me; I released I should be proud of this position and place in the triathlon community, and to keep training no matter hard it is—it will all be worth it in the end.

Pat was my rock throughout the training. He trained with me on those long runs and rides, through rain, 35 km/h winds and fatigue and my whinging and swearing up those hills. Pat deserves a medal for putting up with me. Finally, the day arrived, and I felt good, very nervous and grateful for my beautiful family and friends around me for support.

Everything went perfectly! I felt good for the whole race and smiled, taking it all in. I said to myself, 'I'm really doing this; I can do anything.' From that day on, I knew I was holding myself back from the life I really wanted. I knew this little farming girl had more to give and more things to experience.

Once I achieved the first Half Ironman, I went on to do three more. They too were amazing.

After Cains Half Ironman, I realised I still needed help with my mindset; I needed to grow more.

During the drought of 2017, I decided Pat and I needed to expand our knowledge of our farming business. One day as I was scrolling through Facebook, I come across Farm Owners Academy. The course they were offering was just what we needed. Divine timing, I would say. Andrew Roberts was talking in the video, and I felt he was genuine and knew his stuff. This was the right course and group for me.

Part of this course for farmers is working on yourself. This is how I met Tracy Secombe and her Soul Pleaser course. I listened to her speak and thought it really sounded like me and where I was mentally at the time. So, I had a chat with her about it. I didn't join up straight away as I was a bit afraid, never having done something like this before and being apprehensive what would it bring up. I was in that fear mode again. Tracy's knowledge of people-pleasing and thinking 'I am not good enough' is due to being one herself, so this attracted me because she knows the tools to help others. Tracy's mission is to help me remember who I am, to realign with my soul so I can live my life to my full potential, and to live a life that fulfills me in every way.

Eight months later, I joined Tracy's course. I was ready for the next level on changing limiting beliefs right back from my school days from family, friends and society. This may sound harsh, but it's the truth. I had a lot to learn about myself and the self-sabotage I was inflicting. Going through the course brought up so many emotions from the past and what I truly was doing to myself. The questions I had to answer were very confronting and brought about a lot of tears. But it truly was worth it.

I believe my journey in life has taught me so many lessons in strength, reliance and growth. I have learnt from the people that have come and gone, even the old alcoholic schoolteacher.

The people who said nasty things to me have taught me never to be like them and have allowed me to understand that they are going through some inner turmoil to be that way. All you can do is send them love. The fire was a blessing in a way; it changed everything for me, especially in how I took steps to grow, love and believe in myself again.

These are things I thought I would never say. Just goes to show if you work on yourself and admit something is wrong in your life, you can become a better version of yourself, speak your truth and live the life of your dreams. When I think back, I can't believe how much I used to worry about what others think of me, whether I was good enough, and that I had no confidence in my ability to try new things. It is such a terrible way to live and most of the time you can't see it until things get really bad and you realise you need to change. Once you change, you never want to go back.

My running and triathlon training, personal growth and mindset is always a part of my morning routine. It is my me time. Meditation is a part of the routine I now love, as I initially thought it wouldn't work, but it does. It definitely takes the clutter out of my head and keeps me calm and relaxed. I now really take in what mother nature has to offer while I'm running, she truly does speak to you if you are watching and listening. I have learned to appreciate my intuition and what it is telling me and my ability to read people and their energy.

I never knew much about this until I started working with Tracy, but now realise I always had it, I just choose to ignore it and thought it just a coincidence. I have embraced the true me. I truly live in the present now and live life on my terms. My winding road will always have twists and turns, but I have the tools to drive my way through them. It keeps me learning, growing and building strength and resilience. These tools help me run a better farming business and create a greater balance in life with my family and friends. All I ask of you, the reader, are you living your best life by being your true self? Believe you can and you will. Just take that first step.

ABOUT THE AUTHOR

Marion Drew's journey back to herself began after suffering from post-traumatic stress disorder due to significant loss during bushfires on New Year's Day in 2006.

To heal her mind and body and calm her state of living in fear, Marion took up running and began to focus on her need to grow emotionally and work on her personal growth and mindset.

A confessed people pleaser, Marion had not been her true self in the past and now is her very own soul pleaser. Marion embraces her challenges as her teacher for growth and strength, living her life on her terms with no guilt.

Marion's intuition speaks to her soul and puts her on the right path. She is a humble woman with a warrior spirit, driven by a bigger purpose.

Marion shares her farming life and home with her husband and best friend, Pat. She has two beautiful children and a beloved pet Jack Russell, Muppet.

Her passions include triathlon, running, reading to expand her knowledge, rural photography, working on the farm and bettering their business, spending precious time with family and friends, and travelling to beautiful places.

Marion wants to be the shining example that change is possible for anyone, and that personal development and growth can be found in the most unusual of ways.

Email: marion.drew71@gmail.com
Instagram: www.instagram.com/mariondrew1050

MELISSA CHERNOW

AN ACT OF INTEGRITY

*"I allow myself to receive the abundance of the Universe
for the highest good of all."*

T his is the affirmation I have been dancing with for the past
week. Only seven days, but it feels so right. I have always had
some resistance to affirmations, mostly because they never felt fully
resonant within my body. While the others felt forced, this one found
me. I opened myself to new communities and conversations, weaved
together what I learned and liked, what felt right for me in this now
moment, and I discovered the beauty of this affirmation. It feels right
when I say it, think it, and allow its vibration to fill my body. I am it. I
am allowing.

It was also a main intention in writing this chapter. To open myself as a vessel to
receive the story or guidance that would resonate with your soul in such a way that
you can no longer deny the truth within you: your intuition.

Society is shifting, and this flame is sparked on an individual level of remembering and reclaiming our sovereignty. To all the feelers, seers, and knowers hesitant
to trust your intuitive experiences, I see you. What you feel, see, and know are real.
Thank you for being here and staying receptive and curious.

Below I share stories of my intuition guiding the way. It is easy to think that our intuition arrives solely in extraordinary moments, but our intuition is constantly providing breadcrumbs. It's when we follow them that the extraordinary occurs.

* * *

IT FELT like any other visit up until after we said goodbye. I closed the car door and buckled my seatbelt, looking back at the entrance to his home. Tears streaming down my face, my heart was breaking seemingly prematurely over something I didn't want to believe. It was an odd feeling, but a certain one. I knew it was goodbye.

That was the last time I saw my grandfather. He passed away just over two weeks later, right as I was settling into my semester abroad in Italy. *Something in me two weeks prior knew this was going to happen without knowing why. It made no sense to my logical brain, and I certainly did not want to believe it, but something in me knew.*

Upon receiving the news, my heart so badly wanted to return home for so many reasons. But I looked outside of my heart for guidance on what to do, and almost everyone encouraged me to stay in Italy. I was emotionally exhausted and thought my grandfather would want me to stay. I was conflicted, but after many conversations, I ultimately chose to stay.

As my family gathered in the states for his funeral, I held a little ceremony in my apartment and honored his life, part of which included his favorite evening ritual - a single beer at dinner. I later wept in a friend's lap on a bench under the moon. I felt alone and guilty for not going home. I kept going back to that moment in the car after saying goodbye to him: *something in me knew.*

I spent many nights over the following weeks alone in bed, my body convulsing as cries and grief consumed me. I bought a flannel shirt that reminded me of the ones he wore so I could wrap myself in his embrace. I journaled. I mourned.

He was with me in every ocean breeze, every new adventure I said yes to, and every sailboat that passed by. I said yes to more day trips and experiences than home Melissa likely would have. I felt his presence in every ocean breeze, and I smiled with every sailboat that caught my eye. I found comfort in evening walks to the edge of town to get a clear view of the moonlit sky. He sent me many gifts in many forms to remind me of his presence. He still does.

Upon returning home three months later, hugging my family was bittersweet.

Embracing my mom and grandma was the most emotionally charged, filled with the joys I so eagerly wanted to share about my adventures alongside the sorrow and pain of a loss that suddenly felt brand new. I was on an emotional seesaw, uncertain of what to say.

I recall my grandmother's composure, at one point gently offering, "your grandfather was a man of integrity." A soft smile warmed her face. Both that moment and statement struck me as much for their simplicity as for their truth. There was something both comforting and intriguing about them. Over the next six years, I would come to ponder integrity quite a bit.

* * *

FRESH INTO A NEWLY FORMED MID-MORNING ROUTINE, I found myself at a local park for my daily run. On my cool-down walk around the pond, I thought about how best to spend the rest of my day. Just five weeks prior, I said goodbye to my corporate job, so I had more time on my plate than I was used to, and I was determined to find enjoyment in this time while looking for another, more aligned job.

Walking back to my car, I heard clear as day, "Go to Starbucks." As a walking channel, hearing something like this was not surprising, but I was conflicted. It felt like a good decision in my body, but I had just made a pact with myself to cut unnecessary spending until I found another consistent income source. Coffee shops were top of the "no" list, so I dismissed it as I continued to my car.

Again I heard that voice, to which I once more said no, reciting in my mind the plan I had made to save money.

"Go to Starbucks" came through a third time, just as clear and purposeful as the first time. After what I thought was firmly standing my ground in saying no, I recognized this was the third time receiving this message. I pay attention when things happen in threes: I believe in the power of repetition, and three is that number for me. I was now open to the possibility of going to get tea. I recalled the initial resonance of the statement within my body, knew this guidance and feeling were not derived through rational thought, and I became increasingly intrigued as to why I was receiving this guidance. Still not fully convinced about going (I wanted to stick to my word!), I did what usually do when deciding between two things: I imagined myself in each scenario.

I first imagined myself going home, sticking to my plan of cutting coffee shops from my spending. It felt like a normal day, but a growing part of me was curious as to what the trip to Starbucks was all about. I felt unsatisfied.

Next, I imagined going to Starbucks, which felt far more exciting and adventurous, even without knowing the why behind the decision. There was clearly a reason I was receiving this guidance. I could feel it in my gut.

So, as I parked my car at Starbucks, and before exiting the car, I said, "thank you for the guidance that brought me here. I am open to receiving all that is meant for my highest good."

I stepped out of the car, and within seconds, I saw a friend from high school several yards in front of me. He was speaking to his mentor and the man who would become my next boss.

As soon as the *go to Starbucks* message arrived within me, I knew something felt right about it. But because that feeling went against a personal pact I had made with myself just days prior, I moved away from the feeling and into my mind to decide if it made logical sense even though my body already knew. In many instances, intuition defies logic. Though reasoning and critical thinking help us in many scenarios, evaluating our intuition's guidance with detail and critical thinking is largely unnecessary. Discerning our intuition's communication pathways is far more beneficial.

In going against my logical plan, I created the pathway for a more abundant one by choosing to trust that intuitive nudge. Even though I tried to rationalize my way out of it, I ultimately followed the heart's most subtle pull by returning to the truth in my body.

Following curiosity and taking a $3 leap led me to walk into the most aligned job I have ever had. It was a role I daydreamed about and looked forward to the day it would arrive. Not only was the role itself wildly expansive, but the decision to say yes to my intuition was as well.

This was the prime example: our intuition guides us toward opportunities we might otherwise ignore. In this way, our intuition is one of the most expansive intelligences we have. While the mind attempts to negotiate with the nudges and knowings, the intuition is certain and strong and needs no negotiating. All it takes to lean into this intelligence is trust.

Trust can be difficult when the why is unknown. Sometimes you cannot help but wonder why your soul is speaking what it is. Our intuition often asks us to surrender to the why. In many cases, the why is irrelevant, as it is in choosing to trust our intuition that matters most. And part of trusting is knowing that the why will soon be revealed. It was in walking back to my car, tea and new connection in hand, that I knew exactly why those messages found me at the park earlier that morning.

* * *

JUST ABOUT A YEAR after that initial meeting in the Starbucks parking lot, another gut feeling arose: it was time to say goodbye. It was time for me to leave the job. This time I knew the truth behind the feeling, but I did not want to believe it or accept it. The societal pressure of needing to stay in this role even and my gut feeling to leave seemingly grew stronger by the day. It was a feeling part of me wanted to ignore, but knew I couldn't. In many ways, it felt safer to ignore it, but that is exactly how I knew my ego was involved.

Our ego is a beautiful and necessary mechanism designed to keep us safe. It protects us always. Keeping us safe often means keeping us in the familiar, our comfort zones, or in alignment with social conditioning. It operates based on what we have seen or experienced before, whether in our personal lives or within society.

My ego was on, full protection mode activated. I like to think of the ego as a radar, constantly scanning for threats to our survival. So, I asked what threats it perceived and opened my ears to listen to what it had to say.

"This is the most aligned job you have ever had. You enjoy it. It is meaningful work that people respond favorably to. You're making an impact. You're good at it. You're passionate about the company and its mission. A more aligned job is not guaranteed - you don't know that something better exists."

I noticed a tone of fear. I thanked my ego for doing its job.

Then I tuned into my heart. The heart is true, and this was where I felt the intuitive guidance to leave this role the most, so once more, I listened.

"It's time. You are already creating something in greater alignment. From this space, you will remember and attract everything you need."

What my heart shared was simple and true, and choosing my heart's guidance was an act of trust. It was also an act of integrity. Knowing in your body that something isn't the right fit, whether it be the job or not wanting to attend the party, whatever it is, is your soul speaking. To ignore or dismiss it is to act out of alignment with your soul's truth and desires. To have the knowing or feeling and ignore it is a disservice to your whole self.

My resignation was bittersweet and involved allowing myself to feel the sadness that arose. I remember the moment I officially resigned; I felt freedom in my body. Talk about expansion - I felt like I was a hawk flying in the sky, the wind of my intuition under my wings guiding me forward with ease. My breath was clear, and my body felt alive, and that feeling alone felt like enough of a why.

PART of this decision felt like a door was closing. Even with this truth, our intuition is always expansive. The closing feeling was my ego's fear. After honoring and listening to it, I was able to lean into the unknown with more certainty and excitement, choosing to focus more on this decision's expansive nature. Months prior, I had just experienced how expansive following my intuition proved to be. I trusted that with this door closing, many more were about to open.

Sometimes expansion means walking away from opportunities. It may feel more exciting walking into a new opportunity, but goodbyes can be just as powerful. Regardless of the circumstance, basing that decision on your soul's knowing is what makes that decision inherently aligned and expansive.

We are provided with the comfort and ease of staying small when we ignore the expansive opportunities our intuition leads us toward. It may at times feel easier to ignore gut feelings, stick to the original plan, or choose what we believe society expects from us. The ease may feel comfortable at first, but when your intuition is your integrity, staying small is not easy at all.

Our intuition is giving by nature, offering us countless opportunities every day to listen. Every time we trust its guidance, we see just how much is possible when we align our actions with our intuition. Since leaving that job, I have experienced exponential expansion both personally and professionally. Greater beauty finds us as these moments compound and we strengthen the muscle of trusting our intuition.

We deserve to feel free and alive and excited. We deserve to follow our soul's path. Your intuition may not always go with the status quo, but the choices you make in accordance with your intuition will dictate yours.

THE FOLLOWING framework supports listening to and aligning your actions with your intuition. It is focused on honoring the somatic and is a process that guides us toward more confident intuitive-based decision making.

Pause and breathe. Remember you know the way.

Notice the mind. It's okay, let it speak. What does it have to say?

Offer your gratitude and say *thank you* to your mind.

Now move into your heart. What is your heart saying?

Offer your gratitude and say *thank you* to your heart.

What is the inkling you feel in your body? How is the voice of your intuition presenting itself right now?

A nudge, a knowing, a feeling and goosebumps are common indicators. Perhaps it's one of these, or something unique to you. Trust the information you being is experiencing.

Offer your gratitude and say thank you to the sensations in your body, the voice of your intuition.

What might it feel like to follow this nudge?

Explore the greatness of this opportunity. Notice if you move into your mind. Come back to your heart. It's normal to toggle back and forth, especially in the process of becoming more familiar with the intuitive guidance you receive.

If you are experiencing resistance to your intuitive guidance in the form of doubt or anxiety, take a nourishing breath. Allow this to be playful and move into the imagination as you explore what it would be like to follow your intuition.

Now it's time to discern. Is the decision you are about to make out of fear or love?

The voice of fear will sound restrictive, perhaps strict or judgmental, and you might even feel constriction in your body. The fear-based option will likely feel like a familiar choice. Love will have a freeing, opening element. Sometimes calming and other times exciting, there will be a resonance in your being with this decision that cannot be denied. That's not to say the love-based decision will always be feel-good and free-spirited: sometimes it's scary, but that's likely because it's unfamiliar. Breaking through your comfort zones as you allow your intuition to guide the way can be uncomfortable. Continue aligning with love, trust, and the initial resonance of that intuitive nudge within you.

In moments of fear or doubt, always come back to your breath. Extend yourself the unwavering compassion you would offer a friend. Just like a butterfly coming out of its cocoon, expansive choices can be uncomfortable. Nurture yourself through this process, remembering you are expansive and capable by nature.

Like cultivating any other type of change, the choice between love and fear is a practice that starts with awareness. Navigating between the two requires discernment, patience, curiosity, and compassion. Sometimes the smallest shifts prove to be the greatest change-makers.

Perhaps spiritual teacher and author Sonia Choquette describes it best: "Intuition begins with simple shifts in awareness, followed by simple shifts in action, leading to gloriously positive shifts in experience."

Our intuition is expansive, always. The voice of our soul always has our best interests at heart. We may not logically be able to explain the reasoning behind something, but we know the feeling and we can learn to trust the feeling. Our intuition knows the way forward, and when it communicates this, it is our job to pay attention. It is our job to listen and act in accordance with its guidance. Our natural response may be to contemplate the how or the why, as seen in the stories I have shared, but it is crucial we always come back to the heart.

Just like any other relationship, our relationship with our intuition takes willingness and desire from both parties to co-create. This is a partnership that asks us to trust. It asks us to follow the $3 nudges so when greater leaps present themselves, our foundation of trust is stable and strong. It asks us to leave expectation at the door of possibility. It asks us to trust ourselves. It is a dance we have the honor of practicing moment to moment.

Its guidance comes in all shapes and sizes. Its guidance is unwavering.

THE UNIVERSE IS ABUNDANT, loving, and kind. Listening to your heart, aligning with your intuition, and choosing to trust opens your being to the abundance and beauty of the universe. It is all waiting for you with arms wide open.

Our intuition speaks to us in heart and body knowings. Its guidance is not something we arrive at through thought. Pay attention to the language of your soul. Trust your knowings and the sensations in your body. Take a chance on yourself and detach from the how and the why. Begin to discern whether your decisions are rooted in fear or love. Lean into love. When that feels challenging, reconnect with the love within you that already exists. You don't need to explain or rationalize your intuitive knowings. Acknowledge and thank them. Enjoy the relationship with your intuition - your soul loves to have fun. And keep practicing. Validate your intuition and celebrate your co-creation. Its guidance is ever-present.

Following your intuition is always an act of integrity. It is the wisdom of your soul expressed through your body. To ignore it is to discount your wisdom, your truth. In this way, integrity and intuition become the same. Choosing to align your actions with your soul's wisdom is the ultimate act of integrity.

My grandfather was a man of integrity, and in aligning my decisions with my intuition, I am living in my integrity. It took some personal journeying to affirm this, and it is something we all must decide ourselves, as personal experience and practice are the greatest teachers. Our intuition leads us toward expansion, and our integrity is strengthened in our ability to choose the love already within us.

Breathe into your body. What is your soul saying in this moment?

ABOUT THE AUTHOR

Melissa Chernow is an energy healer, channel, and writer.

Her mentorship allows empaths and heart-centered leaders embody self-trust, freedom, and pleasure through energy healing and channeling. Her grounded, warm energy creates a sacred space for honest transformation.

She channels the precise remedies your soul craves and has a gift for applying spiritual and energetic principles into tangible practices.

Melissa finds joy in many simple pleasures: breathing in fresh air while hiking, the soft sounds on a quiet beach day, the freedom of dancing while cooking, and losing track of time in deep conversation all things spiritual and self-development.

Instagram: *www.instagram.com/melissamelrose_*
Email: *melrosehealing@gmail.com*

MIRIAM SEKANDI

FACED WITH THE TRUTH

Where it started:
"Atanayitaayita, y'atenda nyina okufumba."

hat saying can be loosely translated to mean that the one who
isn't widely travelled, thinks their mother is the best cook.

This was me before travelling to Canada in August 2004. I was born and raised in
a former British colony, Uganda; central Uganda, to be exact. In the suburbs of the
capital city, Kampala. This might not mean much to some, but for context, Uganda is
a country with about 54 tribes and over 40 languages. I grew up in a fusion of collec-
tivistic culture, language and religion. This meant that the group was more important than the individual, and everything we did was aimed at maintaining harmony
within the group. So, to me, that's all I knew and had no clue that there were people
who lived differently.

Key to this collectivism was that we followed the traditional culture and staunch
Christian values passed down to us. Grown-ups were never challenged, deference
was the norm, and so, regardless of how you felt about something, you were expected
to obey, without question. This way of living also permeated the education system.
At school, teachers were not to be challenged, and what they said or taught was the
ultimate truth.

However, for me, this way of life did not sit well. I challenged authority by defying rules and expectations. Any instructions that did not sit well with me, I simply made up my own and, of course, got in lots of trouble. Ultimately, I was shaming the group by wanting to do things outside the norm. So, I was constantly receiving severe punishment from my parents and teachers. Punishments ranged from daily beating, hard labour, being locked in a school cell, anything that would get me humiliated enough to humble me back into following the rules! This infuriated me. I started desiring recognition as a rebel. It became a source of pride for me. And of course, it earned me more punishment and the name "molecule" by the girls. Molecule meant that I was so strong-headed and impossible to crack. This meant that I had achieved my goal. And with each punishment, I was reassured that I had made it! So with each rule that I did not agree with, I created an opposite one because I simply felt that it was unfair that there was never consideration for what I desired as an individual. This drove me nuts! It was stifling!

What, then, was I? Who was I? What was I here for if there was no room for my ideas and desires to flourish? It was kind of like you had to wait your turn to make rules that others follow. But not really, because you still had to make sure that even when your turn came as a grown-up, you had to play within the social, cultural and religious expectations. This was total incarceration! You are free but not really!

I remember my dad saying to me on my 21st birthday, "before becoming an adult, people blame your parents for any misbehaviour you exhibit, when you become an adult, people blame you because they expect you to behave appropriately." (21 is the legal adult age in Uganda.) This sent me into a frenzy! I didn't act out immediately, but I was distraught, not at Dad, but society as a whole. So they push you over the edge by imposing all these expectations, that in my case were totally against who I felt was in my body, now they were going to shame me as an adult for not blending in with everybody else? Gimme a break!

I welcomed adulthood with gusto because legally, it was now my turn. Even though I knew I was going to do my own thing!

THE JOURNEY BACK TO MYSELF

Something I look back on and see total divine intervention, stars aligned and manifestation at its best, was my coming to Canada. I had never longed to travel or live away from my country. My dad had travelled widely, but travel was not on my bucket list. Yet when I needed to get my Masters' degree, I knew travel was inevitable. I learned of possible Canadian Commonwealth Scholarships, and I submitted my application. Incidentally, mine was the first to be received. Hundreds of people submitted their applications, and after gruelling weeks of interviews, (I didn't even think I stood a chance,) they selected six names. Mine was one of them. Months later, two names out of the six were selected, and in August 2004, I left Uganda for Canada.

Remember, "the only cook I knew was my mom!" I encountered a totally different world. A more individualistic world. Without going into the pros and cons of this, I will say, this suited me. I finally had space to express my opinions and people listened. Instead of shutting me down, they pushed me to expand my thoughts about myself and the world. I learned to analyze concepts and ideas critically. Grad school but truly preparing me for the mega eruption.

With unlimited access to the internet, I dove in! I had a burning desire to learn more beyond what I was learning in school! Knowledge was suddenly not limited to the classroom or my socio-cultural group. I could access so much at my finger-tips. Then it happened: I discovered the world of personal development. I had completed my Masters, was expecting my fourth baby, and had months before starting my doctoral program. I consumed so much content that blew my mind! I knew it! When I rejected the suffocating rules that I was raised in, I was right. Everyone was put here on earth for a reason beyond what I was being made to believe. This knowledge expanded beyond the church teachings I was forced to learn, growing up. Church was mandatory. And for me, anything mandatory was automatically optional. Here I discovered that I was born with so much potential than what I was limited to believe. I looked back at my education and realized that all my schooling was decided upon by societal structure. I had been raised to believe that success was going to school, perform very well, go to university, get a degree, get a job and voila. You had arrived. To that add, getting married to a respectable partner from a good family, have children and make sure the cycle continues!

Well, things had already gone sideways for me. I had been sexually abused by my uncle when I was about six or roundabout there. Our house always had many relatives come and go, and I hated it. We had to sleep on the floor, in the sitting room that had no curtains—which was terrifying! Meanwhile, visitors slept in our beds. We sat on the floor to eat when they were around so they could have our seats on the dining table. They were served food before us. Guests were treated better than us!

This made me feel unwanted and less than! During one of these episodes, our uncle, who was living with us, sexually abused me.

As I became a teenager, I heard the talk, "no sex before marriage," or "save yourself for marriage." For me, these did not apply. I didn't have the special something to save before marriage. I was already spoiled goods. So, phrases like, "your body is the temple of the Holy Spirit," or "respect your body" meant nothing. I was already damaged, so there was nothing for me to save. I wasn't like other girls, so there was no need for me to act special. So, this compounded on my rebellious nature. When I became pregnant at 17, I did not even know that sex led to pregnancy. Well, nobody talked to me about boys, sex and pregnancy. All I heard through church was "save yourself for marriage," and I had nothing to save. Additionally, I had lots of male friends, and I recall being beaten lots or yelled at for being seen talking to a boy. No one told me why. Everything was a secret and approached militarily. Do as you are told, no questions asked! And that didn't sit well with me.

Now that I had access to the internet and learned all this stuff, I discovered that most of my childhood and teen life experience left traumatic imprints in my energy. The beatings and punishments, not being seen or heard, sexual abuse... all of that left a lot of gunk in my system! I also learned that it could be passed down to my children and the generations that come after me. Also that I had stuff that had been passed on to me in the form of ancestral trauma. Whatever trauma my parents and their ancestors had experienced, knowingly or unknowingly, had been passed on to me. And the biggest realization was that now that I knew it was my responsibility to stop this trauma in its tracks. That was the beginning of learning my truth!

I realized that the way I had been raised to follow specific behaviour, values and attitudes, was society's way of conditioning. And that this conditioning actually creates some form of institutionalized structure which turns individuals into inmates. The sad situation is that the people caught up in this form of incarceration are so deeply entrenched that they will defend the very thing that holds them down. All because this is all they have known, and anything other than what they know threatens their status quo.

Much as I had been rebellious, it still took me a while to break free from what I had known. I knew it was limiting, but I was afraid of what I did not know. I intended to go back to Uganda after my studies. So I could not change so much that I would not fit in. Even as a rebel, I knew how to compromise to maintain some form of harmony. I did not want to jeopardize that. How would I allow for this newfound truth and still be the same person? Little did I know, this evolution meant that mastering my truth would expose the true version of me that was new to me. She was always inside of me, but she was not even given an opportunity to emerge since birth and in my DNA. The rebelliousness was her trying to escape confinement. She knew even before this was apparent that she did not belong in those shackles.

With the emergence of Facebook, I sought to connect with many of my friends that I was raised with, scattered around the world. I sought to find one very special friend Jacinta that I had met during a brief modeling career stint. Modeling at that time was seen as synonymous with promiscuity. I was a teacher then, but I still pushed past the stigma and made some bucks through modeling. I actually enjoyed it! And I met Jacinta. During my Facebook hunt, I found her! She'd commented on someone's status. I *friended* her and sent a message. At that time, she was struggling and was trying to write a book. I didn't think much of it. We connected a bit. I really wanted to help her, but then she disappeared. A few years later, I tried looking for her. This time, I used google. I found her! She was an author. And she had a PhD! I tracked her down and arranged to go to California to see her. I flew down there, and when I met her, she was different.

She spoke "energy speak." The stuff I had heard on YouTube. She was a healer, a coach, something-something. I was mesmerized. I asked her many questions that had come into my head as I had listened to YouTube videos. Knowing where I had come from, she knew exactly what was going on. She explained the trauma, and even though I didn't get everything, I told her I needed her help. She was hesitant because she didn't know if I was ready. She said she would consult her guides. Whatever that meant! In church, anything that was not God, the Father, Son and Holy Spirit was satanic and ungodly. But this felt different. I felt my heart rip open and ready to receive more. I also felt a ton of heaviness leave my system as soon as I surrendered to this opportunity for expansion. Something about this moment felt so real. Like I had arrived. I didn't have to be anything else. I didn't have to contort myself into anything. I just needed to merge with whatever this was.

Next day, Jacinta told me her guides had consented to her taking me through the process. Honestly, some of the stuff is blur, but I recall being covered in a blanket, and I was asked to pray for my children and me. She had some incense (I didn't know what it was then) on charcoal and I prayed for my children one by one, praying for protection and preservation, and as I got to the last one, the clay bowl holding the charcoal exploded into pieces. I was terrified! She was so happy that something had been released, and I recall spending the rest of the day sobbing. I don't know, what that was then but now I know I released a ton of stuff and broke generational vows that had taken residence in my system. I recommend everyone to get ancestral release work done!

I guess going into the "promiscuous" modeling career earned me a friend that took me through a process I would never have gone into without knowing much about it! During that weekend, I broke free and started my healing from many self and societally inflicted wounds. I did more digging; my life changed, the way I parented changed, the way I approached my marriage shifted, I was never the same again. I could not unlearn what I had learnt. I knew that something had been trying to escape all along. There was a reason I was not simply blending in with other students at school. There was a reason rules did not sit well with me. There was finally an explanation as to why I never felt I belonged. That way of being was limiting. It did not see me for who I was. It did not see my potential. It measured me against a yardstick that was too short for what I was built for. It bypassed all my juiciness, gifts, calling, purpose, and reason for being placed on planet earth. It ignored my truth. And I was now more than ever ready to defy anything that stood in my way. I was not going to let anything come between me and my truth. I was going to seek my truth and express it, and I was determined to make it my life's work to help others who have been shut down and stifled through socio-cultural conditioning to discover their true essence.

One thing Jacinta kept saying to me was that I was being called to help others heal. She said she could see how powerful I was going to be. I didn't know what that meant. And months later other healers kept telling me the same. I discovered that although I now knew who I was, I had just opened a can of worms at Jacinta's. I was shown how much stuff I had to work on: my self-esteem, self-worth, self-belief, personal power, emotional intelligence, womanhood, sexual and physical trauma, emotional trauma, layers upon layers of stuff. I learned to be patient with myself and worked on each layer as it emerged. I discovered that some things I had taken to be part of my normal lifestyle were actually wounds that needed healing. One of these was the money wound.

I had no clue that I had money wounds or trauma around money! What did that even mean? It started with my consumption of so much free content that my head almost blew open. I realized that I could buy low-ended coaching programs. I went in, and they left me needing to pay more. Then I would stop. I have programs I bought that are very good now that I return to them, but I didn't know their value back then. But what I realized, I hesitated. Even when I felt it in my gut, I hesitated. When I contacted friends, they discouraged me from buying the programs.

I also discovered that my day jobs were not as financially fulfilling as I desired. I loved working with individuals recovering from traumatic situations, refugees, at-risk youth, etc. The money, however, was a problem. I was making more than most people, but I didn't feel the money reflected my worth. I learned that my worth could not be monetized. If I put a monetary figure on my worth, it would be in millions! But I didn't dare. I stopped seeing my job as something meant to meet my financial needs. My job was simply part of the work I am here to do. The money is just that, what comes to me on payday.

But it was not enough. And although I had healed a lot of wounds, here I was facing my money wound. I didn't even know I had a money wound. Gosh! Then I started on the journey. I took some money courses, but nothing changed. In fact, my expenses went up, and not as much more money came in. If you are working a day job, there are only so many hours you can work and so much you can make. And I had already realized that this money thing was not to be solved by a day job. So, I embarked on the quest of healing my money wounds.

I went back to my childhood, where it usually all begins. I recall being told to stay away from rich people's kids because hanging out with them meant I would become a failure in school, and not be successful in life. How were the two or three related? As I mentioned earlier, success meant finishing school, getting a job, a husband and children. I had all. *In fact, I have my doctorate a husband and kids. I should be successful, I guess?* So, what I had learned that had probably been passed on to my parents was that money = failure. No wonder, I had failed at securing enough of it! Also, a lot had been told to us that money doesn't buy happiness; money is the root of all evil, etc. So without knowing it, I had energetically repelled money because of deep-seated unconscious beliefs about money!

As a kid, I recall dancing at parties, and received money from the adults watching, as was the custom then. You dance, and people shower you with cash. I would take the money home, buy candy, and I remember being beaten for wasting money. I must have learnt that it was a waste to spend my money on (1) things I desire and (2) on myself. So, I would not really prioritize myself as a grown-up. I didn't want to waste money. That was a crazy realization.

I then realized how I echoed my parents when I spoke about money. Saying, "I don't have money," "I cannot afford it," "I don't have enough money." Especially saying these things to my children. I was passing down my money wounds! Realizing this took on a whole new meaning. I had repelled money with the energy of my words. I had not created space for money in my life. At this time, I have shifted my mindset around money and healed my money wounds, I feel so light around money now, whilst before it was a heavy topic that even caused big fights between my husband, children and I! I now know that money is energy. I too am energy. So if we are both energy, then money isn't separate from me! It took me a while to get here, but I did. And this has opened up money possibilities for me in ways that would never have been possible if I saw money as I did before!

NOW

Knowing my truth today has taken on a significant turn. I had to make a big decision. To complete my doctorate and return to Uganda and fade away into teaching and academia, or drop out and pursue a life of liberating others as I was feeling strongly called to do. Completing the doctorate wasn't easy. I completed it because I wanted to be true to my word. I had started it; I needed to finish it. I summoned all in me and completed it. But I knew it stood for everything I now stood against. Institutionaliza- tion. I only reveled in the fact that through my doctorate, I had been encouraged to express myself in my work. I really liked that. But there were still rules to follow. And I am a rule breaker! It is now behind me, and I am thankful for all it taught me. In the culture I was raised in, a doctorate is *success*. To me, it was the beginning. On my way to fulfil my destiny. So, I embarked on the journey of supporting individuals to heal, uncover their truth and reason for being and break free from socio-cultural incarceration. It all started with me knowing my truth, discovering who I was at my inner core and healing what wasn't mine.

Knowing my truth lies in me being fully expressed as me. With all the wisdom I have acquired and the medicine that is flowing out of me, I am now devoted to liber- ating others through their healing and evolution so that they can align with their life's mission. I help them awaken to the magic within them. To release the medicine within! To peel away the layers of social, cultural and religious conditioning and discover their true identity. I challenge individuals who declare that they "are a child of God, daughter or son of the Most High," to reflect on what those words actually mean. I encourage them to stand in the knowledge that if your Father God created and owns everything, as His child, you cannot lack! I take them from struggling due to subscribing to socio-cultural beliefs that keep them shackled to a life of collective socio-cultural and ancestral wounds and help them break free to a healed, whole and purposeful life. They heal from self and societally inflicted wounds and trauma and extract the medicine from these wounds that they are meant to bring to the world.

I have only shared a snippet of what my life was. There is a lot more coming up in other books. I am sharing this not to shame anyone because that goes against everything I believe in. I am opening up to highlight ways we can be misled by collective ideas to which an entire society or even a family subscribes. This is even more wounding for individuals who feel unable to fit in for various reasons. I have worked with individuals who are unable to fit family or societal molds because feel different. They don't see themselves as the family sees them and are therefore cast aside. Their ideas are dismissed, and anything they do is simply disregarded. If you have ever found that you are a proverbial black sheep in a family or a group generally, first off, you are not alone. Secondly, there is nothing wrong with you. There is more going for you than what everyone else knows. Thirdly, do not buy into the idea that you don't count because you are different. *Therein lies your medicine.* You are unique for a reason, and you are bound to do great things.

I also realized that most people prefer not to ruffle feathers. Some confess to simply acting quiet and compliant in deference to parents and teachers. Others say they are just naturally quiet and felt it best to keep the peace that way. Of course, some people are natural introverts. But being an introvert does not mean you lack your own ideas and should not express yourself. Carrying along as if there is nothing wrong and being a people pleaser doesn't free you of the unhealed wounds and trauma. Sadly, quiet, introverted kids are usually regarded as the well-behaved ones, while the loud, extroverted ones are considered to have questionable behaviour. In school the quite kids were recognized for their good behaviour while us the loud ones received extreme punishment. I even recall being denied a prefect position that I had applied for because I was considered too much! Ha! As they say, *not all that glitters is gold.* Those quiet individuals could be very traumatized but would never say a word.

I also realized that not all I went through was meant for me to suffer. The trauma, the modeling, the scholarship, the internet, Jacinta, all happened to me for a reason—to point me towards my life purpose work. But I could have carried on with my childhood's teachings as the ultimate truth if I had not chosen to be curious. I did not settle for the status quo. I allowed myself to be split open and to not only break free and release my medicine but to be sculpted into the being I was always meant to be. If I had not surrendered to the process, if I had not created room for my healing, growth and evolution, I would still be the rebel that society had created. I would still be complaining about unfairness and poor treatment by others. I chose to stop seeing the rebel and started seeing the person. I saw *me* in all my glory. And I know I know I have not reached the quintessence of my beingness, but I am well on my way. This is why I have devoted my life's work to helping others heal, grow, and evolve.

We all have the opportunity to awaken to who we are and to our truth. One has to get to a place of no return. A place where you are ready to cut your losses. To lose friends who loved you because you aligned with who they are and what they believe. To be estranged from family when you highlight situations where they let you down. If you hold on to the shackles in the form of societal structures that held you down, you can never be free. It's easier to hold onto the known than let go and plunge into the unknown. But when you know everything works together for your good, you trust that when you let go of what doesn't belong to you, what does will emerge for you to grasp.

ABOUT THE AUTHOR

Dr. Miriam Sekandi is an Intuitive Energy healer, Empowerment Coach and Spiritual Teacher. Born and raised in Uganda, she has overcome childhood abuse and trauma.

Miriam struggled to fit into the strict upbringing throughout her childhood. She rebelled against the stringent societal rules in a bid to establish herself. She endured years of emotional and physical punishment, under the guise of discipline. Unfortunately, it registered as trauma in her body.

Decades later, Miriam moved to Canada to pursue graduate studies and awakened to the truth that past trauma and programming had created a disconnect between who she was at the time and who she was meant to be. After years of healing and mentoring, she broke free and decided to help others overcome similar experiences.

Miriam created Break Free Zone, a sacred space where individuals are empowered to overcome conscious and unconscious, ancestral and childhood trauma and coding using trauma-informed approaches. She offers liberation and decoding group and one-to-one healing, belief clearing, and mentoring sessions. She also conducts personal development training for corporate groups, space clearings, and family group healings. Dr. Miriam is also an aspiring speaker and writer.

Dr. Miriam Sekandi offers meet and greet sessions through her website.

Website: *www.breakfreezone.com*
LinkedIn: *www.linkedin.com/in/miriamsekandi*
Facebook: *www.facebook.com/msekandi*
Twitter: *www.twitter.com/breakfreezone4*
Instagram: *www.instagram.com/breakfreezone4*
Telegram: *www.t.me/breakfreezone*

NICOLE CABASSI

CONNECTING CHILDREN WITH THEIR
INTUITION

I want you to know that while the start of my story has its darkness, I feel it is a necessary place to start. I want to take you to the light that has filled my life and raised me to a higher plane to show you that even the darkest start can flourish into the most beautiful existence and that there is always hope.

Like most, my formative years consisted of trials and trauma that left me vulnerable, isolated, misunderstood, and wanting to withdraw from the people meant to protect me always. Constant loss, abandonment, and deception filled my childhood, and worst of it all, I was sexually abused at only four years old. I felt scared and didn't know who to talk to. Hell, at that age, I didn't even know what had actually happened, what to do about it, let alone what to say or that it was utterly wrong.

My dad left when I was very young too. All these events changed me. I withdrew, became shy and developed insecurities, and ultimately, I felt like the kid that no one wanted. When my brother got older, he was diagnosed with ADHD with Hyperactivity and naturally, this consumed a lot of my mum's time. My mum's attention was in such high demand that I took on being independent and getting myself sorted because I knew it was necessary to help my mum and help myself. However, as much I will always love my mum, there was one person who recognized that I needed someone to focus on me: my nan! She was my rock, my constant love and support that never faltered.

At the age of sixteen, I was looking for love in all the wrong places. I chose friendships that were not healthy for my psyche or me. I felt that I had to adapt to be loved and accepted. I put other people ahead of my family and myself. At that vulnerable time, the disconnection from my family and home, found me wandering from place to place searching for the love and safety that I craved. The disconnection caused me significant hurt and trauma. While my parents may have been trying to teach me, it sent me into the harsh reality of unfathomable pain and turmoil. My walls were finally up. I built a cage around my heart, as it was easier than the constant hurt I felt subjected to.

As an adult, I can look back to these events to understand why such things happen. That's not to justify or condone the mistreatment that anyone experiences, but it is a reality that we must all face. To gain a deeper understanding, I created a little internal peace.

In my older years, this pain and trauma continued to follow me. I continued to choose people that were only there to benefit themselves. The manipulation and deception tarnished me further, and I felt so alone. My marriage broke down, and once again, the insecurities of being unwanted and unworthy began to rise. However, amongst all this darkness, I was blessed with two beautiful children who inspire me to be better and to do better every day!

Now, I don't want you to think that it has all been doom and gloom in my life. While all these events built a wall, the size of the Great Wall of China around my heart—I think even the International space Station could see it—this beautiful man came into my life. He knocked the

wall down one brick at a time. He laid them aside, showed me that he would be there even in my worst moments and inspired me to look within and see my worth.

From here, I began to flourish. I worked on my internal self so that I could project it outwards. The first mantra I started to recite was 'as within, so without.' As I became confident in myself, I began to address the trauma of my past. While I will never forget the pain I have been through, I have found that I can put my experience to good use, helping people address their trauma and overcome it, help lift them to a higher existence and become their true selves. So now that I have shared a little bit of the rawest moments in my life, and why I have come to this junction of wanting to connect with the younger generations to inspire them to experience their higher existence unashamedly, overcome the hard times they have experienced and help them transform like the lotus flower. Out of the murky water of life, it grows into pure beauty, trusting in its own unfolding.

For those close to me, it is a well-known fact that you would always find me engaging with children at social gatherings; they just made more sense to me, and it was a place of comfort—the innocent exchange of two souls with no agenda. Our interactions left me with sublime happiness. My soul felt enriched by their laughter and joy. There were even moments when I was at the shopping center or walking down the street, and my gaze would meet with a child. We connected on another level, they would smile or wave, babies would start smiling or cooing at me, and it was then that I knew I had this unique connection with children.

After high school, I studied and obtained my Bachelor's degree in Nursing and began working as a registered nurse. While this experience lifted me in many ways, I always felt that it was not my true calling. Being able to help heal people was rewarding and a time of my life I would never trade, but deep within my heart, this type of healing was not where I wanted to be. After my 23 years as a nurse, I decided to follow my truth and passion. It was then that I commenced my studies as a Medical Intuitive practitioner, through the Medical Intuition School, under the guidance of Emma Turton. This experience has truly opened me up to the possibility that I can achieve anything my heart desires. I have learnt how our energetic systems communicate with our thoughts, beliefs and behavioural patterns through a language of frequency, an idea that excited me to my core.

I now have a good understanding of the energetic flow within our cellular structures, and to maintain it, we must consciously connect with our metaphysical selves. However, depending on our emotional state, the stagnant negative energy accumulates in the appropriate Chakra centers and can manifest itself in the form of physical symptoms, illness or disease. Through the meditation and breathing techniques I have learnt through my spiritual journey, I have realized the power that we hold within, the power to change our vibrational frequency in ourselves, and attract the things we want most. That does not mean that if you think it will arrive on your doorstep the next day; it means that through practice and commitment you will have the ability to change your vibrational frequency to move in the direction your soul desires.

Additionally, the thought of being empowered to prevent illness, by being in control of our thought patterns and behaviours, has given me a new direction in my approach to healing and preventative health care, and overall awareness of how powerful the mind is. Through my personal experiences and recent intuitive studies, I could see the potential and benefits of

connecting children to their intuition, to overcome those hardships they may have experienced, at a young age. The potential to see them flourish, instead of wither for so long as I did was a no brainer for me. Even having access to children that have had minimal emotional trauma, being able to show them how to reach their full potential and blossom into adulthood with these skills is just mind-blowing. As mothers, we all have fears that we have done the right thing by our children; we have instilled in them the values and principles that will get them through their lives. That we have disciplined them fairly and have not impacted their emotional psyche to the point that it impedes their ability to function as an adult. We also have to step back and allow them to fly with the knowledge that we have done all we can.

We have different and various experiences during childhood, some good and some not so good. When there is negative emotion connected to the experience, we tend to lose a little part of ourselves, which continues as we grow and develop into adulthood. I believe that when we are born, we are born perfect, a clean slate. As we progress through our lifetime, sub-optimal events occur. The first time they occur, the soul is shaken, but stable. The next time, or a few times after that, our metaphorical armour dents. Sometimes, the events occur so frequently that they tear our armour. When the event is so traumatic, the tear occurs instantly, leaving us with fear, isolation, vulnerability and insecurity, to mention a few. When we reach adulthood, we have parts of us missing on a metaphysical level, or chinks in our armour, leaving a part of us in those negative experiences. By working on the metaphysical and bringing yourself back to your divine self, your soul will eventually know the peace you experienced as a child. However, if this negative experience and dormant energy are not dealt with on a metaphysical level, it can trigger physical or psychological challenges throughout our lives.

A child can also carry trauma from the previous generation and not even be aware of how it impacts their life. When I work with children, it is imperative to have a parent/guardian present to ensure the child's safety and comfort. When I interact with a child, I see them as perfect because I see their soul first, prior to any physical, psychological or behavioural assessment. The benefit of working with children is the ability to connect with them energetically and teach them the principles and benefits of how their little bodies store this energy, at a level that they understand. I believe this is paramount to their successful physical, emotional and spiritual development.

I have an inner calling to work with children and connect them to their intuition. This calling comes from a place of divine love and compassion, knowing that energy in its purest form is a frequency of unconditional love. And so, I aim at connecting with a child's true soul first, as perfect as the day that they were born. Any adverse behaviours are seen as an extension of circumstances that have left them with an inability to regulate their emotional state, causing confusion, anger, frustration, shame, or guilt. These feelings can be associated with experiencing trauma, powerlessness, and a sense of not feeling safe. I endeavour to create a space that promotes caring, understanding, building trust and respectful boundaries so that the child can intuitively know that they are in a safe space, free of judgment. By sensing the child's energetic frequency through my intuition, I can connect with children on a metaphysical level and determine any points of energetic blockages. From there, we commence working on the emotional connection to those experiences, to guide them to acknowledge the situation and shift the thought patterns from negative to positive.

For context, this doesn't mean that a teenager that has been in a horrific accident and unable to walk is going to experience the accident any differently or feel that everything is honey and roses. The aim is to enlighten them to think about circumstances in a different way that no longer hinders their current reality and uplifts them to seek more experience, to see themselves as more, to find gratitude in even the smallest life events and to share themselves in a way that helps them to overcome this trauma.

Ultimately, people will always choose their own path and reality. For instance, like siblings, two people who have experienced the exact same life changing events can have vastly different reactions and go on different paths. One may become destructive, filled with anger, rebellious or begin to abuse the body through drugs and alcohol, and even blame everyone else for their circumstances. On the other hand, those same experiences can drive the other sibling to want to achieve more, be independent, strong and grow spiritually, increase their awareness and understanding the hermetic laws of the universe to serve others helping them overcome their hardships. There is a no one-size-fits-all, and there never will be, but there is always a light no matter which path you choose to take if you are willing to commit and acknowledge your experiences every obstacle can be overcome.

I am so invested in this approach to wellness and healing that I have now entered the most supreme and fulfilling challenge of my life: working with children, from pre-teens to teenagers, who have endured the most detrimental and potentially traumatic experiences, at such an innocent and powerless stage of their lives. These children will one day grow to be adults and be supported with the tools to live independently within the community. Although this approach provides the necessities to everyday life, the problems can arise when alone, and the monkey mind starts its chatting—triggering fears and insecurities related to their trauma. These could spiral them into an emotional mindset altering their cellular energy frequency, potentially causing illness and disease. By passing on my intuitive skills and knowledge and teaching these children to overcome those moments, silence the mind and open the heart. Knowing when and how to use these skills in their everyday life and overcoming these hard times will continue to lead them through their adulthood with an open heart and an enriched life.

Spiritual self-esteem is the ultimate form of self-empowerment and freedom from the energetic entrapment that the negative circumstances have triggered. Having experienced parental abandonment and sexual abuse, I know the impact this emotional trauma has had on me, at a physical, psychological and energetic level. I kept the abuse and abandonment locked away in my energy centers, from the age of four. I never told a soul about the sexual abuse until in my thirties when I had my first child. The emotional connection to the sexual abuse continued to haunt me and followed me like a dark shadow, hovering in the background. Damaging memories, taking me back to my childhood home where the trauma was initiated. Triggers would ignite flashbacks of confusion, shame and a feeling of shutting down. Even the coming out was as traumatic as the abuse. My validity was questioned by the relevant parties, emphasizing the self-thought pattern, that I didn't matter, I was worthless and had no value.

The parental abandonment had catastrophic effects on my self-worth and self-love, decision making and physical and social development. It is incredible how you learn to fake it, making out everything was ok all the while I was dying a slow death inside. Using food as my comfort, never feeling like I really fit in or that I was good enough, struggling to speak my truth, therefore

putting others above me, making poor decisions when it came to relationships and intimacy, and always looking for love in the wrong places so I could experience that feeling of belonging somewhere or to someone.

The above emotional patterns had a long time to manifest in my cellular energy centers. If I had dealt with it at an earlier period of my life, I could have saved myself from so much despair, trauma and adverse health reactions. However, it would not have led me to where I am today and my truest of callings. They say our purpose for living life is already planned, and for the past five years, I have been working on finding out what that is. The spiritual healing journey has allowed me to find the missing pieces that I had lost along the way and be in a state of complete forgiveness in my heart. I am so genuinely grateful for the lessons that I could find, amongst the confusion and frustration when I visited those dark places. I am now in the most loving and healthy relationship and thank the universe every day for my husband's presence in my life.

As a Medical Intuitive Practitioner, it is my calling and dream to guide people to find their spiritual self-esteem and clear any energetic trauma lying dormant and holding them back from being their true unique self.

I have now come to the point of acknowledging my pain and suffering. While unfortunate, that had a divine purpose in this world, or it would not have led me to where I am today and being able to help connect people with their true selves. If my suffering is a necessary part of enriching others, like children and helping them overcome the difficulties in their lives and achieve contentment and inner peace, then I am grateful for every step that has led me here to this moment. My hope is that by reading this you will connect with my story in a way that helps you to take the next step in your journey, bringing you closer to wanting to tap into your divine self of pure love, cutting off the things that do not serve you or just waking up in the morning feeling like you are definitely worth it.

ABOUT THE AUTHOR

Nicole Cabassi, RN, Medical Intuitive Practitioner is an Intuitive Guide for Children — Connecting Children with their Courageous selves. Youth Worker- Supporting Children who have Experienced Trauma.

For the past five years, Nicole has been on a spiritual development journey, getting to know herself and finding the love that she never knew existed. This included advanced meditation, retreats, spiritual education, bonding friendships, and life-changing experiences granting Nicole the clarity of where her true purpose in life is. Medical intuition has ignited a fire in Nicole to connect children with their intuition and guide them to spiritual self-esteem to become the best version of themselves.

Nicole's journey has reached the ultimate privilege of serving children in child protection services. These children have been exposed to incredibly dark experiences. I see my service contract as an intuitive guide that provides spiritual direction to reclaim their wholeness and empowerment once again.

Nicole saids she married to an incredible man and a blended family of five children and five grandchildren. They live together on eighty acres of natural, beautiful bushland. Connecting with mother nature and taking every opportunity to ground. Nicole has two dogs and if they aren't off camping, you will find them in the vegetable garden, in the kitchen cooking up a storm or just relaxing reading a book. A daily, self-care ritual is completed to clear any negative energy and meditate to maintain healthy chakra centres.

Email: nicolecabassi@gmail.com
Facebook:
www.facebook.com/nicolecabassimedicalintuitivepractitioner

OLGA BOYLAN

COMING HOME

There weren't a lot of young people in Cameron estate, so when Sharon Keane moved into the house around the corner, I quickly went to introduce myself. "Hi, I'm Olga. Welcome to the neighbourhood. I just live around the corner." Smack! She punched me in the face. That was the start of almost four decades of friendship and an indication of how my relationships would be for most of my life.

I was a middle child of three girls. My poor dad was surrounded by female energy. Actually, this probably suited him quite well. My dad has a lot more of the watery female energy than my mom. She definitely was in charge of the family. She was and still is that strong matriarchal figure that glues us together.

I was born in a working class neighborhood in the northside of Dublin in the mid 70s. Back then, there was no talk of feelings or emotions. There was a lot of poverty, abuse, alcoholism, and trauma, but no one talked about it. You just got on with it. Count yourself lucky; what about those poor children in Africa? There was no room or space for intuition back then. It was instinct and action that got you through, not intuition.

My nanny Josie was also that strong, hardcore Irish woman. She had ten kids that survived; one died in childbirth. She brought them up all by herself as my granddad died when my mom was very young. This can't have been easy, but you never heard her complain. She just got on with it. The "just get on with it" energy was passed down to my mom and subsequently to my generation. My sisters seemed to do okay with this, but I was deep, emotional, and sensitive and needed to talk about feelings more and discuss obscure things like the big bang theory and collective consciousness. I possibly didn't get parented the way my soul longed for deep down. I voiced this to my sister recently, and she had a different view. Both my sisters saw me as the golden child. Yet, they didn't know that something deep inside of me felt like I never belonged. I never felt like I fit in.

I have chosen a different path now and live in Australia, and have a soulful parenting approach. Maybe it is not what my kids need as a parenting style; only time will tell. Don't get me wrong, my parents are awesome and did their very best for my siblings and me. They always motivated us and told us how we could achieve anything we put our minds to, but the truth was that things were a struggle. Growing up, we didn't have a surplus of money. My dad worked two or three jobs to provide for us. They sent us to a private Catholic school to give us the best education they could.

At the age of 8, we moved house to a "nicer" neighbourhood. It was an estate with many older people, and I remember being eternally bored as a kid. So when Sharon moved in, I was delighted at the chance of making friends with someone my age in the neighborhood. She had just moved from the inner city too, how exciting! That's just exactly what I craved, something outside of myself to create some excitement in my life. The craving for dopamine hits began years of chaos. I could not stand "the moment" as it was. I always wanted things to be different; more exciting, more dangerous, more free. I was uncomfortable in my skin and searched outside of myself for things to change how I felt, whether that was people, music, places, drugs or alcohol.

At school, I craved drama, and I was a constant source of disruption in the classroom to my poor teachers and fellow students. I just couldn't sit still. I couldn't stand the moment. I wanted to burst out of the moment,

I had this deep compulsion to act out on this, and I was often in the principal's office. I don't think I could attend English or maths class for almost a year due to my poor behaviour. My long-suffering mother was consistently down at the school defending me or fighting my corner. I had been a straight "A" student for all my life before my teenage years. However, once I had to sit down to study and retain information, that all changed.

I remember poor Miss Kearns, the music teacher, struggling to keep control of the class as I jumped from desk to desk before burning a cross into my arm with match sticks. (What a looper)! When she asked us what the smell was, I showed her the cross shape on my arm. She ran from the classroom on more than one occasion due to my antics.

This compulsion for chaos and excitement was so strong and stemmed from this deep belief system I had of "I am not good enough, I am not lovable." At the age of 14, that was not what I was saying. I am not even sure if I knew that I felt that myself then. Hindsight is a wonderful thing.

As an adult, I was diagnosed with ADHD, and with this knowledge and under-standing, a lot of my behaviour from back then makes sense. A misty haze of confusion is how I would describe it. It was deeply frustrating. I tried hard to study for my final school exams, which involved me trying to work with my brain that seemed to have too many tabs open. Why did others find this so easy? Am I stupid? Will my parents find out I'm a fraud, and I'm not as smart as they think I am? I am broken. This feeling of overwhelm was so intense.

I wanted an escape route, and I used drugs and alcohol as a break from this feeling. I stopped going to school. There were no ADHD interventions back then. When I got my diagnosis last year, I grieved for what could have been. I always wanted to be a doctor. However, I now know that this was not part of my life journey. Every moment in my life was as it was meant to be as it has allowed me to learn so many lessons along the way.

I was 17 years of age with the world at my feet, but my self-esteem was at an all-time low. Cue an older guy to walk into my life and tell me how special I was. He told me I was misunderstood, and for the first time, I felt like someone "got me." Fast forward six months, and I'm living in a drug den hovel in a pretty low socioeconomic area in Dublin. I was so naïve. He worked as a security guard in the local mall, and he used to come home and tell me stories of saving babies and mothers whilst being held at gunpoint. What a hero :).

The rave scene was taking off in Dublin, and we used to go and dance the night away fueled with what we called "recreational" drugs. At this stage, I was selling bingo cards on Henry Street in the city to make ends meet. I had completely turned my back on my loving family, as they did not support my relationship with this guy. I had this deeply misplaced sense of loyalty to him, and if they could not support us, then I was off. It became evident how toxic and unhealthy this relationship was, but I was in too deep, or so I felt at the time.

He threatened to kill himself if I ever left him, which got harder with each violent outburst. A turning point in this phase of my life was what happened on a sunny Sunday morning in a leafy suburb in North Dublin. I could hear church bells ringing, and smell the cut grass, and had a metallic taste in my mouth. I don't remember much after the first punch. When I woke up, he was gone. I had blood gushing from my face and managed to stumble down the road to my friend's house.

It was not the first time he beat me up, but it was the last time. My parents brought me to the hospital. He had broken my cheekbones, and I had bruises and black eyes, but the real pain was hidden deep inside me, not to be acknowledged for a long time.

What I used to say was, " Oh, look, it (the physical abuse) made me who I am. I'm a stronger person now. I just get on with it." And I did get on with numbing the pain and attracting more abusive relationships and carnage until I finally did the healing I needed in the last few years. Before now, I was trying to fill a void within me that I didn't have the tools and strength to fill by myself.

When I was 19, I went to a wedding in France in Normandy at a family friend's house called La Maison d'Amities. My family and I used to love going there. One of the family members that owned it was getting married. I was upstairs getting my hair done in this beautiful house, and this man drove through the property on a motor-bike. I looked out of the window, and I thought it was a vision. He was a gorgeous looking Frenchman. I was 19 and easily impressed. Despite my lack of knowledge of French, we found a way to communicate. Before you know it, I am off to Paris with this much older Frenchman. Bye, Mum. Bye, Dad. Bye, everybody. Enjoy the rest of the wedding celebrations. I'm off with this Frenchman who is going to make everything in my life better.

It did for a while, but the monkey on my back was always there waiting to sabotage me. What a beautiful and wonderful romance that was. The Frenchman brought me to Paris and showed me around. My return to Dublin didn't last long. I remember Sharon and myself smoking doobies in her garden, reading his letters, and translating French into English. "Your eyes are like the blue of the ocean," and then we would fall around the place laughing. We debriefed on my time in Paris. Sharon kept saying, "and that was all in French?" She couldn't believe it. I seemed to understand French intuitively.

Once I followed my heart to Paris, I spent almost four years living there with him while consistently going back to Dublin to party and practically living a double life. I tired of trying to be "good" and leapt from that relationship to another one that was certainly not as healthy and was fuelled by a lot of alcohol, risky behaviour, and bad decisions.

Festivals were a big part of life at this stage, and I was always surrounded by drugs and alcohol; forever the life and soul of the party, the one who never wanted to go home. I was one who would buy drugs for everyone and take them all myself and not really understand why people were upset with me. I was unpredictable. There was a lot of drink driving, many crashes, fights, many lost phones, wallets, etc., and one night out might end up being a three-month binge of partying. Life was chaotic, but I did not know any different. I thought this was normal. If I had stayed in Dublin, I am not sure I would be alive right now. Many of the people I partied with in the early days have passed away through misadventure or alcohol fuelled accidents.

I was out for my birthday one night when I was 27. It was an 80's night at this bar in Dublin, and there were probably 20 of my friends there all dressed up and ready to party. One of the guys had brought a friend with him who was a pretty good-looking guy. We partied together, and I ended up back in his place that night. On this first night we spent together, he said to me: "do you want to come to Australia with me?" For about a year before this, I had been considering a move to Australia.

In the beginning, he was full of compliments like: "You are the most incredible woman I know!" These compliments were great for my low self-esteem, and nine months later, we moved to Australia together. I since married that man, and we had two incredible kids. I am now divorced. That is a whole other story in itself. It started and ended with a lot of substance abuse and partying until we grew further and further apart, and I didn't know who either of us was. I lost my voice, and near the end, I had lost the will to live. The only thing that kept me alive was my beautiful boys. I believed the horrible things that I was told daily: "You are useless! You are dangerous! You are crazy." Two sick people together are not ideal.

Something big happened near the end of my marriage. Let's call it "the event." At the time, this event was so harrowing. I had to move out quickly, set up a home for my boys and myself, and start again. I can now look back and see that it was probably one of the best things that could have happened. It forced me to see what was really going on and to have the courage to take the step into the unknown. Sometimes the most painful things in life are the things that bring the most growth.

Single parenting is a tough gig, and the only thing that kept me going was my glass of wine at the end of the day. That glass turned into a bottle; that bottle turned into a couple of bottles. My rules around only bingeing and being hungover when I did not have the kids lapsed. I was so irritable and angry, and the only thing that cured this was a drink until it didn't anymore. The party was well and truly over. Alcohol was no longer working for me.

Two and a half years ago (to this day, as I am writing this), I found myself in a place of complete despair and loneliness. My body was screaming out for me to stop. I found myself in the hospital more than a few times with allergic reactions where my face and eyes would swell up so badly that I could not see or breathe. My body was rejecting my lifestyle. I spent mornings lying on the cool floor to try and bring down my body temperature. I felt like I was constantly overheating. My anxiety was at an all-time high. After a night of binge drinking in Melbourne, we were going shopping, and I had to get the taxi to stop and let me out on a busy motorway as I had a panic attack. Life was not fun—physically, mentally, or spiritually. I found myself at the jumping-off place, and I knew that things were going rapidly downhill. My life was only going to get worse if I continued. I found myself on my knees, crying out for help. My soul was dead. My body was a vessel, I felt empty and void of anything real and worthwhile, I could not even get joy from my kids near the end. I believe that I let a power greater than myself into my spirit at that moment, and I had my first true surrender.

Since then, I have not touched a drink or a drug and got into a 12 step recovery program. Embodying the program's wisdom has been a journey from my head to my heart and hugely instrumental in quieting my mind and allowing me to connect more deeply with my higher self and my intuition. The ability to communicate to Spirit has always been there, but as I have raised my vibrations, my psychic ability has increased, and now my intuition flows smoothly. I had a connection to Spirit for as long as I can remember. We all have this talent in us, and if we choose to exercise this muscle, our intuition strengthens.

I wanted to develop this skill and "intuitively" knew that meditation was the way to do this. My friend and I were driving by a local healing centre that we had never noticed before then. There was a sign outside for meditation classes and psychic readings. It was a moment of profound significance and synchronicity in both our lives. I attended meditation and spiritual development classes in this centre, and when the time was right, I asked the owners if I could work there. Their names were Tony and

Lucia, which are also my parents' names! I enjoyed years of helping others deepen their intuition and meditation practice and provided many healings and psychic readings within that centre's walls. In fact, I went on to buy that business with a partner. Although I am not part of it anymore, I know that the physical sign I saw advertising meditation classes undoubtedly changed the course of my life forever.

The sharpening of my intuition has accelerated since I got sober. I have raised my vibrations by self-reflection and acknowledging and healing any painful trauma I had spent my life trying to avoid. Early sobriety is not for the faint-hearted. All my suppressed feelings came to the surface, and I had to feel them to heal them. I stopped growing emotionally around the age of 14, so I am way behind the average, "normal" people in this regard. I work daily on pausing before reacting. What I used to see as a significant disadvantage I now see as my superpower. If you are an Empath and a super-sensitive soul like me, we have an important role to play in this world. With the right tools and a program for living a full life, we can share and spread our light and use our powers to do good in the world. Life does not need to be an uphill battle. You do not need to feel like you are fighting the tide of life, no matter your circumstances.

My life now is very different from the chaos and carnage of before. My insides match my outsides. I always presented as happy, joyous, and free, but I can honestly say that I feel this way now. I have stopped trying to run my life and plan how things will turn out and instead have surrendered to the fact that God, the universe, spirit, or wherever you want to call it "has my back." Trusting this allows me to really live in the moment and, wow, what a life changer that is. The transformation from a *shouty* mom to a patient and loving mom has been real. It is the small, simple moments that matter now; how flowers smell, the feeling of the wind on my face, the sound of the ocean, the feeling of my little boy's hands in mine! The heart-bursting moments I have with my boys are my fuel for life and make every difficult moment worth it.

We were just back from a mini-break in the Blue Mountains and had a special moment there to remember. We ended up down a very steep track searching for an elusive waterfall. Down the bottom, instead of a waterfall waiting for us, there was a mossy, slippy rock which resulted in lots of falling and crying, and that was just from me! I thought, "Christ, what have I done? How the hell are we going to get back up the top?" I paused and cleared my mind, and it came to me what to do. When we reached the top, I turned around to the boys and said, "look how far we have come...? Well done, boys. You did not complain once." I let them look after me, my youngest son on one side holding my hand and my eldest son on the other side holding my other hand and encouraging me by saying: "Come on, Mommy, you can do it." Because they were not thinking of themselves, they were helping someone else (me), they forgot about their own struggle and got up with ease. I was crying with gratitude and love, and we had a family hug. My heart was pulsating out of my chest with love.

The beauty of where I am now is that I am in a place where I can help others. You cannot give what you do not have yourself. I have an abundance of peace and joy in my life, and I love to share my light and help others get to a place where they can truly accept and enjoy the moment as it is. I no longer want to change the moment. The moment is all I have.

The moment gives me that feeling of "being home," that comforting feeling that I only ever got in meditation or by drinking or using substances. There is no separation from the moment, the divine, God, the universe, other people, or nature. We are all one. Our heart is the chamber for our soul. The answer is always within us—once you connect to this power, open and share your heart. The world needs reminding.

"The knowledge of the heart is in no book. Who looks outside dreams; who looks inside, awakens." - Carl Jung

Some key learnings in my journey of life so far have been;

- Trust in the process. What is for you won't pass you. The universe has your back. Surrender to the moment and allow what is meant to be to come in. If things are too hard, they are probably not meant to be. Listen to the signs of the universe. If in doubt, ask the universe or spirit for a sign. Each time I have doubted my intuition and have asked my guides for help, they have always come good. When I was preparing to do a reading, I asked them to give me definite signs, as this client was a doubter. The next words that came out of my mouth were, "Who is the female energy called Maria-Clara coming through that seems to have difficulty breathing." It was her mother that had just passed from a respiratory illness. Once I tapped into that energy and got validation, I was further able to delve in and be a clear channel for this client, allowing her to reach a place of healing and acceptance.

- Be still! You are a human being, not a human doing. Allow the space for your intuition to be cultivated. Tend to your soul garden with tools like mindfulness, meditation, love, and kindness. A good question to ask is: "How would love respond to this?" If you operate from the soul and tap into the non-physical world, you access a vastness of wisdom beyond this life.
- Be authentic. There is no-one quite like you. Don't be afraid to share your heart and vulnerability with others. It permits others to be them.

ABOUT THE AUTHOR

Olga Boylan is a proud Irish woman that harnesses deep Celtic energy in her work. She has overcome life challenges like abusive relationships, addiction, divorce, single parenting and a diagnosis of ADHD as an adult.

Olga sits in two worlds; the corporate world as an HR professional and qualified executive coach, and the spiritual world as a holder of space, a meditation facilitator, a mindfulness coach, an energy healer, a psychic intuitive and medium, a sobriety coach, writer and a spiritual being living a glorious awakened existence as a human being.

Olga offers one to one and group sessions and a tailored soul connection program. She provides clarity and healing, enabling clients to live a more connected and soulful existence. She is gifting potential clients an introductory free guided meditation to start their journey.

Website: www.psychicsydney.net.au

PAYAL KAKRIA

DIVINE GUIDANCE

Let me take you back to a winter night in the year 2005

JANUARY 21:

A pleasant breeze brushed past my fancy wedding dress as I walked past the peachy drapes with fairy lights and the bright chandelier. The brass white and gold sofa stood out so gracefully and added to the vintage vibes, which blended serenely with the decor. It had taken months of hard work for my parents to choose the perfect setup for their eldest daughter, who was about to get married.

As I was walking towards the red-carpeted stage, my heart fluttered. With the fanciest lights, mesmerizing decorations, and traditional Indian music playing in the background, I felt phenomenal. Everyone had their eyes on me and there were all praising me for how pretty I looked in my deep red lehenga choli, in raw silk, with hand embossed embroidery adorned with beads and zardozi work. I had this weird feeling of excitement and nervousness all at the same time, stirring inside of me. So, with all these butterflies in my stomach, I gathered the strength to step into a whole new world that was waiting for me. As I approached the stage, my husband to be awaited me. I looked into his eyes filled with love as he held my hand.

The day had finally come, 22nd of January 2005. It was a bright and cheerful morning, and the sun rays beamed through the curtains. I got ready to leave for the airport with all my bags packed. The amount of luggage I had was so massive that I had to bring it through cargo. I was making sure that I had everything I needed for the journey and I didn't leave anything behind. I was in such a hurry that I had to gobble up my breakfast within seconds. I hugged everyone in the house and took blessings from the elders. By touching their feet, an old-aged Indian tradition. Jingle, jingle my bangles went, as I rushed down the stairs in my sky-blue jeans and white sneakers. The birds chirped while tears rolled down my cheeks as the feeling of separation kicked in. As I sat in the car, I took my handkerchief out from my red Gucci bag to wipe my tears. With a heavy heart, I was leaving my family and my life behind. It was hard to believe that the place I grew up in and made so many memories in was actually not going to be with me anymore. The reality was hitting hard at that moment. I was on the journey to Australia, boarding the flight from International Airport Delhi at 8:15 that morning.

After all the security checks it was finally time to board my flight. I could feel a constant fluttering in my heart as I handed the boarding pass to the cabin crew. One of the young ladies guided me to my designated seat. I handed my luggage to my husband, to store in the overhead compartment. There was a constant chatter that surrounded me. Babies crying and people were talking. The air hostess handed me a packet of salted peanuts and a warm towel. I let out a sigh of relief as I spread the warm relieving towel across my face. I was so exhausted; I rested my head on my husband's shoulder that I magically drifted into a deep sleep. I woke by the loud thud of the plane as it hit the runway. I opened my eyes to the heavenly view of the clouds as I gazed through the window. The bright blue sky brought a spark of happiness to my face. I was excited for the new chapter of my life.

Everything brand new for me. New country, new lifestyle, new thinking, new people. A few months passed by and I was almost done setting up my new home. I was trying to learn how everything works in this country and in the process of settling down into the new routine and lifestyle, suddenly the days started feeling longer. I was unable to pass my time and got bored easily. I started to lose interest in many things. On top of that, I was missing my family like hell. It was practically impossible to talk to them every day. I wanted to tell them that I was missing everyone so much. I want4ed to tell them that I was feeling sad and depressed. My life was not fitting into the frame of what I had dreamt of. It was getting harder for me to bear the pain with each passing day. If I wanted to talk to my family, I had to purchase a calling card from the local shops to call them, and that was not always practical. Slowly, life started feeling like a burden. The internet wasn't freely accessible at that time and apps like FaceTime and WhatsApp didn't even exist.

As a newlywed bride, I was fairly reserved and scared to share my true feelings with both my family and my husband. How could I tell them that everything in my little world had totally changed from light to darkness. I was consistently missing the love and care that used to be freely accessible to me twenty-four seven. I would often lie and tell my parents that I'm very happy and settled in my new home as I didn't want them to worry about me too much. I had this feeling deep down in my heart, that if I told them what I really was going through they would get the shock of their lives and will not be able to bear it. I was trying to be strong all by myself, trying to fight this war. I was broken and I was failing miserably trying to put myself together. I slowly lost interest in dressing up and going out. I did not feel like meeting anyone. I stopped eating at the right time and started sleeping in more often.

It was an arranged marriage, and it made it even harder for me to truthfully open up to my husband as we were still in the process of getting to know each other fully. I kept my walls closed and kept them locked. It often became hard to express exactly what I was feeling in those moments. With each passing day, this loneliness got worse. I felt a deep hollow emptiness inside of me. There came a time in my life where there wasn't a single day that would pass without tears of pain rolling down my cheeks. I cried my heart out. That deficit of love created such a void in my heart. I stopped thinking straight. The loneliness overshadowed me. I felt trapped in a cage with no escape. Whenever I tried to ask myself how did this happen to me? I couldn't find an answer. All I knew and all I felt was lack of love and this killed me from inside. It started affecting my health. I could not leave my new marriage and go back to my parents just to fulfill the void that I was experiencing. My husband's love was not feeling enough.

This silence hit me like an arrow stabbing my heart so deep that I could barely speak. The thought of ending my life crossed my mind many times. I often felt that something is dreadfully wrong with me. I remembered that I *used* to be such a cheerful, vibrant and vivacious girl who sparked light and happiness. I had such a great sense of humour and I was a super energetic person. *What was happening to me?* Every time I met someone, I had to mask myself with a fake smile and act like everything is okay as if there was nothing wrong with me. I felt like a failure. I became such an expert at hiding my true feelings that even my family members didn't realise what I was going through.

I just knew that I still had a voice inside of my heart that kept telling me I have the ability to come out of it. I was totally clueless about who would be able to help me in such a situation, and then one night when I was self-reflecting, something really hit me. Hit me hard. It was my intuition talking to me. It struck me hard like a lightning strike. I had stayed in a constant state of denial and disbelief. I realised there is a door to other dimensions. We are not linear beings, living a linear life. We are multidimensional beings living a multidimensional life. That experience altered my identity. I got insights of reading the books Bhagavad Gita and Patanjali Yoga Sutra and many more ancient Indian texts.

In that moment I chose to trust my inner guidance. I had an instant realisation that I can't go back to being the same person again. I had experienced the divine in that moment. There was an arousal that took place, inside of me. The energy that I felt was outside of normal. It was so profound, that I couldn't have missed it. This channelling of light created a state of complete bliss. It felt like a union with the divine. The whole *me* lit up from within.

"The more you believe in miracles the more miraculous your life will be" - *Rumi*

After that insight, I gathered courage and could see that there is something bigger than me that had been constantly helping me, guiding me and reminding me to trust that I am always being looked after. I started seeing light at the end of the tunnel. I realised that life is so precious, and I can't just take it for granted and that I have come on this Earth for a higher purpose.

I am enough.

I now started to feel like dressing up, going out and meeting people. Slowly I was becoming who I truly am. I had transformed through the process. I started feeling strong from inside and I could pick myself up when I fell down. I carefully started observing myself and started being more conscious of what I was thinking and feeling at an emotional and spiritual level. The more I learnt and gained clarity about myself the stronger I felt. Life started feeling little easier. In this process of getting healed I conceived and got to know that I was carrying twins. My whole life changed as I was carrying these two precious beings inside of me. It was my duty to take care of these two souls that have chosen me as their mother, and I would do anything and everything under the sun to make sure that I am a strong role model for them. I have learnt that no challenge is so big that we can't overcome it. If we have the right mindset and we are aware and conscious, our soul knows the way and guides us each and every moment so we can stay on track.

Some lessons I want to share with you all ~

As I bid farewell to my old self and welcome a whole new me, I'm taking this opportunity to share my story of transition with you all. I've successfully been able to shed my limiting beliefs, and empowered myself to move forward in life, and made room for a whole new paradigm.

With immense hard work, sacrifice, and feeling extremely uncomfortable most of the time, I managed to level up with the help of books my deep spiritual practices and taking guidance from my higher self and the universe which has taken me more than a decade. I have finally shed my cocoon and turned into a butterfly where I feel light and free. I don't feel heavy, tied up or weighed down anymore. I can't hold all the knowledge I have gained inside of me anymore and have got the divine guidance to share it with the world as there are many souls who are waiting for this light to be shown to them. Be so deeply committed to your growth that you're willing to say no without guilt and yes without fear.

For me, It feels as if a whole new birth has taken place, so if you know the old me, I am very sorry to say that she doesn't exist anymore, there has been a radical shift in me if you've known me from the past. I'm here and ready to present the new me to everyone. So, if you still remember my old self, delete the older version of me as it has expired, and I will not be able to fit into my old image anymore. With this new version downloaded inside of me, I am ready and fully capable of helping anyone who is waiting and wanting to become a new version of themselves. I know and can feel some of you have been struggling and wanting to change many things in your life but are unable to do so. I have worked very hard on my personal and spiritual growth and I guarantee you I have all the tools and experience to take you out of the rut if you are feeling stuck in any area of your life.

Trust me, I know how it feels like to be in that place, I have been through many sleepless nights, been in unbearable pain countless number of times, tons of depressing thoughts, have overshadowed me a million times and yes, I have experienced them all first-hand so I can exactly feel where you are coming from

I am not saying the change is easy, but I can assure you, in the end, is all worth the effort. If you allow yourself to be known and heard in your own authentic way, you were born to do greater things, so believe in yourself. I believe that We all can be an inspiration to each other in our own little ways, so whatever you are not changing today, you are choosing for yourself. So, choose wisely. We all need an upgrade at some time in our life, and it's high time to that we take this note seriously, as the new earth is helping all of us in its own unique ways if you are ready to resonate with our own higher self in the 5d there's no stopping for you. Just remember to remain kind and humble to your own self. During these times.

Being honest and being authentic is the new powerful. So, you just need to get out of your own way and stand up for your own self and know that the universe is always there to support and guide you. Surround yourself with people who can uplift you. Everything that you have lost until now, or will lose in the coming journey, will be replaced with something better or higher, trust the transition as it's going to add magic to your life. If your life is getting harder right now, believe you are levelling up. Do a reality check to see where you are, who you are, what you want to be, and what you want to do. The universe is guiding you each and every second, but nothing will change if you don't show up. If you're not in alignment with yourself, you already know it or are aware of it, or getting subtle signs from your inner voice that you need to change, something, somewhere, somehow. Your soul is dying to be in alignment with you so that what you have dreamt of you can deliver to the world in the way you want. Don't be afraid of losing anything, because there is nothing to lose but only to gain from life.

Just be aware that if you still stick to your old version it will be very difficult for you to survive into the coming times. You can either lead with fear or intuition. Also remember that when you set out on a journey, do not seek advice from people who have never been there, let me help you to the next version that life requires you to be. It will be a total game changer if you take the responsibility for giving yourself the life you want. I trust my instinct that my story would inspire and encourage millions of people across the globe to transform to unbelievable levels. Unleash the power within you, so that you can create a better you. The energies and people you surround yourself with, will eventually become a part of you. Let me help you turn the power within you, which is lying in a dormant state, to turn into a superpower for you. With the expertise that I possess, I have all the means to empower you. Once you find yourself, its only then you can start working on yourself.

"What you seek is already seeking you" - Rumi

The next version of you is waiting to meet you with open arms. The higher self and the divine is always helping, protecting, guiding and loving me. As the awakening started, I was no more a torn page in my own book. I became a ray of hope. I am able to add light to the world. My intuition and inner guidance saved me from drowning. I felt liberated, empowered, and inspired.

I touched the peeks of self-realisation, channelling messages straight from the divine, tapping into my vortex, my soul guided me towards my true purpose. I now feel like a tree, loaded with fruits, to give shade to the needy and for those who are starving, give oxygen to the breathless, with roots grounding me to the core. Love is all I am, and love is all I can give. Love has given my power. love has given me hope. Love is the highest vibration. Once you touch the peak of self-realisation, the truth will unfold itself, you just need to take a leap of faith.

ABOUT THE AUTHOR

Payal Kakria is an intuitive healer and consciousness mentor. She is a mother of three beautiful children and has been living in Australia for the past twenty years. She comes from an Indian heritage where she was raised and brought up.

Payal went through many challenges in her life but has been successful in overcoming them by tapping into her intuition and trusting the voice within. This has helped her to become a stronger and more powerful woman. After she experienced self-realisation, she has been able to find her true purpose.

Payal wants to help humanity reach a higher level of consciousness. She reaches people through her podcast: Soul Sessions with Payal and she has her own coaching and mentoring program.

Payal posts uplifting and positive videos on social media. She also owns her own healing clinic where she helps people to release any pain or trauma.

LinkedIn: *www.linkedin.com/in/payalkakria*
Instagram: *www.instagram.com/paayal_kakria*

RAJALAKSHMI JEYABALAN

TINTED NOT TAINTED

He said, "Hmmm, it looks like a small growth. However, it is not life-threatening. Nothing to worry about. I could still see you again tomorrow to proceed with a small surgery on it."

Dr. Sean was still holding on to my hand. A conversation I thought was not going to take long took longer than I expected. He moved closer and peered onto the two-centimetre-long growth on my right bicep.

He then placed his inner thighs outside my knees to close them together.

The vibe I was feeling from him and his body language made me feel like a child in restraint with no wiggle room moments before receiving an injection.

Each time he started to explain after inspecting the zit-like growth on my right arm, I slid my hand out of his hand. He took my hand into his hands three times in the pretence to inspect and explain his diagnosis. Each time he reached out for my hand, I slid it away.

As he commenced to explain after his first examination, I freed my legs from his inner thigh grip without losing eye contact and pretended to listen to him attentively. I was anxious that he would grab me sexually, so I did not want to set the alarm for him to react that way in desperation, which was the internal vibe I felt. I could not help notice how green his eyes were, and the curiosity to know his cultural origin was overwhelmed me. My logical mind kicked in to wonder if it was normal for men from his culture to hold a patient's hand while giving their diagnosis. I wondered if his age, which seemed like in his early 50s, projected him to behave in a controlling way during his medical practice.

When he became conscious of my escape gestures by the third time, his expression showed extreme disappointment. Feeling his change of emotion seemed familiar to me for some reason.

His sense of disappointment came across like a child who did not get a lolly despite his persistent efforts to ask for them politely. I would not fall for his intimidating body language, which was no longer seeming within legal boundaries. Wishing not to give him the power by reacting, I counted my blessings that it did not end up with a sexual request or being sexually violated in his room.

Before I stepped out of his room, he asked where I was formerly from. I replied, "I am from Singapore," however, just as I asked him the same question back out of reciprocity of curiosity, a voice in me said, "Egypt." My intuition said to me that he is from there, and that he played a huge role in the ending of my past life.

As I stepped out of the room, I started to see visions of him in a black and navy-blue cloak. A sense of knowing that this is the final puzzle of that past life. A past life that carried the key to my purpose in this birth.

2017

I stepped into the world of personal development, knowing little to nothing about how it would make any difference in my life. The words: "What is your innermost dominant thought?" got me thinking of every area in my life that has made me choose second best instead of the best. Growing up in an environment where I witnessed physical abuse, arguments, expectations, and constant tug of war in my parents' marriage caused a certain level of low self-esteem within me.

At the age of 12, I witnessed a huge argument between my parents, and an overwhelming sense of anger and fear rose from my feet upwards, which made me stop my father from hitting my mother. I screamed at him when I gathered the courage to say: "Don't you dare touch my mother."

However, little did I expect that this situation had programmed a deep imprint in my subconscious mind, causing it to repeat in my marriage too. My first epiphany in my first personal development journey was based on this event, which showed me how I was mirroring my mother's defensive gesture towards my ex-husband, Sathish, just like my mother did during the argument I witnessed. I was filled with gratitude that my parents showed how not to be in a marriage and that I do have a voice to express my disagreement on marriage antics.

A month into my epiphany, I decided to tell my ex-husband that I could no longer pretend to be happy in the marriage. I had realized that I became asexual growing up as I resented men and their desires for intimacy. I craved for the sense of touch of a man and his kiss but the act of intimacy numbed me. I played the blame game that my husband was not helping this neuro condition of mine to heal and does not have the interest to as he had kept me on the shelf of no sex for 3 years. As we flew back to Perth from Singapore after visiting family, I bawled my eyes out, expressing how empty I felt in the marriage, and decided to take time away from our union for six months. My ex-husband was clueless about why I was crying like a child who had lost a doll and desperately wanted it back. Let alone he neglected to understand how I was truly feeling within about myself. It certainly was a feeling that I had lost something, and it was going to be difficult or even impossible to retrieve my life as I was holding on to the better choices I may have unwisely declined and years I had lost. Although I was visiting and on vacation, it seemed like a trip to heal myself at the place I grew up and created most of my childhood programming.

During the six months of separation from the marriage, I had dived deeper into personal growth as the universe seemed to be providing me financially to get the inner child healing work done. I only understood the basics of the law of attraction, neurolinguistics, and quantum physics, but somehow, things started to unfold unexpectedly because I was becoming a junkie of "The Power of Letting Go." It was becoming a drug as I was beginning to fuel my low self-esteem with the little things I discovered about my hidden thoughts and perceptions. I still played victim as I only realized the effects of the causes on a surface level.

However, the universe threw a curveball on my decision to leave the marriage by sending Sathish, my ex back onto my path to ask for reconciliation.

As it seemed easy to return to default and stay in comfort, I agreed to work on the marriage again.

2018

After graduating from my first personal development course in December 2017, I stepped into 2018 with lots of hope that the marriage would escalate to a whole new level of success. That I could work on my asexual realization and try to become more intimate with my husband. I created a vision board filled with materials and vacations as per what he had promised upon the reconciliation. My expectations towards my growth became ego-driven that I had done the inner healing work, played by the universe's rules of letting go so the overconfidence that I am in the universe's good books. What I perceived as success was statutory in the material world. We upgraded our car, and we decided to go on a flashy vacation that we had never done so in our nine years of marriage; basically, we wanted to go back to pretending to be a happy family in the 3D world of external gratification fuelled environment.

The universe had other plans for me. Let us just say that 2018 became the year that the universe decided to drag me, face down, on the gravel to see what I was refusing to see with clarity and listen to my intuition.

I went down the rabbit hole of spirituality and studied the art of Reiki. Being a stay home mother who is a wife to a FIFO worker who worked away in the mines of WA, Perth, I was grounded to be in stillness. The universe well-orchestrated it for me to become more aligned by forcefully becoming homebound, a domestic goddess. This was a title I never wished upon myself. However, I became her, due to circumstances. This forceful grounding state started to show me visions, screenshots of a woman with long black hair, kneeled on dunes before an reddish orange stained fortress, with her neck bowed down. I felt a sense of familiarity towards her, although I was unable to view her face. My indoctrinated mind started to fear if it was a spirit following me in my dreams, so I used reiki to block her from showing up in my mind. I finished the basic and advanced courses on reiki, hoping that it would elevate me in my spirituality as I feared to see spirits of any sort.

By now, cracks were starting to reappear in the marriage. I decided to channel that sense of void in the marriage into a career, back to the workforce.

2019

As I came down the staff lift of the hotel, I walked into the human resources office. I took a deep breath as I knocked on the office door of the human resources officer who was busy on a call. I handed in my badge as an employee of the hotel and said, "thank you, I quit."

She wore a face of shock and anxiously gestured me to wait; however, my mind was made up that I would not turn around to be convinced to stay.

I walked up the slope that led to the majestic glass door by the street and into the unknown world of my future.

As I pushed the door and felt the change of environment, the hustle-bustle, the traffic, the birds chirping, I heard the loudest piercing ringing in my ears, which was deafening every other sound of nature around me.

That was the sound of change, the sound of saying "No" to chaos, the sound of letting go for my better good for the first time in my life.

As I walked towards my car, I still had a niggling feeling that I had to let go of one more thing in my life. Before I could start the car, a flow of thought came through: *my marriage. I must let go of my husband.*

I picked up my phone and said, "Dear, I am letting you go," without any hesitation or stutter. He was just as surprised as the human resources officer.

He replied: "Ok, as you wish."

His voice projected a sense of relief in his tone. A relief that he no longer needs to provide me with explanations about his folly anymore, which I used to pick up on during our union constantly. It made him feel like a child being caught red-handed. He tied the knot with a woman who resembled his mother, one whom he resented for the same reasons.

As time went by after I pulled the plug in my marriage, many around us who saw us as a loving, successful couple who created two bright children and was rising in the game of the 3D world with our materials, could not wrap their head around what was wrong in the marriage.

No one could guess the void, the big white elephant staring at us constantly into our marriage which was stifling each other in our ascension as individuals.

There were lots of speculations on what could have happened, but no one could guess that we no longer loved each other and became friends playing happy family to cover the untold truth embedded in my mind for so long that I am asexual and equally married to a man who does not touch me sexually anymore.

The 18th of May 2008, the day we tied the knot traditionally before relatives and friends: as I was removing my heavily decked up accessories close to midnight upon returning to my in-laws home, my husband entered the room smiling. However, I was in tears.

The next thing I knew was I was slammed against the wall and told to shut up and almost landed a punch on my left cheek, but he controlled his temper and decided to land his fist on the wall behind me. Surely, I did shut up because all I could think of was, "what just happened? Who is this monster?"

"Am I going to die on my wedding night?"

"He is supposed to be a kind man like his father."

"He comes from a respectable family; this does not look right."

A month after our wedding, we moved to Perth, Australia, where he attained a promising job with a 4-year contract as a mobile mechanic.

I thought this would be amazing and a brand-new beginning because the stress inflicted by family would take the monster I saw on the wedding night in him.

How wrong I was. The cracks started to show.

In Dec 2008, six months into moving to a new land, I dialled 000 from the bathroom of our one-bedroom apartment, where I felt the safest at the moment. The monster in him was back—however, this time the worst and in action to charge. I waited in the darkness of the bathroom, and even while hiding, he said to me, "I am sorry, please come out. I didn't know what I was doing." When the police arrived and assured me it was them and that it was safe to open the door, I was shocked to see blood all over my clothes when I switched on the light in the bathroom. That evening I was hospitalized with a broken nose and a bruised eye because I walked away from an argument I perceived was pointless.

I received numerous calls from his father asking, "Are you going to leave my son." Every time he called throughout the night, I hoped his question would instead be, "Are you ok?" The voice of my father-in-law had a tone that felt he was questioning my loyalty to him. I was obliged to pay back his loyalty as he gave me the privilege to be his one and only daughter in law. His kindness before our marriage and all that he had provided me to marry into their family was pulling me away from deciding on righteousness.

The next morning, I returned home from being discharged from the hospital into our one-bedroom apartment which we had just moved into two weeks ago. Feeling the emptiness and cluelessness of what had happened the night before, I lay on my side of the bed, turning away from my husband's side, not wanting to acknowledge his absence and the possibility that he will never lay beside me again.

Shortly after, my phone rang, and on the other side was my husband bleeding his victimhood onto me that he wanted to be forgiven.

I gave in to loyalty towards his family and their reputation and forgave my husband that morning, which was the most significant setback in my life.

Upon opening the door for him, he was shocked to see the damage he had done. He could not believe that he had hurt me that badly. It seemed like he believed that someone else took over his soul at that moment. This was when I started seeing the cracks in his mental state.

Sathish affirmed to me that he would evolve and turn into a new leaf. His dedicated visits to his anger management classes were superficially blinding me to the mask he wore.

This mask created a man who decided to control me in ways I least knew that fell into the category of narcissism. He controlled me with his silence and emotional absence.

To save the marriage and fill the void between us, we decided to start a family, and we created our firstborn three years after our marriage to each other, a calm and obedient child, our daughter showed up to brighten our life . He proved to be a great father who was hands-on and treasured her like his prized possession, but I did not notice his control even then.

He started to deny me my self-worth as a woman and wife. I was not allowed to pleasure him sexually, nor did he feel he had to love me that way.

When I would tap him on his shoulder to show me love sexually, he would nudge it off with reasons that he was tired or felt too cold during winter. I kept searching for ways to please him in ways he would notice me. I cooked sumptuous meals to feel loved, to no avail. I dressed well to be planted a gaze of amazement from him to no avail either. I worked out at the gym, diligently attending classes at least six times a week after my 2nd child's birth, a miracle who was conceived on a one-night stand with Sathish after two years of a dry spell, of no lovemaking. It made the situation worst.

It made him feel that I was even more untouchable—that I was starting to look too good for him physically, which gave him more of a reason not to feel worthy of me.

I was forgotten. Eventually, my cries for attention came out in the forms of chaos to be loved.

The day I decided to free him from and any further attempt to save this marriage was the day I realised; his silence controlled me.

Some nights I woke up from a repeated nightmare of hearing the news of my husband's death from the mine site which he worked at, but it was images of the desert much like the red earth on the mine site. It felt real, as if I have been there and experienced being informed that I am now officially a young widow aged 29.

I questioned why I was still feeling incomplete and needed answers and further work. It was then I was introduced to the world of subconscious reprogramming and rewiring combined with trauma release. I plunged two feet in when a friend introduced this elite programme conducted completely online, something I had a limiting belief towards as my logical mind was moulded to think that work must be physical hard labour, face-to-face. I genuinely wanted answers to why I experienced domestic violence in my marriage, my true purpose, the pattern of my financial flow, which was always irregular, disconnect from my own family, and the sense of constantly feeling misunderstood.

Growing up in an Asian culture of heavy indoctrinations of religion, it was also intertwined with hypocrisy that abusing a child physically was a form of discipline, something inevitable. Capital punishment with a rattan cane was normal and this is a concealed taboo topic in Singapore. Most prison sentences are included with capital punishment of a few strokes from a 50cm-long cane.

If the law was setting a role model for discipline, it was certainly being practiced at homes as a form of curbing a child who did not behave as expected. As a child, I experienced physical abuse on multiple occasions and because of these events, I was unable to accept the home environment I grew up in as it did not resonate with me to attain tiding for poor grades. As lots of importance was given to academics, I was certainly perceived as a rebel for my poorer grades in comparison to my sisters.

This comparison was the thief of my life, and always felt alienated from my sisters, who were four years older than me and grew up with different perceptions.

I developed dyslexia at the age of six, and staying focused on reading, or long duration of examinations were a true challenge for me. My sisters would spell words out to prevent me from hearing their conversations. This occurred due to my creation of resentment towards my family which disciplined me with a cane. Over the years, I invited criticisms that I was blunt and bitter especially when I started my career as front office reception at the age of 21.

In the journey of finding my purpose and values, to my surprise, physical abuse was a repetition of a past life event. This past life that kept flashing as a vision since 2018, carried perceptions of anger, control, and deep sense of feeling misunderstood

At the age of five, my dad had closed me in a dark room to prevent me from running out of the house to stay with my grandmother, who was preparing to head to her own home. Those moments of sitting in the room feeling lonely and trapped, and feeling resentment towards my father was a recreation from my past life in the jail. I could not believe my eyes because it was the same feeling as I had felt when I was five.

A former friend, who was a karmic connection and is no longer in my circle, also showed up in the hypnosis as the chambermaid, named Jamilah who gullibly gave information of me to the court investigators of the Queen that I was engaging in mysterious acts and rituals. She advised them that I was usually up late, praying and performing rituals especially around the full moon phases. As there was a belief that the moon carried strong energy, my rituals were perceived as evil and used as evidence to frame me for treason. As a single parent who had a son to support, just like in this birth, she did it for the monetary reward she was offered if she told on me.

Growing up, my mother always asked why I felt I was very misunderstood, and this was something I carried with me since young. Little did I expect that these were fragments my soul carried from my deeply wounded past life in a place called Tubak , close to Egypt , in BC 624.

Going deeper into this past-life hypnosis in Aug 2020, I watched 3D visuals of myself and how I was imprisoned for treason and during my imprisonment prior to my execution day, I experienced sexual and physical abuse; being whipped and brutally assaulted by soldiers. This too explained why I yearned to feel loved but not any sexual act as this is what my soul resented . In this past life was when I was married to my ex-husband who died on battlefield and never returned. We were not blessed with children in that birth

. After his death, I was offered to work in the fortress as I was known to be a healer in the village I resided in so to fill the void of my loneliness, I took up the offer. The offer was to become a Sacred Prostitute which was believed to be a highly powerful way of healing men. However, I had found myself falling in love with a particular soldier and this led to my doom's day.

As a sacred prostitute my designation was to only use sexual pleasure to heal men who returned from battlefield, not to fall in love which we were warned against. I had emotionally attached myself to a soldier in the palace and was starting to refrain from healing other soldiers who needed healing as I felt guilt being sexual with other men. This in a way caused my death as I had refused to heal a palace medicine man, Dr. Sean in this birth, who had approached me for sex not with the intention to attain healing. He certainly did not qualify to attain sexual healing. He sabotaged me to the higher authorities that I was not a genuine priestess and was breaching my duties as a sacred prostitute, also using the information Jamilah had provided. I was kept in jail for days, being whipped to speak the truth of my rituals I was framed as practicing secretively.

Being able to meet her through a deep hypnosis made me realize that her last moments on the dune before she was executed with a bow and arrow to her back, she was not angry for what happened to her but more determined to prove her innocence and that her work was pure.

Knowing this allowed me to understand why certain events happened in my life and no longer resent the people who carried out the physical abuses as they were enacting out the imprints of my soul's memory. Something that they would not have known either but were made to make me come to awareness through their actions.

It allowed me to come to peace with what happened in this birth. I realized that everyone around me showed me what was played out in my most recent past life, which took a while to reincarnate due to the impact of the emotion felt. I had learnt through quantum physics that the more the negative impression was created during the death, the longer the soul gets to reincarnate. This is what we label as an old soul and an old soul I indeed was with a birthmark on my back that grew with me, believed to be my execution point.

Using my intuitions to find myself throughout this journey of self-discovery was the best yellow brick road I had ever detoured on to. Every step towards healing my past life wounds was guided by my intuition, and if I happened to take a detour from the path, I was always pulled back to it with a harsh lesson from the universe.

Whenever I channelled into my intuition, I could even find directions without using a navigator to guide me to my destination. I was starting to notice people whom I am familiar with instantaneously as they would be right behind as I turn with a sense of knowing that they were. The icing on the cake was when I crossed paths with the soldier I loved in that past life after engaging in the inner child healing program. His energy was completely familiar—a man who was well built and carried lots of pride over his religion, upbringing, and career. The old version would have instantly fallen for his looks and his choice of sweet words. He poured to me about the caste he came from , his growing wealth and his assets. Although I instantly rejected his proposal , my intuition said I had to allow him to come into my life and so I did. In a month of knowing him, I realised he was not what I preferred internally, certainly not in this birth. Realising why we crossed paths and how we shared similar visions during meditations, allowed us to understand our journey. We were not meant to love in this birth and clearly the perception that this is forbidden love was eliminated. It is not all the time that when we cross paths with someone from our past life that we are meant to unite as a couple. Letting him go in this birth allowed me to step into my power more as I was not bound to what the visions were showing me and used my intuition to guide me on my decision to end the courtship eventually.

The biggest lesson was that love is about connection and the mutual emotional understanding and not about one's stature, which was what I was attracted to in my past life as well as before I healed my inner child wounds in this birth.

It has become a necessary tool to use in business and social environments that a day without tapping into my intuition made me feel misaligned.

Three years of peeling the layers to my intuition has led me to find true passion in helping others. I am currently pursuing my traditional education to become a case manager, preferably in helping women who have experienced domestic violence, while running my own business as a Subconscious Mind Reprogrammer and Time-line Trauma Release Practitioner . Eventually, my main goal is to incorporate my professional and clinical knowledge together to be able to serve the community I reside within. This is where I was guided to serve and could not agree less on that decision from my intuition, my higher self.

All credits go to the collaboration of the power of letting go and intuition.

My void of feeling anger, having grown up with physical abuse has made me find my true value and passion in life. I would not change anything about the way I experienced life as a child as if it were any different, I would not have found the answers I was looking for all my life.

ABOUT THE AUTHOR

Rajalakshmi Jeyabalan is a mother of two beautiful young girls, aged 9 and 5. She is currently a subconscious mind re-programmer managing an online business, Tinted Not Tainted. She was born in Singapore and moved to Perth, Australia, at the age of 26, a month after her marriage. Within five months of her marriage, she was a victim of domestic violence and felt trapped and obliged to stay in her marriage since then. Although the marriage no longer was violent, she knew she was unhappy. Through her journey of self-discovery, she decided to take the executive decision to free each other from the marriage because she was ready to stand on her own feet. With the professional knowledge of subconscious reprogramming, she mainly specialises in Timeline Trauma Release and Past-life Regression using holistic techniques such as Reiki during the sessions with clients. She is also currently pursuing her professional education in Community Services to work towards becoming a Clinical Psychologist and specialise in Women Services. She wishes to guide women using the reprogramming tools she has learnt to step out of their victimhood and to be able to stand up again with courage after their life's experience and realize that they have the power within to create a better future themselves and that it's not the end but the beginning.

Email: rajijeyanair@gmail.com

SALLY-ANNE KEARNS

INTUITION + NUTRITION = ULTIMATE VITALITY

I n this chapter, I'm going to take you on your very own personal health journey. It's safe to say most of you will be confused, curious, enlightened, and excited along the way. By the end, you'll have some new ideas about nutrition and individuality that will forever free you from the lies you've been told about what you eat and how you feel about it.

Have you ever:

- Made a food choice then felt weak, bad, or wrong?
- Given into a craving and then been overwhelmed with guilt?
- Started a diet or fad without sticking to it?
- Suffered digestive reactions after food choices, bloating, diarrhea, cramping?
- Known something felt off with your health, yet test results come back 'normal'?

I have. All of these. That is until I learned that I had been brainwashed about food, at an unconscious level, since birth.

One thing I'll ask is that you keep an open mind about what I am about to share.

What if I suggested that everything you knew about food was, in fact, a lie, the biggest marketing hoax that the world has ever played? We have all been indoctrinated so well in the last 60 years that everything we now believe about food is wrong.

How do I know? Nutritional qualifications aside, I bought into all of it! Every last bite. I adopted beliefs around food choices with no consideration for what my own body needed. I ate blindly, each meal and beverage choice taking me further away from what I truly needed; ultimate vitality. More on that later.

How is it possible that people are just eating based on marketing programming? Examine the evidence by looking at the people around you. Do you see many with a healthy waistline, bright eyes, flawless clear plump skin (without Botox)? Or people who don't complain about pain and inflammation? Or tiredness? Poor sleep? Stress? Mental health obstacles? Neither do I.

We have been tricked. Most of us lead unhealthy lifestyles; I know I did. I ate for convenience, lathered myself in expensive facial creams and perfumes. I used fancy cleaning products, bought the latest throw-away fashion and furniture, all treated with fire retardants and volatile organic compounds. I never considered what those purchases were doing to my health or the planet. Why? Because that is what the marketing insinuated I do to be 'happy,' just like everyone else. But are we?

I do not recall the specific moment I realised I had been hoodwinked, but I imagine myself starting to wake from that marketing hypnosis when I began listening to my body. When I began nourishing it physically and mentally, that's when I started to understand the juiciest secret of all: The person with the power to truly nourish myself is ME.

I'm going to share some simple tools that can debunk the million-dollar marketing campaigns and turn you from a number, on some corporate spreadsheet, to someone aligned in both body and soul.

If I can make it to that balanced place, anyone can. You see, my upbringing is what most would call 'colourful.' Rife with alcohol addiction, nicotine addiction, sex addictions, drug addictions, betrayal, abandonment, domestic violence. A terrible drama series with me as the lead character. It's no wonder I developed into quite an anxious person.

My chaos was so all-consuming that it never occurred to me that I had the power to make myself feel better at any point in time. I didn't know that decisions about what foods went into my mouth or that environment and lifestyle changes could manifest into better mental, physical and spiritual health.

There is no one to blame, not the many schools I attended, not my twisted upbringing, not the system, or longstanding Irish family history. The simple fact is, I never learned how to nourish myself or how food can make me feel one way or another. But let's go back to the beginning.

Growing up in the 1980s, the Western food Pyramid infiltrated cooking decisions with a vengeance. The cholesterol myth had taken its grip on the Australian culture creating a universal fear of this silent killer. All fats were vilified. We were taught that the best defence meant filling your trolley with cereals, synthetic margarine, and highly processed vegetable oils. Surely these things would protect our blessed beating hearts from that very threat.

Wheat-based bricks, flaked corn for breakfast, white bread, margarine abound. MSG-laden chicken crisps were so well-marketed that science was out, except for propping up a good fear campaign with statistics (often with studies funded by the food processors themselves). Fear and overwhelm collided with busy lives to market the new version of convenient healthy.

Let us pause here and remember that no foods are *good* or *bad*, just nutrient-dense or nutrient void. You're not a *good* or a *bad* person for what you choose to eat. We can reframe that type of thinking by learning to eat according to what our bodies need to live a life of ultimate vitality. To do this, we need to unravel our unconscious beliefs around food and aim to nourish ourselves, one plate at a time.

Read through these questions and answer them in your mind:

- Why do you eat the foods you eat?
- How do you know that the foods you eat support your health?
- What system do you have to know that every plate you eat has well-balanced macro and micronutrients?
- Who taught you the foundational approach to eating to assist you with ultimate vitality?
- Do you constantly eat with intention and purpose and in a parasympathetic state?
- How do you feel after meals? Satiated, empty, bloated, brain fog, exhaustion?

Some of these questions may seem confusing, but you can begin to unlock emotional healing and spiritual purpose once you learn how to answer them.

We must first work on our nutrition, the physical element of our relationship with food and our environment. This is one of the paths to achieving your ultimate vitality.

I've mentioned Ultimate Vitality a few times, so what is it exactly? It means being healthy enough to fulfil your life's purpose. Without health as an obstacle, you can reach your dreams and achieve your desires while being completely supported. One sure way to get there is to foster an awareness and deep connection to our body.

As I look back at my personal story, now it's easy to see how my struggles made me stronger. How listening to my inner voice saved my life many times. It may not have been the life I would choose again, but it made me the person I am today, and I know it's vital to stay present, look forward and learn from the past.

MY STORY

As a 16-year-old, I took any opportunity to leave the monotony of school that frankly taught no life skills, gave no support, no understanding of the troubled young woman I was inside. I stopped caring about school very early on because no one seemed to notice the trauma I experienced at home.

I recall arriving late to school one time after being belted black and blue that morning. I wore tracksuit pants under my dress to hide the purple bruises covering my skin and bony knees, even though it was a hot Australian morning. I was a broken, confused seven-year-old girl, yet the teacher decided to punish me for my tardiness.

He forced me to stand inside a large metal rubbish bin in the middle of the room. My classmates stared; I had nowhere to avoid eye contact, like a lighthouse flashing in the middle of the room, heart pounding in my chest. The lesson resumed as I stood in that stinky bin for what seemed like half-a-century.

Growing up, I didn't know my mother was addicted to alcohol, nicotine, drugs, and a party lifestyle, or that she birthed me ten weeks premature at the age of 20, having arrived in Australia from Ireland nine years prior. She told me one night, of course whilst drunk, that a family friend sexually abused her. I am yet to verify this story, and I'm unsure I need to. My mother was traumatised by living, so she attempted to kill herself with alcohol, drugs, and the wrong men.

My health decline started around school age when I had a severe reaction to a vaccination. I was hospitalised for a few weeks in the cancer ward where the specialists thought I had leukemia. It turns out it was Idiopathic Thrombocytopenic Purpura, a now known and named side effect of vaccines.

After being poked and prodded for weeks on end with bone marrow extractions, heavy medication, and regular weekly blood-tests, I started developing unexplained food aversions and allergies to eggs, and shellfish where I would break out in hives, and that would not be the end of my troubles.

Perhaps not having anyone to nourish me as a child, emotionally, physically, or mentally contributed to the health tsunami I faced in my 20's and 30's. A series of unexplainable circumstances lead me to this point now as I'm about to turn 40, a prize for surviving this far for one important reason, my ability to ask questions.

I made it through the turmoil of my early life in my tiny life raft without a map, simply because I listened to this whisper of a voice in my mind, like an invisible bird sitting on my right shoulder guiding me to safety. 'Turn left here, Sal,' it would say, 'Now, if you just avoid this large iceberg in front of you...', 'Oh no, we are running low on water and rations, we need to find the island quick!', 'Sharks up ahead Sal, paddle, paddle.' Continuously attempting to avoid danger is exhausting, but I always listened.

That little voice protecting me I now know as my inner truth. My *intuition*.

I am grateful to have left school early and landed a clerical traineeship; my wages of $160 per week gave me a freedom I had never before experienced. My confidence grew, and I could make better decisions. That first paycheck proved I had value beyond the child standing in the bin.

Still, I struggled in early adulthood. I developed an eating disorder, continuously falling ill with tonsilitis, colds, gastroenteritis. My menstrual cycle was out of control and rife with pain. I was often hospitalized, thinking I would die with anxiety attacks and pain.

None of the doctors mentioned my diet as a factor, even when I asked about it. They offered me the contraceptive pill over and over again. One doctor suggested my symptoms were because I was approaching 30 and I didn't have children. He may as well have said, "It's all in your head, dear." My lab results, brain MRIs, countless blood tests all came back in 'normal range.' Yet my inner voice told me otherwise.

Daily pain made it hell to manage my work and life even though outsiders probably thought I was just fine. It appeared I had my life 'together,' as I worked in my successful real-estate business, managing multi-million-dollar property assets. On the inside, a different story. I felt terrified of the next spell or attack. It spiralled into an

239

unhealthy co-dependency on codeine; I popped them like lollies to relax my body and relieve the pain and spacey feelings around my menstrual cycle.

I moved into an apartment with some friends in Redfern that was covered in mould. There, my alcohol dependence became destructive because I believed that my life was a mess and that I should give up on love. I felt lonely, tired, and empty.

When I met someone nice, not marriage material but good company, we started kicking around together to pass the time, then he suicided. At 33, my world was as out of control as the mould in our apartment, and I couldn't find my way to any sort of inner peace. Only I could make a change, and that's exactly what I did.

The choice to move into a better apartment in a nicer neighbourhood caused a chain reaction of better decisions. My building had a pool and gym facilities, so I started exercising, which made me want to eat more vegetables. I cut down on smoking and went to see alternative therapists for advice, hair tests, Chinese medicine doctors, massage, and started meditating.

I cooked myself soul-warming chicken soup, eating at home more. I walked around the bay and journaled my thoughts. Business was good, so my partners and I started plans to expand our offices in Sydney. Children didn't seem like an option for me, so I focused on learning to love myself, staying single, and getting to know my true self, away from any drama.

I booked a meditation retreat in Bali called Return to Soul. It felt like something I needed to do, that little bird on the shoulder pushing me toward it. I had already done a Vipassana meditation retreat and learnt how to manage my busy mind better. I didn't know my life would change forever before that trip.

One of my best friends called me and wanted to introduce me to someone, only he lived in Melbourne, a state away. I took a chance, and we exchanged phone numbers, which started endless conversations with this new and exciting person.

Strangely enough, he would also be in Indonesia for his 40th birthday while I was at my meditation retreat, so our first face-to-face meeting would be in a foreign country! I felt with my whole being that he was the one. On the night we met, I blurted over dinner, 'I'm going to marry you.'

Eight months later, we were travelling through Asia and fell pregnant. Everything felt right for the first time ever, though unconventional and coincidental. The puzzle pieces of my life were finally falling into place. I sold my real estate business whilst heavily pregnant, and we moved to Melbourne. Unfortunately, it was not the happy ending I hoped for.

Whilst pregnant, the autoimmune condition Idiopathic thrombocytopenic purpura returned, and my platelets plummeted. Should I have complications during birth, I could bleed out due to lack of clotting. This was a serious risk for both the baby and me.

The questions I asked the medical team during my pregnancy were met with a lack of enthusiasm. I wanted to know if diet played a role in my wellbeing, but no deeper dives were done on the nutrition front. When I asked the general practitioners if gluten played a role in my health, I was met with near laughter. You see, I started making the connections between the food going in, my inputs, relating to my outputs, and my overall health. I knew there was more to it, even if no one would tell me if food played a role in autoimmune conditions. Frustrated, I went down the podcast rabbit hole, implemented a whole foods dietary approach and went gluten-free.

After my son arrived, postnatal depression came hard and fast. It was a numbness like I was in a fog cloud. Yes, I loved my baby, however the daily grind of parenting activities grated on me. Birthing my sons and marrying my husband helped to open my heart to love myself and others with an intensity previously unknown, and it felt overwhelming at times.

As I slowly opened my heart and embraced the love from my family, I also started to heal myself, one meal decision at a time. I started to come alive as a parent when nourishing my children, and this was when I truly started to nourish myself as a consequence.

The compounded effect of my nutrient-void-existence until my mid 30's meant that my body was severely postnatally depleted, my essential fatty acids status was almost non-existent, I had what is referred to as leaky gut, all foods were acting as inflammatory and putting my body into a state of stress response.

I had further healing work to do. After researching and reading, listening to endless podcasts, and researching some more, I came up with a solution. Reluctantly, I commenced GAPS protocol (a limited diet) to detoxify my system and improve my mental health. As difficult as it was to follow, it started working.

Boom, just like that, we fell pregnant with our second son, born 26 months after our first. I believe my body was still in a state of shock, particularly as an older mother of 37. With the second newborn, my sleep-deprivation brought back postnatal depression with a vengeance. I became chronically anxious about everything, and this morphed into monthly suicidal episodes that were unexplainable and terrifying.

My health story is a game of snakes and ladders. Unfortunately, healing is not often linear. If I am the character in the game, I was playing blindfolded. But you don't have to. Sometimes you just need to ask the right person for help. No matter what, do not give up!

Somehow after navigating the GAPS diet, I found another wholefood supplement that really helped my mental health and energy. I started to exercise at home and get in more meditation to support sleep. Around the same time, we had a several friends suicide, high flying executive friends who told my husband that they never saw their children during the workweek. Life felt imbalanced. My husband was leaving the house before 7 am and arriving home at 7 pm. Days passed when he would only see the children when they were asleep.

I had a vivid dream; I was an eagle flying through the mountains following a tree line that met the start of a hill. When I woke, I had a compelling desire to relocate. Urgently. I told my husband how I felt, and we took a long drive to Mudgee in regional NSW and spent a week there with our children. My husband spontaneously applied for a job online, and we were surprised to find that he secured the position. We packed up our newly renovated Melbourne home and moved to Mudgee.

Shortly after moving, with my husband home more, I decided to study to become a functional nutritional therapy practitioner. The studies were intense and deep. When I signed up for the course, the goal was to continue my own healing journey and what I gained is so much more.

I wish I knew the importance of nutrient-dense food growing up; I wish someone had taught me about food and its role in my own body and for my mind. I wish someone had shown me how to know a particular food is right for me and not creating an allergic propensity in the body, distracting my body from its primary digestive or immune functions of taking nutrient-dense foods, breaking it down adequately then absorbing it for nutrients, energy, vitality, and youth. But all those 'mistakes' I made allowed me to understand what my clients are going through. I know what it feels like to be undernourished, and I know what it feels like to heal.

Becoming a functional nutritional therapy practitioner gave me the education I needed to start a healing process. Moving to our regenerative farm is a powerful metaphor for that change and has also helped me understand myself better. I observe the landscape like I'm now able to observe myself. Every scoop of regenerative soil takes love and patience, pouring it back into the Earth, which will eventually reward us with her fruits. Connecting to nature helps me with the patience to understand the cycles of my own body and wellness. The answers are there for you in your life, too—you just need to find them. Be kind enough to yourself to look.

There is one tool I would love to share if you suspect you might be struggling with food intolerances like I was. This is called a pulse test. Something you can do for yourself in a matter of minutes to truly know if a particular food is supporting you in your health journey or holding you back. This tool works to support you in tuning into your intuition and what your body needs to heal.

PULSE TEST INSTRUCTIONS

PURPOSE: A simple 2 ½ minute self-test to determine if a particular food or supplement causes a stressful reaction.

Note: This test may not be valid if you are taking a drug that controls your heart rate, such as a calcium channel blocker or a beta-blocker.

PROCEDURE:

1. Sit down, take a deep breath, and relax.

2. Establish your baseline pulse by counting your heartbeat via your wrist or neck for one full minute and record your pulse on a piece of paper, as "Before."

3. Put a sample of a particular food to evaluate in your mouth (on your tongue). You may chew but refrain from swallowing. You need to taste it for approximately 30 seconds.

Note: The sensory information taste signals from your mouth will inform your central nervous system (brain) about the nature of the test substance. If the test substance is stressful to the body, you will have a brief reaction that causes your heart to beat faster. Test only one food at a time. Testing individual ingredients will yield specific information, compared with testing foods containing multiple ingredients. Testing a banana, for example, yields more specific, and therefore more valuable, information than testing banana bread.

4. Retake your pulse with the food or supplement still in your mouth. Write down your "After" pulse.

Note: An increase of 6 or more is considered the result of a stressful reaction. The greater the degree of stressfulness or reactivity, the higher the heart rate will be.

5. Discard the tested ingredient (do not swallow) and repeat the procedure to test

other foods or supplements. Repeat the procedure as frequently as you like, as long as you always return to your normal pulse before testing the next food.

Note: If a reaction occurred, rinse your mouth out with some purified water and spit the water out. Wait two minutes, and then you can retest your pulse to see if it has returned to its baseline. If it hasn't, wait a couple more minutes and retest. Continue to retest until you have returned to your normal pulse. Once your pulse has returned to its normal rate, you can test the next food.

There are many other ways you can support your lifestyle with diet and nutrition. I believe everyone deserves the personalised information so that health is not an obstacle to living your life.

This chapter intends to illustrate that you have within you the power to find what foods are most nourishing for you and which are not, so that you can achieve ultimate vitality, for life, effortlessly, without feeling deprived.

We are all bio-individual, which means all our bodies function differently. There are no cookie-cutter solutions- one diet may work for one person at one point in their life and not another. Vegan, vegetarian, keto, paleo, and pescatarian, when some of these 'diets' morph into lifestyles, can be hard to navigate and understand.

There has never been a time in history where we need more energy to conduct our daily lives. Yet, the foods that we are choosing to support this highly-energetic existence are not nourishing enough. They are actually the opposite! Most convenience foods are void of nutrition and substance; they can even be toxic in some cases. The time it takes to read a food label is astounding; most words on the labels these days I hardly comprehend without a dictionary.

When we switch our habits to eating nutrient-dense, locally sourced, whole foods, eradicate the environmental toxins and make deliberate choices, we not only support our lifestyles as conscious humans, but we also support our ultimate vitality, and in turn, that of our planet.

We can reverse society's brainwashing. What it tells us is 'healthy' often is not in our best interest. When you wipe this programmed-slate clean, you'll find that your body will innately communicate to you what it needs to support your healing journey. We have this powerful, magic-like ability to tune into what our mind, body, and spirit needs to support our ultimate vitality.

I had not anticipated that working on my nutrition status and nourishing my physical self would create a clear path to my deeply-needed emotional healing. I now know that I matter. That I am enough, even on my bad days. And that I deserve a life of love and abundance, a life with absolute vitality. My inner knowing is loud now. I have tools that I share with my clients on how to listen to and honour our bodies- it gives us clues for us every day! Our physical-selves tell us how to heal our inner-selves; we only need to learn to be better listeners.

My gift is my ability to communicate with the innate intelligence of the body. This helps me identify the body's priorities and allows me to reconnect clients back to themselves. Helping them make this connection is powerful and a privilege. It's always my goal to set them on the right path to be empowered to navigate their lives and reach their goals successfully.

It's a bit of a choose-your-own-adventure at this point. Maybe you're at the early stages of listening to the whisper of your inner voice, perhaps you need to do more research, or maybe you're ready to find a health professional who will truly listen. Whichever choice you make, it's all meant to be part of your journey.

By working on your physical self, nourishing your body and mind as you so dearly deserve, by supporting your own healing journey, the path is there waiting for you to walk it, to heal emotionally and spiritually. Intuition combined with nutrition will result in your absolute vitality.

ABOUT THE AUTHOR

Sally-Anne Kearns is a certified Functional Nutritional Therapy Practitioner (FNTP) with a farm-stay clinic, operating from her regenerative farm in Mudgee regional, NSW. She believes from experience that we all have the capacity to heal, physically and emotionally.

After 35 years of health obstacles and falling through the conventional medical system cracks, Sally-Anne had her first child. Post-natal depression and an auto-immune condition swooped in and stole her spark.

Tracing back the myriad of health concerns over her life, it became obvious there was no intuition involved with her food choices, no awareness of how lifestyle impacted her wellbeing, and how true it is that we are what we absorb.

Sally-Anne prides herself on her empathy and being able to meet clients at whatever stage they are in their health journey. Functional Nutrition is a unique approach to health as it assesses the bodies symptoms to understand root causes.

All people are bio individual and deserve personalised solutions.

Sally-Anne's passion is implementing simple nutrition and sustainable lifestyle solutions for women who want to show up in their lives. She would be honoured if you let her hold your hand to wellness.

Website: www.holdinghandswellness.com.au
Phone: 026373 2193
Mobile: 0400 203 203

SAMANTHA LESKE

WOUNDED HEALER

The room was spinning. I had this overwhelming need to vomit. My husband of 11 months and three weeks had just screamed at me that it was over.

I didn't see it coming because we rarely argued. I could count on a few fingers when we had in the past three and a half years. I was in shock. I thought I had created a healthier relationship this time. Having so many trauma lines running through you enables the unfortunate attraction of things, people, and situations to show you something that still requires healing exists within you. This was the first man in many years I had trusted enough to let in fully. I had felt safe with him. He loved me as much as I did him. He accepted me as I was and was even proud of who I was. I had never experienced this before. Daily, we looked each other in the eyes and declared our love and gratitude for having found each other. We had merged our worlds. His kids called me Mum; mine called him Dad. I thought I had it all.

His angry words swam through my head. I sat on the bathroom floor shaking, my whole being in shock. I could not believe that I had chosen someone who could treat me this way again, disregarding me with such little care or thought. He was ending our marriage without even a discussion or explanation as to why. Shock and disbelief were all I could feel.

You see, I had a trauma pattern that stemmed from my childhood. I was the first-born of three. My mum was 17 when she had me and was not ready to be a mum, spending most of my life buried in depression. Not all at her hands; there was no abuse that I didn't experience as a child. This was the perfect ground-work to create a wounded healer.

This kind of childhood set me up to be attracted to narcissistic people (or not see an issue with their behaviour). I was told consistently that something was wrong with me, and I had no idea what a boundary was if I had tried to assert one—well, it just wasn't something I was brave enough to do. All laced with lines of addiction (from both sides), all set inside of a nice container of self-doubt and loathing. I knew that trusting people was unsafe. I had grown up with those who had loved me, throwing me under the bus whenever it was needed. Add to that a nice dose of catholic shame, guilt, and victim all piled on top. (As I said, wounded healer.)

My teenage years were pretty rough. I know it was by the grace of God and my spirit team on the other side, I'm still alive. My intuition and the voice of those on my team I heard in moments of true danger saved my life several times. Growing up, our nan cared for us often. She was a devout Catholic. My siblings and I were all baptised and went to church regularly with her. In my mid 20's, I renounced my religion. I could not connect myself to a belief that not only hid so much paedophilia but also condoned it and protected the people who performed these horrendous acts. I reconnected with God on my own terms when my spirituality opened up a little down the track, and my connection to Him is personal and not created or supported through any organised religious group. Now, I can sit in gratitude; all my experiences allow me to do the work I do now, supporting clients with whatever still binds them, judgement-free.

I managed to get through my teenage years and settle down with a guy—the passion with this man was crazy. So much was hidden, I wasn't ready to see, know or understand. I just didn't have the skill set yet. I felt safe (or what I thought was safe) with him for the first time in a long time. Life was a little more stable. I had the protection of a strong man. We bought a house together and began our family. During our ten years together, we had a son and twin daughters. As much as we loved each other, our families were meddlers, concerned with themselves, not with us as individuals or the health of our created family. Neither were kind or supportive.

We didn't know how to communicate with each other, we were both products of our childhoods, and my trauma was always sitting in the background, ready to gift me another panic or anxiety attack at any minute. He had no idea what this was or what to do with it, and neither did I.

When our twin girls were seven months old, trauma hit our already unstable family unit. Neither of us was responsible for it, but neither of us had the skill set to deal with it either. It left us on opposite sides of the table—we were both in shock, and me feeling like I had to protect my children at all costs. I found myself a single parent with a three and half-year-old and seven-month-old twins. I walked away from EVERYONE to guarantee my children's safety. I went into full protection mode. I chose to be a single mum and focussed upon my children and their needs. I knew my vision needed to expand: my understanding of people, who they really were, and what makes them tick. I learned to read people like never before; my children's safety required me to master this skill. My intuition became an integral part of me to meet my children's needs, from who is around us and what I need to know that I am not being told.

When my girls were four and a half, I met my ex-husband. I finally felt ready to welcome someone into our lives. My children were a little older now and able to communicate with me. He was a widow with three children. He appeared to be the kindest man I had ever met: thoughtful, not scared to embrace change, and calm. I could not move past how calm he was, not an experience I'd had to date. I was so used to tempers and, at times, outright violence.

We embraced each-others' children as if they were our own. He taught my son how to kick a footy, ride a motorbike, sandboard, surf... the list went on. I was so grateful to have been gifted three more children I could love on while their mum watched from heaven. The following three and a half years were a fairy-tale; we blended our families, went on adventures, and bought a massive house to hold our very large tribe. I often had those around me tell me how lucky I was, and I felt that too. We appeared to be the couple that had it all.

I had begun my spiritual journey when I first stepped into the solo parent gig. I kept putting my back out from picking up my girls at the same time. It was then I started getting a little self-care in the form of massages. A few things quickly began to change for me. A therapist was balancing my chakras as I started to feel relief from things that had plagued me for years. I started to see green around my hands, and I decided to commit to seeing what else I could work on within myself to feel better. The battle daily battle in my head at this time was huge. Panic attacks were only moments away. I could see very quickly from the small amount of work that was done how much relief it had given me. I also decided to educate myself in this while continuing to do my personal work. I wanted to learn everything I could. I became a spiritual course junkie. For every course I took, I was gifted another lot of freedom and in-depth knowledge about how trauma lines and energy work and how to help others that this related to. I knew that the world was full of people having the same experience as me. If only I could share this with them, they would see other options, other than the often prescribed medications for the daily battle they were facing. Right through to my soul, I knew that so many didn't know what this style of work could do for them, removing the daily battle and the solid belief that exists for many that this is their "lot" and they just have to make the best of it. I had discovered that there was another option, one that frees you from your childhood! For the first time in many years, I wasn't living with anxiety anymore.

Just before I met my husband, I had discovered my ability to read crystals—Lemurians, to be exact. These little beauties are a form of record keepers that hold vast amounts of information; the ones I have read to date are all about the past. Weeks before I met him, I purchased a few new ones. They had been mine previously in a past life, and I was excited because they contained information about my previous relationship with him. This reading showed me the life I lived in Atlantis. I was one of the Singing Ladies of Atlantis who would sing in divine language to huge crowds of people offering healing and vibrational support. There was a huge team of us; I was one of many. I was also shown the downfall of Atlantis, everyone running for their lives. I could see myself grabbing loads of Lemurian crystals, programming them, and then diving into the sea as Atlantis crumbled all around me. I was shown my ex-husband "rescuing" me from the desert where I had collapsed. He had come along, picked me up, slung me over his camel, and taken me back to his place in the middle of the desert. Following scenes were at a later date where we had two children together, one boy, one girl. I was in hiding, and my abilities were to be kept a secret. If someone saw my children using them or me, we would be in danger, our lives at risk. I could see myself sitting at the kitchen table while my daughter played on the floor with her blocks, she was all of two. She was levitating them in the air. I could see myself telling her that we couldn't do that because it wasn't safe. This, little did I know, was the beginning of me birthing a timeline.

With this, as a psychic vision, stepping back into real 3D life, I thought that I had been blessed in physical 3D life with a calm, kind man and that our past life history together was blessed. It wasn't until later I discovered the frustrating reality that the relationship I had was all about clearing up karma of the past. Past lives are always worth looking at to know the depths of a relationship. However, sometimes we are not shown *all* of the circumstances. We are shown what we need to see to support us to clean up (or understand) our soul mission. Just like pieces of a jigsaw puzzle, sometimes we don't have them all yet.

Stepping back into the night I was told it was over, I was slumped on the bathroom floor. I dragged myself to the couch and passed out there for the night. The next morning he left with his kids, and that was the last time I saw him. When I asked him why, his only response was, "I will tell you after it is all done."

The next 12 months, he fought me for everything. He shut me out of the bank accounts, put the house up for sale, and tried his best to financially drain me so I couldn't even fight for what I went into the relationship with. He never told me why.

A year after the date, I had just woken up in my new rental, and my spiritual team told me that he was triggered over his first wife's death. He was emotionally raw and didn't know how to connect with me or ask for help. His reaction was so large and disrespectful, he didn't think there was a way out other than to run. My team told me this is why it happened. The man I trusted with my heart and my children's chose behaviour that hurt us all. He broke my trust. I also know that hurt people, hurt people, and I forgive him.

It seemed that from the moment he left, two big things happened: the true story of Atlantis was born, and I learnt to love myself unconditionally. Really, truly unconditionally. This is such a powerful timeline, so many of us were involved. As my separation became final with all of those uncomfortable things you need to face, I was shown details, visions, and information regularly about Atlantis, as I was able to process it and hold it. I was shown who was responsible for the falling of Atlantis. It was in this life where the masculine took control with ego and greed being big contributing factors. When you combine the misuse of powers with the ability to tap into very powerful energy, it could create a recipe for disaster if it falls into the wrong hands.

I started in my 3D waking life to have women who were with me through the Atlantis trauma, appearing in my real life as clients ready and willing to work on, and release their particular part in the story.

As I worked with each woman, many would look at me and say, "Sam! Are you talking about my life now or my life in Atlantis?" I was always talking about their experience during Atlantis, but because it was their energetic experience, it is an energy that has stayed with them. Energy that has continued to cycle out for them, life after life, as it created a trauma imprint.

My full Atlantis story—Yes, the experiences I have already mentioned happened, but the context was not gifted to me before I married this man; it was gifted after he left. The misuse of crystals, people, their energy, and powers were taking place. In Atlantis, my mum had a set of twins—myself and my sister (funnily enough, I know this woman in this life, and we both have twins). We were raised with our full knowledge of energy, we both had individual nannies that cared for us and supported us, learning our full abilities and talents. Our mum knew that Atlantis was going to fall. She knew what was going to happen because she was aware of what took place behind the scenes. To keep us safe, she "sold" us to the respective men we ended up with. Mine "found" me in the desert, our mother was trying to guarantee our safety. I was shown a vision early on where they brutally removed our teeth, sitting them in jars along the front of the local market's tabletops, selling them as lucky tokens. The ladies of Atlantis tied up behind the table were also sold as house or sex slaves, while others were killed on the spot. While I avoided this fate, I still had my own. My husband was waiting for me where he knew I would be. It looked like he was rescuing me, but really he was collecting the bride he had paid for. I was taken to his tents and given the contract. I would be his wife for X amount of lives or die. It was my choice.

For someone like my husband, I was a valuable commodity. He had his sear write the contract, and I could see that underneath there was a whole heap of underhanded things written in. I held the belief at the time that magic was only ever used in love and free will, so all I believed I could do was to write love all through it, so if I had to experience it, it would be weaved with love. My life with him in Atlantis was not a bad one. I could see myself making the best of a not-so-great situation. I did love him, and I did love our babies. I was shown that he was captured, and they knew, that he knew, where I was. He was tortured to death in this life, protecting me.

Later through the timeline birthing process, I was shown other scenes that let me know and understand just how much I needed to hide, and the vows I took to correct the wrongdoing we all endured. I saw scenes of myself in the local market place doing my weekly shopping. My head was covered with a scarf and clothes to hide me as much as possible. I was left with the feeling that my physical self and my energy needed to be as well hidden as possible. I could see myself refraining from making eye contact as much as possible. Following visions showed me that my feelings on this were correct. I could see myself, while deep in the trauma of Atlantis, taking on a vow to find my fellow sisters who had been hurt by this and helping them to heal. I was then shown visions of travelling the world to find these women who were once my sisters in following lives. Two specific images have stayed with me since. One where I travelled to the top of a mountain to find one of my sisters—when I arrived she had no idea who I was, she was happily married and had children. I can still see her playing with them as I accepted that I could not share with her why I was there in this particular life. I have had the pleasure of connecting her in this life, connecting her to her experience and supporting her to free herself. Another vision gifted to me was walking into a monastery. The person I was there to see came outside, greeted me, and told me to leave, saying that now is not the time. They knew who I was and what I was there for, again I have had the pleasure of connecting with this soul in this life and correcting the energy.

So, while I was going through so much turmoil in my 3D life, that seemed so private and personal, it seemed the more of the timeline I birthed to be connected to my life and experience in Atlantis. Many women stepped forward during this time and due to this, enough trauma was healed and released from the timeline, allowing it to crash. It no longer exists.

The biggest gift I was given during that whole experience was learning to love myself unconditionally. When my husband walked out with no explanation, there was a part of me that knew he left because of what was going on in his own head. Through this experience, I learnt it is really important to not just identify that a man isn't violent when angry but that he has a skill set to feel and process his own emotions. When men can't do this, they are as dangerous as a violent man. They become unpredictable. Your whole life can change overnight because an emotion they don't know how to deal with has risen. They don't know how to deal with it, and they don't know how to be vulnerable and ask for help. They can even assume that because you are psychic that you should not only know what they are going through, but deal with it for them. Healthy people know this is not a fair request, you can't help or support someone who won't communicate with you.

When he left, I was in shock for days, still functioning because I had young kids that needed me, but numb nonetheless. I was left rattled. How could I attract someone like this again? He was just another version, slightly less cruel but still nasty when it really mattered. I felt embarrassed, betrayed, violated, abandoned, confused and downright angry, and still grappling to understand how we went from "I love you and I'm grateful to have you in my world every day" to "it's over and I'll tell you why after."

I have lived in shame for most of my life, never feeling worthy, like I have to hide who I am to be accepted. This latest experience took me to a new level of survival and shame. I was back on unemployment benefits, looking for a rental, making phone call after phone call explaining my situation trying to get extensions, etc. It was hell. I was barely surviving. I knew it was going to be a long road to recovery. When your whole life is decimated, starting from the ground up, is no small task.

I began with a notebook by my bed. I made myself write three things every day that I was grateful for—some days it was as simple as "my heart is beating."

I also decided and knew it would be a long time before I would trust a man again, if ever, and I wasn't prepared to wait to feel love again. I waited my whole life to feel love from another. I couldn't accept that I would not feel it again until I was in another relationship. I decided to start loving myself right where I was—full train wreck mode. Every morning I would wake up, set my intention for the day and fill my body with love. Each night I would forgive myself for whatever happened during the day and tell myself "I love you, I am proud of you." Every day I did this, every day, I still do.

I knew from my ability to read others that most people don't love themselves, how can I ask or expect someone who doesn't love themselves to love me unconditionally? I can't. So now, I love me, warts and all. I am still a work in progress, but I know myself better than ever. I understand my own trauma, I gift myself what I need to heal and will continue to do so, as it is an ever evolving process. I learnt through this whole process to listen to myself to let go of the shame when it rises within. To choose self-love in all situations that rise. Sometimes that means saying *yes* to new experiences, and sometimes it means saying *no* to someone's bullshit and selfish expectations of me. It means knowing my boundaries and honouring myself when new ones arise, and defending them as fiercely as I would one of my children from danger.

What I know for sure is that self-love is a skill set. Many of our parents did not know what it was, or if they did it was classed as arrogance. When we become healthy, we know what self-love is, and we have no shame in living it as one of our true expressions of self. *Loving Me* has become for me, not only a lifestyle, where I am as kind to myself as I am to everyone I meet, but I teach it. Self-love is weaved into every aspect of our lives, every choice we make.

I want to leave you with two take-aways:

1. You can (without question) heal from your childhood. You had no choice while you were growing, now as an adult you do. You do not need to live the rest of your life doing the best you can with what you have. You do get the choice to thrive if you want.
2. You deserve to be loved, unconditionally, by you. You are worthy of your own love—know this to your soul. No one will give you permission, it is a choice you and only you can make. Self-Love is THE game changer.

ABOUT THE AUTHOR

Samantha Leske is a spiritual healer who has worked professionally for the last ten years, supporting her clients to understand themselves better, release the chains of the past, and learn the skills of loving themselves unconditionally. One of her biggest joys is seeing clients released from the trauma that has plagued them for a long time.

Educated through the University of Life, Samantha has also gained many, many certificates and qualifications in various energy modalities over the years.

This has allowed her to gain a very in-depth understanding of how energy lines run, how trauma works and needs to be released, and what is created when certain lines run and how to heal them. While her abilities grew over the years, she discovered she has a unique ability to birth timelines from the past, supporting them to be heard, seen, or understood until they can collapse, freeing those energetically caught in them (Atlantis, being one example).

Samantha lives in the Adelaide Hills with her children, horses, and dog. You can connect with her and her work through the channels below.

Website: *www.nurtureyouhealyou.com*
Facebook: *www.facebook.com/HealYouNurtureYou*
Instagram: *www.instagram.com/nurture_you_heal_you*
YouTube:
www.youtube.com/channel/UCEJi9tOugDyQ3WKQLlBKy0g

SAOIRSE CONNOLLY

EMBRACING RADICAL VULNERABILITY TO
BIRTH, LIVE AND DIE FEARLESSLY

As I sat by my beloved grandmother's hospice bed, I could feel her unconditional love wash over us as I clung on to her gentle touch.

Her hands were warm, her heart beating strong but her breath was shallow and slow.

The precious life force energy that we all too often take for granted was about to leave her frail, fragile body and I remember thinking how brave she was in the face of such adversity.

My gran's fears never grew old, her vulnerability was always a sight to behold, yet in this moment she was at peace. She was showing her strength and her weakness.

She had lived, laughed, loved and lost. She had said yes to life with an open heart, even in the knowing that everything could fall apart.

And then it clicked, her vulnerability was not to be resisted; it was to be revered.

This was a superpower, in life and in death, to radically embrace our vulnerability with trust, knowing that we could get hurt or die in the process but being in the courage of it anyway.

She kept repeating my own limiting belief back to me, "I don't know," a phrase I had spent my life telling myself, and yet in that moment it was okay not to know.

I reminded her that I didn't know either, none of us knew, but by surrendering control and the need to know she was free to move from a space of not knowing to not knowing – the ultimate path—unafraid, fully engaged in the present moment, because that is all we have.

Her borrowed body's work was done and her eternal spirit was getting ready to move on. She had birthed and raised eight children and spent her life being of the highest service to her family and humanity.

Now I could feel in every cell of my being that it was time for me to continue her legacy so I asked my gran to help me call in my baby.

FINDING MEANING IN MISCARRIAGE

Only a week before I had been on my hands and knees on the bathroom floor of a hotel room in Ibiza. My womb was pierced with excruciating pain and then the clots came.

I didn't even know I was pregnant but in that moment I knew that I wasn't anymore. I felt numb. I took some painkillers and after a while it was like nothing even happened. It was easier to pretend that anyway than to face up to the reality.

When I got home from holiday the shame and blame started to sink in. We had been partying like rock stars and I wouldn't have given this little life half a chance.

Up until this point, I was playing the game of the eternal teenager and I didn't feel ready, but losing what I never knew I had made me realise how much I wanted to start a family so bad.

As much as I loved my life I was a little lost and confused. On the outside I was bursting with love and light but on the inside my intuition was drowned out by fear and self-doubt.

It was time to let go of who I thought I was, to become who I was born to be.

It was time to be brave and embrace my vulnerability.

But first I had to burn down the fearful, wounded walls that trapped my love inside. No longer would I run, numb and hide.

And so began my healing journey. I faced off with the shame and blame I was experiencing and allowed myself to be fully seen and held in my grieving while vowing to give up my partying ways and get intentional about creating a healthy vessel that could carry life and legacy.

I was finally ready and in a breath-work session a little girl came to me and danced with me in a garden full of daisies. I felt light, love, laughter and true liberation and all my fears around becoming mother melted away.

A week later I discovered I was pregnant. I believe it was always my daughter's soul choosing me to be her mammy. She was just waiting for the conditions to be 100 percent ready before committing to sticking around for the journey.

DROPPING THE MASKS

Once I started digging deep and asking myself why I did the things I did, I realised I had been using drinking and partying as an escapism from the story that I didn't feel worthy of love and belonging.

I truly believed that if I wasn't the life and soul of the party, I had nothing to offer anyone. I had become attached to the tools I used to fit in and the identity I created to make me feel like I belonged.

Peeling back this mask, while painful, was a huge revelation for me. For the first time in my life, I could choose to honour my body, say no to things that did not serve me and be authentically me. I felt so free.

I was finally able to see how I was allowing stories and feelings of shame, lack, isolation, separation and unworthiness keep me from expressing myself freely.

The wound of unworthiness will have us believe that to be loved we need to hide who we truly are so we make ourselves smaller for fear of being seen. We put others on pedestals and trust in their opinions instead of ourselves and our intuition.

This is the legacy of our conditioning. From inter-generational and childhood trauma to being women living in a misogynistic culture that programs us from an early age to believe we are not good enough or worthy of love, so we feel self-conscious and ashamed to take up space and own our place.

With this new awareness and sense of responsibility to feel my feelings and stop distracting myself with shiny things I felt fire in my belly and a wild awakening stirring deep within me.

I had the power of choice. I got to decide the stories that looped in my mind. I could tend to the little girl inside me who felt unworthy and rewrite my story while making conscious decisions about how I would live my life moving forward.

In a world hell bent on training and taming me, I would fight for my full humanity and that of this beautiful baby girl growing and flowing inside me. I would be a model for her from the womb to the world on how to live wholeheartedly.

INITIATION AND TRANSFORMATION

At 35 and pregnant I had no idea what lay ahead of me. The only experience I had of birth was memories of my childhood friends who had babies in their teens and had traumatic and drug-induced experiences, which was the norm where I was from in Ireland.

It was my yoga teacher, who was also a doula, who opened my eyes to birth as ceremony rather than medical emergency. On her recommendation I read *Spiritual Midwifery* by Ina May Gaskin. From that moment I was hooked on the wonder of birth and creating a sacred space that would honour my initiation into motherhood.

I also felt a deep desire to share what I was learning with other women because I woke up to how we had been brainwashed to believe birth was a traumatic and terrifying experience.

I answered the call of my soul and threw myself into a doula and pre/postnatal yoga teacher training to fully embody the wisdom for my pregnancy and help other women enjoy rather than endure their journey.

In some subtle yet profound way, I could feel the hands of both my grandmothers' on my womb space and hear their whispers to step up and hold space for my sisters.

I began to widen, not because of the ever-growing baby inside me but because I was unlearning the version of birthing and motherhood that I had been led to believe.

I discovered that birth is big business and a third or more of all women are coming out of their births traumatised, with interventions on the rise.

Intuitively, I knew if I didn't get in the driving seat and take radical responsibility I could be robbed of this life-enhancing opportunity to birth powerfully and positively.

DOING THE INNER WORK

I began to imagine the most passionate, powerful, playful birth possible and set about turning over all the stones inside myself that could get in the way of me making my dream a reality.

Increased psychic awareness is common during pregnancy. I delved into the opportunity to communicate with my baby, making space every day to sit in silence and send messages of love, trust, gratitude and guidance.

I scripted my birth story, wrote letters to her, sang and chanted to her and visualised my birth and the changes my body needed to make including talking to my cervix and encouraging her to open when the time was ripe.

Slowing down and turning off the doing mode so we can be in the art of surrender is a powerful way to strengthen our intuition, allowing us to hear and obey the signals that our body and baby is sending us and trusting in the subtle messages.

By witnessing the fears, stories and tendencies that made me react in certain ways, I cultivated safety in my body and felt so connected to myself, my baby and my own divinity.

EMBRACING RADICAL VULNERABILITY TO BIRTH FEARLESSLY

In order to feel connection we must allow ourselves to be seen, to be open, to be vulnerable. By embracing my vulnerability in birth, just like my gran did in death, I became a vessel like a midwife in formation, supporting an energy coming through instead of commanding that I knew.

Anytime we hold on to something, we are blocking the energy flow so birth (and life in general) is about learning how to let go and allowing ourselves to come back into alignment with the present moment.

I surrendered into myself, melting into the experience, becoming one with it instead of resisting it, reminding myself over and over again that I was safe. Fear was safe.

After more than 40 hours labouring at home, I intuitively felt the call to go to the birthing centre where I would be having my baby – but when we got there, the midwife didn't seem to think that I was anywhere near ready.

She felt cold and uninviting, making me feel unworthy of her attention and care, instead of being empathetic and responsive to my needs and vulnerability at that stage.

When they wanted to carry out a 'routine' examination to determine cervix dilation, I stayed loyal to my intuition and refused so I could remain in 'my' zone.

This was hard to do when the pressure from the medical team to 'know' was so huge but with the loving support of my doula I resisted their incessant moves sending a message to my body and my baby that I trusted in them to lead the way.

When I felt the urge to push, I allowed the midwife to check and I could feel my baby crowning.

Who knows where I would have been if she had checked me in those hours previously, because our thoughts, feelings, comfortability and confidence can help or hinder the dilation process, so not focusing on time and numbers is important.

Doing the inner and outer work during my pregnancy made sure I did not abandon myself in moments of overwhelm and uncertainty.

Yes labour hurt like f%ck, it was intense, overwhelming, and all-consuming at times, but I allowed it all in, I softened to it, breathed and sounded through it, received it, trusted it, and transmuted fear into love in every way I could.

And we had fun. We laughed, we cried, we loved, we hugged, we danced, and we kissed. At times I felt like I was in a hallucinogenic state; at other times I felt primal, sensual, and radiant.

I stayed in the zone. It was orgasmic almost, not in sensation but in the sense of the surrender necessary to orgasm when making love.

By surrendering control and letting go of any resistance or rigidity, I could integrate the flow of energy and keep leaning into the unknown with courage, turning uncertainty into certainty.

Standing on the precipice of not knowing, engaging wholeheartedly in the present moment – because that was the only place to be—just like my gran had done in the face of death 10 months previously.

And now, in birth, here I was connecting to my inner wild woman and maternal lineage. I could feel the pulse of my being, leading from a place of deep body listening, following my own natural rhythms, obeying the signals, deeply engaged in the embodiment of now.

When I heard my baby cry on that final push I was elated, empowered and triumphant. It felt revolutionary even though it had been done by every woman since the beginning of time who came before me on their epic birthing journeys.

My wild blessing Fiadh wasn't just born, it was a cosmic rebirth for me too, and it is my wish that every birthing Mother gets to fully embody this powerful and spiritual experience. This is our rite of passage and we are worthy and capable of it.

KNOWING MY TRUTH

Birth as a rite of passage teaches us life changing lessons about who we are, what we are capable of and what we need to face or learn to transform into the mothers our children need.

But what I have come to know is that too many women are emerging from their births feeling far from transformed and instead, they feel traumatised, violated, not listened to, shameful and remorseful.

We live in a culture that wants to make the uncertain, certain and control all outcomes but with conception and birth, the less we control the better.

A birthing mother needs to feel safe to be exposed in the most real, raw and vulnerable way so she can open up to the task of birthing her baby.

Many women who experience birth interventions and birth trauma have been led to believe they were let down by their bodies and those who did plan and work for a 'natural' birth feel shame or regret for getting their hopes up.

These feelings of failure and not having choice or control is not something that women should have to hold because it is not their bodies that failed them but the system that was supposed to entrust and support them with the right environment to give birth in.

Instead, it often feels like we are being pushed through a conveyor belt of boxes being ticked, clocks being watched, monitors being attached and 'routine' examinations undertaken, while lacking empathy, warmth and emotion.

We seem to have de-humanised birth with a one size fits all approach. We need a shift in consciousness where birthing women feel connected to their bodies and birthing choices while trusting in their babies and their innate abilities.

TALKING ABOUT A BIRTH REVOLUTION

As women, we have been disconnected from our inner power, wisdom and intuition. Many of the limiting beliefs and blocks we feel and experience daily are the result of thousands of years of conditioning, living in a patriarchal system designed to disconnect us from the truth of who we are.

Our culture was built upon and still benefits from the control of women, and what better way to maintain control than to convince us that we must control ourselves.

Our conditioning begins from an early age when we are told to be quiet, be good, don't ask questions or ask for too much, be pretty, be polite, be passive. All of these trained 'good girl' traits spill over into our birth room experience.

We learn to mistrust ourselves and our own big feelings and become afraid to express ourselves freely as we try to fit into the cages society has made for us.

We learn to mistrust and feel disgust for our bodies thanks to the beauty and diet industries.

We learn to mistrust our own curiosity from childhood stories of girls getting eaten by wolves if they dare venture into the woods.

We learn to mistrust our own ideas, visions and intuition because we are encouraged to value professionals, politicians or institutions' opinions.

We learn to mistrust our own choices and abilities when it comes to our own reproductive systems.

We learn to mistrust our own memories and experiences because we've been convinced that we were either responsible somehow or should be grateful for it.

And we learn to rely on religion as a means of salvation instead of trusting that the only one who can save us is ourselves.

The truth is we have been fed lie after lie after lie and our mistrust of birth is no different.

Fear of birth is so engrained in our society that it is hindering our ability to embrace this transformational experience impacting on how we bond with our babies and increasing the risk of post-natal depression and feelings of disconnection.

This truth is the fuel for the fire in my womb that makes me so passionate about joining the birth revolution. Even when writing this chapter has brought up so many old stories and doubts within me for fear of saying the wrong thing and hurting birthing women or even having the audacity to have an opinion.

But I will not try to put the fire out; I will sit in the flames and burn to the ground until we can rise from the ashes, hand-in-hand, if that's what it takes to help women awaken to their full female power and potential and ensure women can trust their maternal instincts and lead with their intuitions in conception, birth and motherhood.

THE HISTORY OF BIRTH

Birth matters and women embodying trust and receiving others' trust to make the right choices for themselves and their babies' matters.

Many birthing women have been led to believe that birth is so unpredictable it's not worth preparing for or they don't know they have choices and rights so feel powerless.

In Milli Hill's truth-bomb book *Give Birth like a Feminist*, she traces the roots of this powerlessness back to the fourteenth to sixteenth century when the divine feminine, once revered, was suppressed and oppressed in place of the patriarchy.

Women's role in creating life was diminished with religious texts referring to us as nothing more than host bodies, robbing us of our humanity – the legacy of which still lives on today in our struggle for autonomy of our own bodies.

The Church and State came together to torture and burn millions of women or 'witches' – many of them healers and midwives and at the same time men were established as scientific experts with women in birth relegated to 'old-wives.'

From there, money-making tools including the forceps, were introduced and the billion-dollar drugs industry turned women into medical patients at a time when they should be upright, empowered and experiencing their full female strength.

While we have a lot to be thankful for when it comes to medical advances for women and babies who need medical support and the staff who provide such excellent care, it is the structure and system under which they work that gets to be challenged because we seem to have lost sight of what birth is or could be for the majority of birthing women.

The influence of institutional patriarchy is alive and well in our maternity care systems and even in a female-dominated profession such as midwifery, it can be powerful and pervasive, leading to many unnecessary birth interventions.

But we do have rights and we can reclaim our bodies and feminine power through the portal of birth by educating ourselves so we can make informed decisions and give informed consent or informed refusal in the birth room.

The World Health Organisation has expressed concern that the medicalisation of childbirth with its focus on initiating, monitoring, measuring and controlling has left the question of how women feel about their births completely off the agenda.

This approach, they note, undermines a woman's own capability in giving birth and could negatively impact her experience of what should normally be a positive, life-changing experience.

Birth is not some random, risky, excruciatingly painful event that we have to endure.

Yes it might turn into an emergency and that's when the medical system can come in handy but if we are given the right environment, support, trust and love then the need for interventions and pain relief is hugely reduced.

Whether a woman chooses an elective caesarean or a free birth, medicated or un-medicated, in hospital or at home, it's all perfect once they are making conscious and confident decisions and feel safe, seen, loved and listened to in the process.

HEALING AFTER UNEXPECTED OUTCOMES

For those women who may not have had the experience they desired, I see you, I feel you, I honour you and I am holding space for your healing.

As the formidable womb witch, Jane Hardwicke Collings says, *"we have the births we need to have to teach us what we need to know about ourselves, to take us to the next place on our life journey, our journey to wholeness."*

After a traumatic birth, it is so beneficial to look at your trauma and suppressed emotions by working with your body to release them and ask yourself the hard questions like what did this experience teach you?

What qualities were maybe lacking and if you couldn't access them then, can you call upon them now? Often this is the quality that you get to bring into your life and mothering.

You don't have to do this work alone, seek help, talk to your loved ones, don't judge, and have compassion, kindness and patience with yourself and your process.

Grief and pain are the fuel of revolution. Can you sit in the fire of your feelings, burn down the fortress walls surrounding you and from the scattered ashes reassemble yourself piece by piece to emerge anew?

And remember loving ourselves through the process of owning our story is the bravest thing we will ever do.

BIRTHING THE NEW EARTH

I hold the vison of a world where every woman feels strong, powerful and vital as she crosses the threshold to motherhood.

A world where we stop controlling ourselves and start trusting ourselves.

A world where we stop resisting and start listening to the voice within.

A world where we stop fearing ourselves and start loving ourselves.

A world where we are not afraid of our own big feelings and inner healing.

A world where we are in total embodiment of our experience.

COMING HOME TO THE TEMPLE OF OUR BODY

It is my wish that this New Earth starts right here and now with every woman reading this.

Heart-to-heart, womb to womb may you remember your brilliance and bow down to yourself in deep reverence? You are a god damn goddess.

You are beautiful, magical, capable and worthy. Come home to your womb and the wisdom of your body.

AWAKENING TO OUR WOMB WISDOM

As women, we can—and must take—our power back and remember who we are beyond the stories we have been told and limiting beliefs we hold.

Awakening to our womb wisdom gifts us infinite and expansive energy and helps us rekindle love and acceptance for ourselves while trusting in our journey whole-heartedly.

It is not just connecting to ourselves but it is connecting to the mother – It's a descent into the womb of the earth allowing us to listen, learn, feel and heal what is here for us.

WE ARE THE GRANDDAUGHTERS OF THE WITCHES THEY COULDN'T BURN

Womb healing gives us access to the guidance of our ancestors and reignites our own ancient innate wisdom reminding us that everything we need to know is already inside us.

The power of the divine feminine longs to be remembered and awakened in every woman.

By working with our wombs, we can release ancestral trauma or family karma and cut ties to imprints and stories that no longer serve us so we can step forth into a new beginning free from past programming and societal conditioning.

On my own womb awakening journey, calling in our second baby, I got clear transmissions to love myself deeply and own my gifts completely because it's my duty to my grandmothers' and their grandmothers who didn't have access to the tools and opportunities that we do today to heal themselves from the suffering and situations they faced along the way.

But we do. When we speak our truth we liberate the women in our lineage who had to remain silent and when we listen to our intuition we liberate those who could not use their magic. When we heal ourselves we heal the trauma of inter-generations, ensuring our children's roots stem from solid foundations.

The womb is the birthplace of all our creative abilities and as we heal and transform our wombs we heal and transform our world.

So this is a call to come home to your power, to the seat of all creation. Trust in her. Descend into the depths of her darkness and transmute all that is not yours into the highest frequency so you can free yourself from shame and stand in your sovereignty.

We own our bodies and bear its fruits.

We rise with the depths of our desire to inspire truth.

Meet me at the altar of transformation that is birth.

Together let us use this sacred initiation as an opportunity for our own salvation.

Let us rewrite her-story and reclaim this magical rite of passage by unbecoming everything we thought we were to become the women we were born to be – held, wild and free.

Let us bravely and fiercely embrace our own naked vulnerability, trusting in our own miraculous capabilities as the only force powerful enough to navigate unborn spirits onto this earth.

Let us remember our worth.

Try these practices to reconnect to your intuition and reawaken to your womb wisdom no matter where you are on your motherhood journey.

RECONNECT

Take some breaths to drop into your womb space, close your eyes and feel your breath move down into your belly. Allow your exhale to be audible, noticing what happens when you make sounds, your womb and pelvis relaxes. With your root chakra, open and receptive, imagine roots coming from your womb, plugging you into the womb of the earth beneath you. As you breathe in allow yourself to receive this incredibly nourishing, loving and activating earth energy back up into your womb space. Notice how she feels. Maybe there is pain, discomfort, electricity, aliveness, numbness, just allow all of your senses to receive her information, sensations, vibrations, even irritations and make an intention to get to know her better, opening up to her wisdom and noticing after these few moments of connection how she responds to your attention, she loves to be honoured and revered. The deeper you go, the deeper the gold.

REALIGN

Our desire to feel safe, loved, expansive and alive relies on our ability to connect and love ourselves wholeheartedly. Make peace with your body and love on her unconditionally for everything she does for you by adding this powerful self-love mirror practice to your morning ritual. Stand in front of the mirror and admire your body for the temple she is, looking deep into your eyes and seeing past the physical deep down into your soul, embracing your essence, dancing with your own divinity, smiling to all parts of you that make you and whispering lovingly that you are so worthy. Dancing naked is nice too. Allow the soft animal of your body to move you. Witness your feelings, if you feel contracted or repulsed, can you alchemize these feelings from self-judgement into self-love. The more devotion you bestow on your body the more she will reward you in return.

REWIRE

Make space in your life for silence. We have two internal voices, our ego and our intuition. Our ego moves like fear, it's loud, jumpy and messy projecting so many different outcomes and catastrophes that rarely happen. Our intuition moves like love, it's calm, grounding and always offers the same nurturing advice. Our intuition is our superpower in conception, pregnancy and birth. Get to know her by creating space for silence, use the breath as your anchor, extending the exhale to slow down the nervous system and bring you into a rest and digest state. Listen for the still, small voice of your intuition rather than focusing on the loud fear based thoughts that limit our capacity to navigate our journey courageously and wholeheartedly. You are an alchemist. You can transmute worry into wonder and fear into faith. It's always a choice. Choose love.

REWILD

Many of us miss out on our evolution because we are too afraid to feel big feelings that arise in our body and instead numb, hide or consume our way out of them. We label our emotions good or bad and want to only feel joyful and happy instead of sadness, shame and rage but by pushing the hard feelings away we become disconnected from our emotional intelligence and miss out on the full experience of what our emotions are here to teach us. Now is the time to end the cycle of avoidance and embrace our emotions as the juice of life. Tune in and feel where your emotions might be in your body, ask them what they have to say and once you receive the message send it love and let it go by dancing or shaking it out in an embodied way.

ABOUT THE AUTHOR

Saoirse Connolly is a wild and free woman, here to hold a loving mirror up so you can remember who you are.

She is a feminine embodiment and empowerment guide, womb alchemist, birth and postnatal doula, yoga facilitator and fierce and fearless lover and leader who will advocate to the ends of the earth for the women she works with to have an empowered pregnancy and birth.

Through her online coaching container, *The Liberated Womban*, she supports women calling in a baby or embarking on their pregnancy and motherhood journey.

Women experiencing self-doubt and disconnection from their bodies and their babies and would like to tap into their womb wisdom and intuition, remember who they are, and unleash their full feminine power and potential by using this sacred initiation as an opportunity for their greatest transformation.

Women who work with her feel seen, supported, heard, held and deeply loved through the sacred container of conception, pregnancy, birth and motherhood.

Saoirse (meaning freedom in Irish) is daughter of Marie, grand-daughter of Marie and Madeline and mother of Fiadh with another star seed in her womb due to be birthed at home in April 2021.

Born and raised in Dublin, Ireland, she now lives and loves on Gadigal Land in Sydney, Australia, with her twin flame Darragh.

Instagram: www.instagram.com/sessionswithsaoirse
Facebook: www.facebook.com/saoirse.connolly.5
Website: www.saoirseconnolly.com

SARAH BEALE

UNTAMED CHILDREN, WILD HEART

Where to start? Right here, I think. The last 24 hours that led me to these words nicely show how I've come to live in a deep relationship with my intuition and how quickly things fall into place when we sit in trust with ourselves.

Two nights ago, I went to bed feeling relaxed and a little excited. I'd been working towards something for many weeks, and it was finally coming to fruition. Because it had been hard work for me, emotionally, I was relieved that my instinct wasn't letting me down (I think it's pretty common for people living deeply in intuition to still question it at times). I slept deeply. Until I didn't. It's not unusual for me to wake in the night. Having children has messed up my sleep schedule in perpetuity. If I know I don't have to get up early, I've learnt not to fight it. Wakeful periods give me quiet time, unavailable during the day in a house with four children and a border collie puppy!

However, this wasn't one of my usual awake times, and I felt twitchy—restless. I wasn't able to just lie there with ease. There was something quite specific on my mind, and it hadn't been there when I'd gone to bed. It was this book. This very book that I'd vaguely heard of but not seriously engaged with. I'd stored it at the back of my mind thinking, 'maybe someday I'll do something like that. But not now. DEFINITELY NOT NOW.' If asked, I'd have said I didn't have the capacity and wasn't in the right place.

I lay there, quite awake now—shocked awake, I'd say—as the first thought hadn't been totally lucid. I think I'd woken myself up saying 'what the *"@#!!!!' At 6 am (thank you village clock). I had this exact thought: 'I am going to message Brigid and ask to be in her book,' followed closely by: 'I'm certain she'll say yes.'

And I did. And she did. And here I am. I hope the beauty of that intuitive unfolding isn't lost on you, the reader.

Now, right back to the start. The actual start.

I was raised in a Christian family. I say 'family,' but it was really just my mum. My dad was faking it, I later found out. And my brother and I were only going to church for the cream biscuits after the service. But my mother was and remains devout and convicted (of her faith, not a crime). I continue to admire her for that, but it's taken me many years to recover from the experience of forced spirituality—or, rather, religion. I now know the two are distinctly different.

You see, I also don't like rules. I have a strong aversion to anything arbitrary. Unless it's pancakes for breakfast, even when it's not the weekend—I'm happy to enshrine that in law. So I found myself questioning many aspects of the brand of Christianity I was exposed to.

Why can't we learn about evolution? Where was God before He created the earth? Why aren't we allowed to bring magazines to school? Do I HAVE to go to church?

One day, my grandma said something which has always stuck in my head. It gave me further insights into why I wasn't any more a fan of organised religion than organised fun. My brother and I were squabbling (as siblings do), and she asked, "Why do you two fight? You go to church; you should be nice children." This led me to wonder, firstly, what kind of children were we if we continued to fight (we did), and secondly, had I missed one of the lessons in Sunday School? More broadly, I began to question if I might not fit in at church since I had no intention of being 'like everyone else.' And I wasn't sure I wanted to be 'nice.' Although that programming would remain with me for many years.

At 18, my mum said, "of course, you don't have to go to church if you don't want to," prompting me to consider how many years I'd been attending out of duty. All night partying took priority over an early Sunday morning service, and I rejected everything I associated with church attendance. Like, everything. Ironically my brother and I got on very well and often explored this rejection in each other's company. My grandmother could rest easy as we were also devoted grandchildren and finally being 'nice' to each other.

It was easier, as a teenager, to simply outright reject religion in its entirety. I hadn't yet uncovered the nuance of spirituality vs. religion. It was relatively straight-forward, given I'd spent so much of my life engaged in church activities. I'd also attended a Christian school, so I was surrounded by dogma. They never taught us evolution at school—we were told it was evil and not up for discussion. We were regularly shown end-of-times films and told that rock music, particularly heavy metal, was of the devil. School dances were banned as dancing encouraged promiscuity (Footloose anyone?), and most popular music was embedded with satanic messaging.

This was all presented to students as truths and not up for debate. Status was related to spiritual gifts such as speaking in tongues, which was right up there. My aversion to hierarchy was challenged by what I perceived to be made up rules even at a young age. There was also (and continued to be) disquiet about the notion one had to be involved in the Christian church to access these gifts.

To distance myself from the church, I forged an identity founded on anti-church-dom. This quickly became anti-spirituality.

I've always been intuitive—I see that now. But for a long time, anything that I couldn't explain in absolutes, I relegated to the realm of quasi spirituality and there-fore not for me. And despite my rejection of the organised version of religion I'd experienced growing up, I heard my mum's voice in my head, aligning anything 'not of God' with satan. It was easier to ignore it all and stay grounded in the present and what I could explain. Except I also wasn't terribly grounded in logic. This was a conundrum.

My heart persisted, though with many signs that my intuition was indeed alive and well. Yet I couldn't name it. Personality test after personality test put me firmly in the category of 'feeling' and 'perceiving.' Possibly, I took some comfort in those official determinants of my nature. It was affirming that deciding to buy a house on the strength of the smell of citrus blossom was explained away by a company-funded development course!

Impulsive. Scatty. Irrational. Easily distracted. All terms that have been used to describe my personality at one time or another. All signs that my intuition continued to knock. This conflict between the heart I was born with and the world we live in that almost demands a measurable kind of logic. Decision making built on risk assessment (or risk aversion) and tangible outcomes. Linear and consistent movement forward. Do exactly THIS and get exactly THAT. But it never made sense to me. Even when I took a very sensible government job at 24 (my first 'proper' job), my intuition was my constant, although unacknowledged, companion.

I've always had a knack for working with people, and it's in the human realm that my intuition has spoken the loudest. Even at the height of my spiritual denial phase, I just could not shut off my deep love for humanity. In my sensible government job, I was quickly designated 'difficult client' officer. I used to think it was because no one else wanted to deal with them and having a 'go-to' made everyone's lives easier. But I suspect it was my knowing that gave me the insight to read people in a way that helped them feel connected and safe. Not judged for their choices or their circumstances. Accepted. This is where intuition really sits.

For intuition to flourish, to be heard, one must quiet the voices that sit in condemnation of others. Attempting to control others with agenda; manipulating others into our way of thinking or doing.

And so I introduce my children, also known as 'Where the real work begins.'

I put a lot of energy and time into preparing for my first birth. I knew it would be important (everyone said so), and I also knew I'd have my baby at home, which would shape how things would be. I read every book on physiological birth that I could get my hands on. I befriended midwives. I took every opportunity to talk with my unborn child; quiet moments with nothing to do were almost always spent hands on belly, feeling her movements; multiple pregnancy yoga classes; generally basking in that pre-baby bliss that comes only once in a life. I couldn't get enough. I was tuning in, and in those months, I can see now I was also practicing tuning out; tuning out the noise; tuning out other people's negativity; tuning out the programming that tells of home birth being unsafe—of women's bodies being incapable.

I went on to have four normal, physiological births at home, and with each one came a new transformation. A slightly altered version of myself. Not new—that would discount what came before, and all of that was important too and is part of who I am—but a new incarnation. I now see that birth IS important, but for me, it was merely practice for what would come next.

And yet, I wasn't able to fully tune out.

Actual life with small children! Beyond birth. Does anyone even think about that? I certainly didn't. Oh, I ironed the cot sheets and arranged the nappies in colour-coded order, purchased and assembled the pram, and imagined my unborn child in the cute (neutral) onesies I'd carefully chosen. Grandmothers are quite good at stoking those fires! But I quite literally couldn't visualise anything beyond the birth itself. I couldn't see the baby IN the nappies, and I couldn't harness what I might feel like actually pushing the (very expensive and highly photographed) pram. I probably thought everything would take care of itself. Of course, it did, but not in the way I expected.

I think I imagined I'd be like a French mother. Well-mannered children in stylish attire, nibbling at baguettes and stinky cheese; polite and intellectual conversation and tripping politely through the streets of Paris. (I've since taken my children to Paris, and I can tell you, they are NOTHING like French children.) I even recall verbalising to a polite enquirer that of course I knew my life would change after having a child, but I was confident they would fit in perfectly to MY life, and I didn't see the need to pander to them.

Dear reader, if you too are a mother, you'll already have laughed at my expense; at my naivety at how I assumed my life as a parent might look. The ease with which I (wrongly—but you know that right?!) thought my children would slot into my life like a new paperback on a bookshelf. You are right to chuckle, and if you knew my children, you'd be downright slapping your thighs.

As it turns out, my children released something in me which I'd forgotten. My heart's voice, consistently but quietly, tapping me in gentle reminder of her existence, was suddenly let out of the box by my wild children. Never to be put back in. Like a naughty genie, like Pandora, like a lioness trapped in a cage for decades and invited to run full speed across the savannah. Like an eagle.

We all expect our children to question things; why is the sky blue; why can't I have lollies for breakfast; do I really have to wear pants? We know they'll go through a phase of saying *no*, determinedly, and, if we're honest, endearingly—when they're two and saying *no* to things like 'would you like extra veggies with your lentil pattie?' But times that by four and extrapolate to things like 'why do grownups get to stay up however late they like?' and 'why do old people try to make us kiss them?' Then apply the 'no's' to situations like hair brushing, dental care, shoe-wearing (we had a long phase of 'no' to clothes wearing full stop with one of the kids), and you'll have some idea of the gifts I've been given in the form of small wild things.

I use the word 'gifts' quite intentionally about the offerings of my children; it's through them I've become reacquainted with my intuition. My inner guides. My heart.

With the benefit of slight detachment, I'm able to imagine how others view my kids and our family life, and I'm sure 'gift' is the last word they'd think of! But each challenge to my perceived authority, each show of their autonomy, each struggle to relate to why on earth it takes 30 minutes to find the perfect pair of socks (only to discard them when we get to the corner), has pushed me deeper inward.

Like many parents, my first real challenge in those early days of motherhood was sleep. Mostly mine. Prompted by hers! I thought I might die. I realised some years later that one can survive on very little sleep. Sure, you might be so exhausted you forget to strap your kids into their car seats; or maybe you forget the actual kids, but I didn't die. I believe I may have wished for it at some point. But what doesn't kill you, and all that. It wasn't the lack of sleep that was the real trigger; it was the fact I couldn't seem to control this small creature. Imagine, only four weeks old and already out of control. She sure didn't seem like that French baby I'd been visualising. So I did the obvious thing and set out to find a book, written by a parenting guru, that would tell me EXACTLY WHAT TO DO. And I did, and it did. And she did—sleep that is. Phew.

But what I'd really done was outsource. And it seemed easier on the surface of it. I sought solutions outside of myself. I shut down my instinct. My intuition. Oh, I still heard it, but I ignored it in preference to external knowledge. I assumed that someone else knew better about my baby than me. Of course, it was easy to do because the oracle of baby sleep that I'd purchased from my local bookstore suited my agenda perfectly. Sleep, on a schedule, consistently. The Holy Grail of parenting. The bonus offer was I got to appear the very ideal of motherhood. I assumed (wrongly) that being in control was the same thing as feeling genuine calm. All I had to do was keep on following the formula. I even believed the lie I told myself that a schedule allowed me to be more flexible—but what I didn't tell myself was it was really about control and my agenda to have my babe fit into my life. I didn't realise that until my third child.

Enter third child. I've just realised that my second born, should he read this, might feel slightly forgotten at this point, but he does enter the story later! Each child really has taken me to deeper levels of connection to myself.

My third babe, and second son, born only 20 months after the previous, showed me how to tap into my mothering instinct. It turns out it was there all along, just below the surface and hidden behind the baby books and societal chattering. I'm sure I would have found it eventually anyway, my Wild Woman, but I'm forever grateful to this child who wouldn't be put down; who wouldn't be held by anyone else; who hardly slept more than 30 minutes at a time and who, by his personality, cast the blueprint for what we now refer to as 'bonkety' in our family. Once he decided he could be put down, he proceeded to live in the spirit of a hurricane. A barefoot hurricane. He was the happiest kid alive and the model exhibit for attachment parenting, into which I threw myself wholly. I was rewarded for my re-acquaintance with my intuition by a child who, by his very nature, demonstrated the wisdom of gentle and attached parenting in its entirety. Sleep with your child in infancy, and they will naturally leave their bed when they are ready; he did at around three years old. Breastfeed on demand, and they will naturally wean when they are ready; he did at about 2, during my fourth pregnancy. Encourage connection, and they will separate with confidence when they instinctively feel independent; by 2 ½ he was confidently scooting barefoot down the road with his long hair blowing behind him.

I know I'm making it sound easy, this switch from sleep training/schedule mum to a doyenne of attachment mothering, but it was far from straightforward and took several months to lean in to. Initially, I thought there must be something wrong with this baby, who was clearly cross with my constant attempts to separate him from me. It was a dear friend that suggested it was "just his personality." I was horrified at the idea of having a baby that was anything other than persistently content. If anything could be said about my previous two, it was that they were 'settled.' Pretty consistently undemanding. Of course, I couldn't see at the time that I'd possibly repressed any other state of being. I think what this friend was really trying to tell me, in a very gentle way, was this was how it was going to be, and I'd better, pretty quickly, get my head around it. And so I did. If I can make any claim about myself, it's that I'm a pretty quick learner, and once I decide on something, I throw myself into it. And so the, by now useless, pram was packed away, and a variety of rainbow coloured baby carriers were purchased. I learnt very quickly to go with the flow—there's not much else to be done with three young and pretty strong-willed children. I knew myself well enough that I didn't have the grit for close control under pressure, and by now, I was discovering the joy of letting go.

The thing about letting go though, is there's always MORE to let go of! My fourth child took me to the next level. I kept thinking, when people commented on her, let's say 'zest for life' that she'd calm down like her brother before her (by 3, he'd just about stopped tipping buckets of water onto the kitchen floor and sticky taping all the chairs together—ok, definitely four). I was confident my attachment parenting ways would, once again, stand me in good stead. I just knew there'd be a payoff for all that bed-sharing and breastfeeding. I mean, my exhaustion would count for something, right? And if not a calm, independent, relaxed child, then what?

'Then what' indeed. It began to slowly dawn on me, in a series of warm LED light moments, I'd been approaching my parenting journey, and thus the relationship with my children, as I'd approached my very sensible and responsible government job. With a set of desired outcomes and a position description. Sure, I was tapping into my instinct in many ways, but I was relating to my children with agenda. Do this, get that. Parent this way, get this kind of child.

My fourth child clearly had not read the attachment parenting handbook, and she tested every part of me. This lovingly parented, gentle birthed, breastfed child who was still very much attached to me was refusing to wear clothes, swearing like a sailor (I've never heard anything like it, prior or since), preparing her own meals, and refusing to do, well, anything I thought she should do. One wouldn't have thought she had much to push against, but what little there was, she did. There was the hair-pulling phase (other children's hair), the scratching phase (again, other children), the no-knickers phase (in retrospect, it wasn't a phase), the eating mandarins at 2 am phase, the 'I will do literally everything myself, and if you forget and accidentally do it for me, I will undo what you've done, take ten steps backwards and do it all again' phase.

This angelic looking child (she looked less angelic when she flipped the bird at strangers) was not merely a pocket rocket. She was a fiery ballistic missile. She called me out on my agenda. Every. Single. Time.

Do you know what agenda does? It controls. Do you know what control does? It prevents connection. It kills it. When we control our kids, we kill our connection with them. When we control ourselves, we kill our connection to ourselves. Our intuition cannot be heard. Oh, it's in there somewhere, desperately trying to wake us up, as mine did. But we remain deaf to it; we don't notice it's desperate (and if I'm honest, more than a little defiant, just like my kids. Coincidence? I think not) cries underneath our insistence that things be just so. Often backed up by society's expectation, no—demand, that things be just so.

As my children's strong desire for autonomy grew, I saw that I had a choice between two options: extinguish the flame of freedom by increasing control, or live with them in partnership, leaning into radical acceptance of who they are and all they would be. It's a distinctly different way of relating to kids. Our world tells us that children are born empty and must be filled with the vast knowledge of adults: teachers, parents, grandparents, experts. To trust them as the perfectly whole beings that I believe them to be requires us to do something quite revolutionary: trust ourselves; hear our heart's voice; lean into KNOWING and BEING. It's a vastly contrasting story to the one we've bought into, of DOING and FIXING. The completely brilliant thing, though, is kids are born with fully developed intuition—it's literally how they survive. We might call it instinct that babies are naturally wakeful, demand frequent feeding and close contact with their parents. Might it be that instinct is just a rose by another name? Might it be that close control, coercion, and manipulation of children, almost from birth, in fact, teaches them to tune out their instinct, their intuition, and instead teach them to outsource their innate knowing to others deemed more expert? First their parents and later on nursery or school teachers. Later still, their peers and employers. Might it be that were babies to be nurtured in their instinct, encouraged to trust their perceptions, that this would develop into fully-fledged and well-developed discernment? Intuition even?

This is certainly what I've found. The deeper I go into trusting my kids, the more they show me I also must trust myself. This is bringing forth many synchronicities for me, and as we all lean into living without force and in our sovereignty, life flows more easily. In the words of Raphael (the Teenage Mutant Ninja Turtle, not the Renaissance painter), 'like the river over stone.' From a pretty young age, we're taught that life should be hard, battles should be fought, and the key to success is following someone else's formula. My inner knowing tells me the opposite is true. By resisting the temptation to control, by embracing our innate wisdom, and living in a state of trust with others, we allow our intuition to unfold. The intuition we are born with.

There have been many 'aha' moments in my mothering journey, but mostly it's been a slow and consistent burn toward a life forged from values as distinct from rules. A life lived without force. A life of alignment to self through which all relationships flow and the most important relationship, the one with ourselves, guides all.

The times we live in call for us to gather, as humans, and as one in our collective humanity. We can best serve others when we tap into our own heart space. Conventionally we are encouraged, as women, to look after others, commonly by sacrificing ourselves; looking outside of our intuition for answers to the questions of our modern time and in doing so, forgetting our ancient wisdom and intuition. But when we ask how best we can thrive, we surely must see that trusting ourselves naturally means trusting others and in a beautiful symbiosis of reliance and giving, a mother doesn't come second to her children, and a child doesn't solely rely on the mother. We each can learn from and obtain succour from one another. It is in this spirit that my children have delivered to me, my transformation, not only into my motherhood but into my intuitive humanity.

ABOUT THE AUTHOR

Sarah Beale is many things. Only one of them is a mother. She is also a collector of kitsch knitwear, a sourdough addict, a bird whisperer (her daughter doesn't believe her), a late-night Netflix viewer, and a somewhat regretful border collie owner (she wanted a lurcher).

Her children have brought out not only the very best of her but her most real self, the self that shows up authentically, lives joyfully, walks barefoot, and sings loudly. In that spirit, she co-founded The Partnership Parenting Movement and now seeks to bring that same sense of connection and playfulness to other families. She supports parents in undertaking the inner work required to live in freedom with their children and advocates for self-directed learning and life without school.

You can find her blogging about all the things rattling around in her brain at *www.radicalthinkingradicalliving.com.*

> **Website:** *www.partnershipparent.com*
> **Facebook:** *https://www.facebook.com/*
> *groups/thepartnershipparentingmovement*

SARU GUPTA

DEEPER THAN PERCEPTION

A s a young child and teenager, I used to stutter. It was not a simple stammer over one word here or there. Every time I opened my mouth, I found it hard to speak without the air rushing in, and words stumbling out. I started fearing to speak.

There were times when I could speak without stuttering, yet it was hard to predict when I would sound normal or embarrass myself by having no control over how I sounded. So, it was easier to remain in my thoughts and feelings than to speak.

I suffered a lot of backlash from other kids, teachers and parents for my poor speech abilities. I did not like going to school. Some would make fun of me all the time, some would scold me, and some would not allow me to do things for fear that I would embarrass myself.

I clearly remember a moment when I was 13 years old. There was an opportunity to make an announcement before an event. I put my hand up but was not selected. Later, my teacher told me that she was protecting me from embarrassment.

It was easier for people to silence me by making fun of me. I would lose my power and ability to stand up for myself. This treatment, by kids and adults alike, crossed boundaries for me and denied me of a childhood where I felt safe to express myself. This meant that I never learnt the abilities kids should develop growing up— to trust their feelings, discover their voice and feel their feelings.

Maybe this abuse of my boundaries, which I was too sacred to speak about, exacerbated my stuttering. I will never know. Our bodies are so intelligent, and they work in strange ways to protect us from pain.

And yet, there was something within me that wanted to express myself, regardless of how others treated me. I must admire my own tenacity for wanting to speak up back then despite how I sounded.

Even though I had many friends, growing up, I always felt different. I thought something was wrong with me.

As I got older, I started to use food as a coping mechanism for the pain I felt about my lack of ability to speak properly. Food became my best friend. It helped me numb my feelings, and I used it as a way to find pleasure and nourishment.

By the time I entered my teen years and started growing into a young woman, I had put on a lot of weight. This meant that now I had also become a 'fat kid' and a 'weird kid' who stuttered.

Like most teenage girls, I wanted to fit in and not be overweight. So I discovered ways to lose weight without having to give up my coping mechanism. I would not eat in the morning or during the day so I could use food at night if I needed to.

Later, I started to use exercise instead of starving myself so I would not put on weight. I had no way to understand life, and I never spoke about my internal struggles to the adults in my life. They were bound to the culture I was born in, and I felt they would not understand what I was going through.

This is no reflection on my parents and the other adults in my life. I know they loved me. They brought me up the best way any parent does. No parent receives a manual on how to raise a child when they are born. Moreover, every child is different and has very different needs.

In hindsight, I can see that my inner child was very critical, harsh and confused. The inner child is the part of us that never grows up. I was looking for the belonging I never felt as a child. That same part made me travel the world to explore so many different things in the hope that I would find some place to fit in. None of this was conscious. She had been driving my life for so long. She did not know or understand herself or what she felt—she kept trying to find ways to soothe herself.

I have learnt that we, humans, automatically move towards healing when the pain becomes excessive. That's why we look for coping mechanisms or distractions, so we don't have to look inwards. I kept trying different things. They would work for a short while until they would not anymore, and I would find that my old patterns would play out again in different situations.

I moved from my childhood home in India to the USA when I turned 21. I studied and had a great career there for the six years that followed. My life looked perfect from the outside, but inside I was lost. It did not seem like that to people. I did not openly stutter anymore, I worked in one of the top consulting firms. I was living alone and had a good life. Yet, there was complete chaos inside me. I was admired by my colleagues for being a high performer, for being a caring friend, for being fun, for being fit. However, if anyone looked inside me, they would see that I was running away from myself.

I still used food as a coping mechanism. Exercise in the morning, a long workday and many nights watching TV and snacking.

Now, looking back, I can see I lacked self-esteem. I was following the motion of life. Trying to find my identity through doing well in the world. To fit in by having an admirable career, a good circle of friends, independence and a good physical appearance.

But then I never fit in. Actually, no one ever fits in. We just try to fit in. I spent my whole life looking for a sense of belonging and fitting that I never had.

Even as I write this chapter, I feel the resistance to write whatever is coming out of me. I want to fit in, with this chapter too. I am worried about seeming weird. I fear getting sympathy from others.

I have to tell this wounded part of me that those who give you sympathy have not been in touch with their own wounds. So, their opinion does not matter.

That wounded part of me, which everyone has, wants to get approval and love from others. The little part that wants to compartmentalise my life, not show my weirdness or speak my truth. The little me who is better at not showing my feelings because they are uncomfortable, and who feels that others will run away when it gets hard for them. It's the same little me who was laughed at when she was young.

After spending over six years in the USA, I moved to Australia and started a different chapter in my life. Despite marrying my childhood sweetheart, married life was not the rosy picture I saw in movies. Now looking back, I can see that I had an image of a picture-perfect life. We are so used to hearing fairy tales growing up, showing us that some prince will come save us from ourselves, and all our life problems will be over. The amount of pressure that puts on the prince!

Those fairy tales or movies never show that the poor prince has his own childhood troubles, and his own fears. He is finding his way in life and also his voice. He is not some fully formed godlike figure who can save us and take away all our troubles.

My marriage and relationship have been the biggest growth and learning periods for me. I love my husband. He is my best friend, and I have learnt so much about life and humanity through this 12-year relationship. At the beginning of our marriage, I used to subconsciously blame him. But over the years, the more I explored myself and got in touch with my patterns, I learnt that I was so far away from my own self that I was projecting a lot on him.

In Australia, I worked in a similar profession to the one I was pursuing in the USA. I tried it for a few years and then changed to another profession in the corporate world. By this time, I was becoming more aware of myself and could see that using food, as a coping mechanism, and denying my true feelings were not working.

I had been working out for almost ten years by then and had explored every workout you could think of. I had also tried every diet possible but still had deep body image issues. Reading psychology articles had become my passion, so I knew that something was amiss. I had been in the corporate world long enough by then and believed work made it hard to be healthy. But I had no desire to give up work altogether as it gave me purpose and was part of my identity.

So with passion and the drive to make the world a better place, I founded my own start-up. I convinced my husband to leave his great-paying job and join me on this adventure. At the end of 2014, we started working to create a holistic health, fitness and mindset app. We left our jobs in Australia and moved to India for a few years.

It was a big project. We had a team of experts helping us create the content and program. An IT team developed the whole app that would allow working professionals to be self-sufficient and achieve balance in their lives. So, it could be a one stop shop, the app was equipped with balanced nutrition, *High Intensity Interval Training (HIIT)* based workouts that took less than 30 minutes a day, daily meditation, and a lot of mindset exercises. Along with that, it featured articles from naturopaths, osteopaths, a running coach, a mindset coach and other experts, which also helped people to understand themselves and their bodies better.

That was the intent. Yet two years into my work, all my issues came up again. As I stepped into my role as a leader and change maker, I found my own world starting to crumble. I was not happy. My life and inside were far from aligned. Even though I had enough knowledge and experience, there was not a complete synchronisation of the different areas of my life and my being.

I had a long list of degrees and personal development courses by then, yet something was not right. My emotions ranged from high to low all the time; I still could not share what I felt and honour my needs. I did not trust myself, my voice, my feelings. I did not stutter anymore, and even though I had tried to look at my life under the microscope through counselling, and had coached many people myself, I did not own my place in the world. I was still hiding like I did as a little girl when life became too much.

I had tried all the new age things like past life regression, hypnosis, courses such as Landmark, counselling, and some speech courses. Yet since my symptoms were defined simply as "THIS IS LIFE," I did not openly speak about them. After all, I was questioning what is considered normal.

I knew that I was just surviving in India and that I had to go back to Australia. So, in November 2016, I left India and left the business with my husband. I moved back to Australia to return to the corporate world. I was born Indian but, in many ways, I am considered "too headstrong" for this culture. Maybe due to my childhood stuttering and the resilience of my soul, I have fought at every level and I never give up.

If someone asked me what the turning point in my life was, I would say it was in May 2017, when I did my first silent meditation course.

It was four days and nights long, and this was the hardest thing I'd ever done. This was a body-based mindfulness/meditation course. I had done yoga and some meditation before, but this time with no distractions—phone/internet, no reading material and complete silence—became my undoing. Giving myself space to be present with my body was too much for me.

I don't even remember how much of the actual meditation techniques I used over those four days. I was given more gentle practices over the weekend under the guidance of the teacher, which made it easier to stay till the end. My only goal was to leave when other participants left, not before.

I must have thought about leaving the retreat every few hours but something in me knew that I had to sit through this.

This was the best decision of my life. As I type this, I am a completely different person from who I was four years ago.

Whatever guided me during that course unfolded a new path for me in life. The next three years took a course of their own and I experienced the biggest roller-coaster ride of my life. Everything that was in my subconscious came out into the open. No area in my life was left untouched. It was intense yet so liberating.

I came out of that course thinking I had not done much, but I got to experience my body fully for the first time. A newfound awareness grew in my body. This might be mind boggling. It can be hard to explain unless one has experienced this.

We all have bodies, but most of us are so focused on our mind and thoughts so we don't know what *being in our bodies* means. Yes, every yoga posture and exercise is done through our body, but it is an automated response. That does not necessarily mean that we can truly feel the sensations of being deeply embodied.

We exercise, breathe, have sex, and do all things that being a human means. However, our society has become so fast paced that even when we are experiencing life thinking we are present, it is usually a mind concept. We are present in our mind and can hardly feel anything below our head.

This new awareness in my body, following my meditation course, was so subtle yet so profound. I had cried and experienced a lot of fear during the course. I could not wait for it to end. Yet a few days after it did end, my world started to change.

All of a sudden, I started to notice more people being magnetised towards me. In the trams, at my new job, in yoga classes, everywhere strangers spoke to me or spoke about me. It was a strange experience. Then a week later, I could hardly sleep, and I did not need much food. I was feeling alive and had so much energy. It was an amazing and intense experience. My awareness of my body and my feelings seemed to have increased. I could not control whatever was happening inside me, it had a life of its own. It was freeing in so many ways yet so scary as well. Everything seemed possible, suddenly. I found myself doing things I would have never said *yes* to otherwise.

I continued to explore more body-based somatic tools, and after speaking to some meditation teachers, I realised that I had a Kundalini awakening. That word is so cliché, I feel. Many people want to experience this kind of awakening and go out of their way to achieve it. In my experience, it was not fun. For months after the meditation course, I felt ungrounded and did not know what was happening to me. Yes, I had tons of energy, more men were attracted to me and I had a kind of aliveness that made me feel I could achieve anything. But looking back now, I did not have the right support in my system to handle this kind of energy. Without many other tools and practices, self-inquiry and questioning, my own mentoring work and the help of other teachers, I would not have experienced the full benefit of how to channel this all-powerful energy.

Yet, I also know that I needed this energy to open me completely and pull my inside out to become the person I am today.

This energy is called *Chi* or *Prana*, which everyone in Chinese medicine and similar traditions talks about. This is an energy that we can cultivate with the right tools.

Once we start to establish strong body-mind practices and silence and work on settling our nervous system, we create foundation and the space to handle this kind of aliveness.

It is the life-force. This gives us the strength and excitement needed to look at our deep-rooted patterns so we can bring about real change in our lives.

I have explored my nutrition, movement, exercise, relationships, career, spirituality, and sexuality my whole life, yet something always felt incomplete. I had already learnt many tools through coaching, neuroscience, psychology, etc. so conceptually it all made sense. I would apply tools and techniques, work with experts, help my clients, yet after a while I was circling back to similar issues again.

Once I started to work with my body-mind connection, silence and my nervous system, along with my ability to see through the bullshit, I realised that it is possible to bring permanent change in all areas of my life.

I started exploring more practices, learning different meditation styles. I sat many seven-day silent meditation retreats and was mentored for over 200 hours by a Buddhist meditation teacher. I started studying positive psychology, stress management, the language of emotions and somatic therapies to understand myself more and bring this powerful work to others.

Over the next three years, my whole life came out inside of me. The stories and miracles that happened were unbelievable. A practical logical woman like me, who worshiped the mind, developed awareness and skills so that I could see beyond any situation. Yet, I had not yet developed the ability to trust my intuition. Over the next year, the more I practiced and the more clearly, I could see, my trust started to develop.

I call this clear seeing. It is deeper than intuition. Intuition is still based on our perception. This clear seeing allows us to develop deep knowing, to develop the ability to listen to our heart. The heart's speech is very different. It comes in silence and gives a gentle nudge. Our heart knows and the path is so clear that things just manifest.

This happens over time when we have the right support and guidance to create deep rest in our nervous system. I worked with many teachers, guides and mentors over those years to develop this ability.

Over those years, I also explored my relationship with my sexuality, with food, with exercise, with others (my family, my husband and friends), and with life. I used to believe life is stressful. Now, I understand that life can be chaotic but that does not mean it has to be stressful. I have developed enough strength in my nervous system through the right tools and practices to handle all that life throws at me and still be able to find joy in life. I have been able to get to the root cause of most of my problems: the so-called stressful symptoms of needing to rush, not reaching out for proper self-care, remaining in situations and relationships that do not serve me and establishing a love for myself.

I have not given up on having occasional drinks or going out with friends, my ambition to be a successful career woman, having an orgasmic relationship with my husband, wanting children and having fun.

I have always been a passionate heart-centred woman, which meant everything could touch me deeply and bring my emotions to the surface for the smallest of things. Yet, because growing up I had not learnt to value my emotions or myself—and I came from a corporate world—I numbed them.

Now I feel safe to wear my heart on my sleeve, eat what I truly desire, feel and look good in my body and connect with the people I want to. I have started to speak my truth while following my heart's nudges, along with working and operating in the corporate world.

Of course, this does not mean that I face fewer life challenges or that life has become all rose-coloured glasses. I still experience challenges, and it can still feel hard from time to time. Yet I have developed enough resources within myself to face anything life throws at me while feeling comfortable with my emotions and not abandoning myself. There are some areas in my life I am still working on to get to the root of the problem. I still have to make difficult decisions, but now my heart is fully involved in my decisions, not just my mind. I am in complete acceptance of my female cyclical nature as I have cultivated strong foundations within myself that support me in valuing the gift of being a strong yet feminine woman.

I desire to conquer the world in my feminine essence while allowing my masculine side to hold me. This is how I choose to connect with others in the world. Not from co-dependency but interdependence.

And from this powerful no-bullshit heart space, I want to support ambitious working women to experience this deep nervous system reset and shift that my clients and I have experienced so they can get in touch with their true essence and thrive in the corporate world.

No more emotional eating.

No more body shaming.

Feeling my feelings and honouring them.

Valuing myself and my voice, no matter how it sounds.

Creating the right kind of self-care routine in my busy life in honour of my body so I can feel and look good in my body.

Enjoying my sexiness and my sensuality.

Allowing for play, joy and juiciness.

Being a powerful, successful busy woman yet having amazing emotional, mental and physical health.

Continuing to nurture my nervous system and work with it to achieve my goals in life.

And letting that aliveness, Prana, Chi and Kundalini serve me and my purpose in life.

This is my mission and my passion!!!

"My foundational work, along with getting to the root cause of every issue in my clients' lives, starts with helping them to reset their nervous system. Pure magic can happen when you work with your body's most intelligent system not only to keep you alive but to thrive in life."

Lessons and take-aways:

1. The biggest take-away that I give anyone is to establish a connection with your body. You might think you already are aware of your body, but I am confident that this is one thing that we can keep deepening. Especially in the world we live in, we are so cut off from nature and, due to the overuse of technology, we have become very mind centred.

If I don't use different tools daily, I feel that I become very head centric, and my body awareness becomes weak.

2. For real life permanent change to happen, you have to work with an expert who can help you to find the right tools for your nervous system. We can't surpass our primal instincts. And the nervous system is as primal and as old as it gets. If I did not have the right support at every step of the way, I would not be where I am today. I am a girl who used to stutter, was made fun of, had an eating disorder, did not trust her feelings and had no faith in herself. Today I am a woman who has stepped into her power and is proud of her past. My past no longer defines me. I know I have taken the lessons from my past and am recreating a foundation in all areas of my life so I can conquer my world with fun.

3. Just meditating and calming yourself is not enough. Yes, it will get you into a calmer state but if you don't take the necessary steps to change your environment, you will be stuck in a vicious circle. Therefore, self-inquiry, looking at your deeper patterns, and addressing all areas of your life is important. Addressing health from mental, emotional, physical and spiritual components allows for real change to happen. It's like a RESET, but then you have to clear the junk and make better choices that become easier because now your body and nervous system will support your choices.

4. Truth, honesty, and clear seeing. Don't distract yourself from the truth. It will keep trying to get your attention in different ways throughout your life if you deny or ignore it. The earlier you bring it to your consciousness, the easier it will be to feel happy and have all your desires met.

ABOUT THE AUTHOR

Saru Gupta is a health and transformation coach, writer, and speaker who sees the truth through the deep patterns that keep people stuck in the same situations in health, relationships, and life. She is a multifaceted woman with over 12 years' corporate consulting experience and a deep passion and knowledge of mindfulness/meditation, embodiment, emotional health care, positive psychology, and somatic therapies.

Saru's willingness to get uncomfortable, grow and challenge the status quo and life experiences across three continents—in the USA, India, and Australia—led her to keep seeking wellness, allowing her to get in touch with the deep knowing within herself. She has been called very intuitive and a great space-holder, allowing people to talk about things they would not normally discuss.

Saru believes we are born intuitive, and we experience this in our day-to-day life. Yet, due to the constant noise of life and mind, we forget how to listen to our deep knowing. Saru's approach centres around embodied change and regulation of the nervous system, so passionate, ambitious women can listen to the subtle messages from their bodies and their environment.

Saru supports corporate and businesswomen living a 24/7 high-pressure life to create wellness in their mental, emotional, physical, and spiritual health by getting to the root cause of stress and empowering them with practical tools to experience deep transformation and aliveness. Her mission is to burst the myth that it is impossible to have a high performing career and amazing health.

Website: *www.sarugupta.com*

SHANNON VAN DEN BERG

THE POWER OF THE HEART

I didn't jump right into this book as I did with my first book, *Wild Woman Rising: Brave Women Who Carved Their Own Path*. I could talk about intuition and tell you stories you would hardly believe all day long.

But I uncharacteristically waited. I struggled with how I would condense what I know and feel about intuition, truth, and trust into one chapter that would help divine feminine leaders claim their sovereignty and power, and use it in a practical way.

I woke up at 2 am and downloaded this chapter to help you feel the power of your intuition and call you to explore it. Feminine leaders have to have their bearings and your intuition is your natural ability to connect with the incredible help you have available to you and your highest, soul self.

This chapter has the real-life, practical journey of how I was a victim of my abilities, how I struggled through the cycle of using my abilities and then shutting them down, then having to reconnect with them and on and on, how my experience with intuition has changed not only the inner and superconscious guidance I receive but how I project it into my life to create with and call in exactly what I desire.

I won't talk about the basics like the nine kinds of "cliars" or sixth chakra openings. You can look those up online, and they don't really matter. Learning to trust yourself and exercising your intuition, and then using it is what will expand your abilities and change your life.

Actually, since we're talking intuition, I have to address the over-hyped spiritual entertainment fad, which is a huge block to learning to use yours. Ouiji boards, psychics, and overly relying on tarot and oracle cards are just distractions from real intuition. Intuition isn't something you chase after for the answers for major life decisions, know your destiny, or have power over your life or others.

Although I was intrigued by Edgar Casey and famous psychics when I was young, I've always thought having a psychic reading was so strange. Another person can only see what is possible from that one moment's perspective, it could totally change the next moment, or with the next choice you make or feeling you have. Most people take the information they receive as a set in stone prophecy instead of a highly changeable snapshot with variables of the person doing the reading's ability and your ability to be read. For instance, I can completely change what someone sees when they read me, just as I can change a pendulum's reading. This is why it's crucial to learn to deepen your intuitive abilities.

Skip the boards, psychics, and cards for now. Tune into yourself, your heart. You are a multi-dimensional being with the ability to navigate with your abilities every moment of your life, focus on yourself, and you will get a lot farther.

Your intuition is your divine gift and your sovereign power. To use it effectively, you have to grow into it, as you'll see in my story. It's your foremost navigation system and connection to help and creativity.

We each have our own journey and unfolding of our intuitive abilities. As you read my story, see what hits you in the heart. What parts excite you? What scares you? What do you wish you could do intuitively?

BEYOND FEAR

Most people come in with age-appropriate blinders on to their gifts. Not me. I came in wide open, and it wasn't easy. The extra things I could hear, see, feel, and knew scared me, and my fear opened me up to opportunistic entities attracted to that fear. I can still feel the terror of being alone in my dark bedroom when I was three years old. One of my first memories was of watching passing car lights go across the wall and ceiling and then seeing dark shapes descend into my room until they merged with the darkness. I could feel them lurking there but couldn't do anything about it.

My family was no help. None of it was real to them besides the fact I was an annoyance. My fear grew, and so did the feeling of being abandoned. Each night turned into its own saga to survive until I would give into my exhaustion or call in my angels, my only vise.

I'd ask my angels to come help me. I'd see them encircling my room with their wings touching so there were no gaps and hovering above and below my room, making a bubble of angelic protection for me. And then sweet relief and sleep were possible. I still use this today. My four-year-old Wesley and I call in angels every night before bedtime, and my older boys also remember it.

My childhood was a struggle. I didn't understand why I was different, and neither did those around me. My grandparents, who raised me, thought I needed help with my "nightmares" and insomnia, so they took me to a series of psychologists who couldn't explain me either. I was labeled intense and learned not to speak up about things that were outside the norm. It was isolating in school and made me feel like a fish out of water. One of the reasons I said yes to this book was I deeply wish I had someone to help me understand my abilities when I was younger, and I feel strongly about helping other women come into their intuitive knowing and power.

In eighth grade, my grandparents brought something back from a trip to South America that would help. They'd been approached by an Incan shaman in Chile who gifted them a one inch long stone for their granddaughter's "nightmares." They gave me the small Imperial Topaz crystal when they got home, and the crystal seemed to sooth me when I held it. It was beautiful, see-through with rainbows, natural facets, and rich gold in color. I carried it with me in the day and slept with it at night. I felt better. The terror-filled nights stopped. And I shut out most of my abilities, which opened me to grow in other ways.

In high school, I pretended I was normal. No abilities. It was easier that way. I was in a new state with total autonomy at boarding school. I learned to tune into my intuition for practical things, like test answers, communicating with my barrel racing horse, staying out of trouble, and knowing when my aunt had passed before I was told. I leaned into my natural tendency to feel my way through my heart, which I reasoned was a different thing than intuition. It made it safe to still connect with my abilities and opened my heart beyond the grief and trauma I'd been through. It wasn't until many years later I learned intuition comes through your heart and *is* your heart intelligence. This whole time I'd been strengthening my abilities like a muscle.

The heart-brain connection blew my mind. As a thinker who used to never shut off my brain, it was a bombshell to learn your brain isn't meant to make decisions. Your heart is. Your brain is meant to be the computer your heart intelligence utilizes as a working tool. When you start using your heart intelligence, you are engaging your intuition in your choices which changes everything. Those changes led me right to finding and marrying my soulmate I've been married to for 23 years and heavily relying on my intuition as a mom.

LEARNING TO TRUST

I got pregnant right after we were married, but at our five-month ultrasound found out the baby had suddenly died. My heart broke, I'd had no warning, and I was angry. Being angry at my abilities wasn't new. I felt like I should have had some type of knowing about it, like when I needed to know the most I was let down. I knew in my bones a big part of my purpose was to be a mom; I had dreamed it many times in the kind of future telling dreams I had.

I had three more miscarriages over the next year, after which the doctors told me I couldn't have children. They had valid reasons. So before I left their office that day, I sat and asked if I would carry and birth my own children. I heard a clear yes. I decided to leave what I had just been told there in that doctor's office and was pregnant again within the next moon cycle.

This pregnancy was different. My intuition seemed heightened, and I could easily tap into my growing baby I named Garrett. I felt like because I had opened myself to receiving help through my intuition, it had expanded.

I was two weeks past my due date when my worrying mind thought inducing labor was a good idea. I was in labor for 26 hours of unnatural pain and stress on my son, who was born pale and needed oxygen at our high elevation.

I stayed with him in the nursery and noticed he was warm to the touch. I asked the nurse to retake his temp, but she refused—she had just taken it. I asked another nurse, and she did. In a few minutes, his fever had gone from normal up to 104 degrees fahrenheit. That nurse told me to never go against my intuition when it came to my baby; I would always be right. Her words have helped me stand in my knowing even when I questioned myself.

I gave birth to Aidan a year later and Caleb a year after that. Aidan was past his due date like Garrett, but this time I waited and went into labor by myself and had a relatively easeful eight-hour labor.

With Caleb, my intuition was tested again. He was two weeks past his due date when I had to fire my doctor because he insisted on labor induction. I hired nurse-midwives instead, had ultrasounds twice a week to check the baby's health, and waited another two weeks before I went into labor myself. He was a month late according to the doctor's perspective, but I knew better. I had a three-hour labor with no interventions and was ready to take my new baby home to meet my toddlers. Caleb was postterm the midwives shared the results of the testing they do on post-term babies to see if they show signs of actually being born past the optimal time for them. Caleb had no signs of being truly post-term, and neither did my other boys when I requested their results. I had been right each time, and science proved it.

Mothering three boys born in 30 months was exhausting. I didn't know all the answers. I did know that I wanted to be a badass, deeply connected, and fully present mom who was absolutely willing to go against the grain and create new ways to mother if that's what was needed. I wanted to model using my intuitive abilities and soon learned that would be easy as I needed my intuition more than ever.

My intuition helped me know when to go to the emergency room and when not to, the

Suddenly, Garrett was in extreme pain one afternoon and had a hard time moving his left leg. It was strange. I knew he had broken something. When we looked him over, his thigh was bruising, so I decided to take him into ER. Sure enough, he had broken his hip through the ball, and the bone had moved three centimeters. The doctors were in a mad dash to *CareFlight* him to Denver and get him into surgery to correct the break. I heavily relied on my intuition about how to support his healing over the next year through the surgery and recovery at Children's hospital, a severe infection, a pic line, medication allergies, and three more surgeries. He made a full recovery and even tested its strength by playing football and riding saddle bronc in rodeos.

CHARTING A NEW COURSE

Fourteen years after Caleb, I learned I was pregnant with Wesley, and again I waited almost a month past his due date before I went into labor myself. I labored at home for four days until I knew something was wrong at 2:30 in the morning. I climbed in the pickup truck for our almost-hour trip from our ranch to the hospital, asking for support from The Mothers. On the way to the hospital, I dilated to nine centimeters!

When I was ready to push, I knew I had to be on my left side—totally not my plan. Wesley was born with his umbilical cord tightly around his neck twice. The doctors told me the umbilical cord around his neck was probably why my labor stalled and could have hurt him if I wasn't in the right position.

In Wesley's second month, he started showing allergies to what I ate, and he got through breastfeeding. A milk protein allergy. So I quit milk. Over the next three years, doctors ran us ragged with weekly weight checks, running to this specialist then that specialist, ongoing blood tests that always resulted in adding more allergies to the list and taking away foods he could eat. He didn't like to eat nor sit still long enough to eat, had 12 foods we omitted, and always had tummy problems. He was getting taller but was not gaining weight. He had sensory processing disorders, wasn't talking and was all over the place behaviorally. We barely slept. He fidgeted all night long, unable to relax, and most nights, we'd sleep in 20-minute intervals between waking, which made morning come way too fast. While studying about him, I heard the words "sun child," so off I googled that.

I found and tapped into the energy of these new "sun" or "golden" kids, several versions after the indigo kids came in. I shifted that day from my sleep-deprived worried mind trying and failing miserably to solve the mystery of what was wrong with Wesley and his allergies into my natural intuitive heart centered perspective. I started to look at what the root causes of the symptoms could be, his nature and gifts, and how to support him.

We stopped going to the doctor and all the specialists. I kept tapping in, and following the energy trail. I called in one holistic practitioner after the next until we had a team working with us instead of against us. I intuited all these challenges we'd been up against were actually about how sensitive he is. He came in like me, wide open. His gut was over sensitive to foods causing inflammation, and he had to acclimate to them. We still avoid the biggies like gluten, dairy, white sugar and corn syrups. We found the Healy frequency device, which gave us biofeedback on what he needed and then could deliver it, and he started feeling better.

When we started homeschooling, he started talking more and sleeping better. I'm still eagerly awaiting the first time he sleeps through the night for sure! As I got more sleep, I was able to use my healing abilities to help too. This huge change all because I trusted myself and listened to where my intuition led. He is happier, eating and growing faster than other kids his age.

INTUITIVE SELF-HEALING

I loved our small town and rural property in southwestern Colorado. The energy was powerful but supportive. The property we lived on was the perfect storm for me, though. I had learned by now that scary movies and real haunted houses were just a bad idea for me. I was still unable to control them opening me up to other dimensions and spirits. I never considered land being a problem for me, but the land we lived on had a lot of spirit activity. I was startled often, and woke up at night by these spirits. My childhood terrors were showing again as I became resistant to feeling and seeing and being open to all of them. I gained a ton of weight, was kind of jealous of my husband who could just peacefully ignore it all, and my babies were being woke up and scared too. I was shutting down as much as I could.

A shaman approached me, and a new phase began. I was resistant. Lord knows I really didn't want to open to my abilities at this point; I was trying to do the opposite! She placed a small amethyst crystal in my hand, and it turned my hand purple from where it felt like it had merged with my hand. This awakening continued as she showed me I was in control of what I allowed.

When I was woke up at night by these random spirits, I would stand on my bed and demand they left. I made a rule that no matter what kind of spirits or guides they were, I could not be startled by their presence in my house, and they were not allowed to bother my children. I learned to transmute my fear that attracted a lot of this attention, use sage to keep myself and space clear, and chose to trek down the path I had chosen before I was born into this lifetime.

I became an initiated shaman. Learned to move and work with and heal with energy, including sound through crystal singing bowls. I learned to work with spirits and non-physical guides, angels, and star beings. My world opened up. I felt at home in my body for the first time. I began to heal with my abilities, got master reiki attunements, connected with plant medicines, Mama Gaia and her cycles, and crystals. My inner witch was happiest in the kitchen making medicines and learning how to use my abilities in traditional and new ways. I took on my role as a healer, medicine woman, channel and shamaness as seriously as I took being a mother and wife. My abilities unfurled as soon as I dropped the fear. I was protected. I did have a purpose for and beyond my beautiful family. My boys would grow up with such a different perspective being homeschooled, having self-trust, stepping into abilities modeled, and having stronger bodies they understood how to work with instead of against.

I began to feel into clients hiring us in our construction business to see if they would be a good fit and our business grew. I had a shamanic singing bowls healing practice that allowed me to stretch and explore my abilities while serving. I learned to channel through ideas, copy and projects including a new way to heal and create with Intuitive Self-Healing.

The next big leap was to share my story in three multi-author book projects. I loved the synergy, collaboration, impact and initiation I had with each one. Clients poured in and I was at the brink of all I could handle when I got the nudge to start my own publishing company and give feminine leaders a platform to share their story and experience becoming a bestselling author. Pretty much everyone important in my life from my husband to my business coach said no to this plan. I trusted my heart and did it anyway. My heart led and I followed.

I created Kiva Publishing and chose the theme for my first book, Magdalene Rising: Feminine Leaders Guided by Her Fierce and Unconditional Wisdom. Everything fell into place and made sense. A book coach showed up, tech help and then perfect heart-centered authors started applying to contribute to the book. It was fun, enjoyable and effortless!

At every decision, fork in the road and precipice, I stop. I listen. I ask my heart. My intuition has never, and I mean never led me astray, not even a little. Every time I can't see how the guidance would make sense, it becomes abundantly clear and opens exponentially into new possibilities.

Listen. Trust. You know.

Tapping Into Your Power

The core of intuitive self-healing is tapping into your heart sourced intuition which is your power and sovereignty.

We are in the midst of a global dark night of the soul, void of collective sovereignty. We march into uncharted territory, darkness and shadow as we witness the labor pains of the New Earth coming into being. Our heart sourced intuition is the only way to get our bearings. The only way to bring in the upgrades and new codes and create from the 5D.

You are part of the long-awaited feminine leaders who chose to be here now at this unprecedented and exciting time of transition on our planet. It's time for you to step into your power, your purpose and your divine feminine leadership.

ACTIVATE YOUR INTUITIVE POWER

Here are the top three ways to activate your intuition:

1. **How you care for and what you feed your body matters when it comes to our intuition.** Your abilities will be stronger when your body is relaxed and well-rested; being in survival mode shuts it down.

The better fuel you put in your body, the more your body is in a vibrating state of expansion and can grow your abilities. For me, this means omitting inflammatory foods like gluten, dairy, fast food, processed food, and white processed sugars and corn syrups. I do eat some meat, but I find alcohol and caffeine limit my connection. I also make sure my food is high quality, and I take magnesium, selenium and trace minerals specifically for my intuition.

2. **You need space to increase the flow of your intuition**. This means space in your body, which I didn't understand until I lost over 150 pounds and opening your space with movement. I love belly dancing, Buti Yoga, paddle boarding, horseback riding and my ranch chores to get in my movement every day. This also means space in your heart, letting go and releasing the past. Forgiveness and EFT tapping is huge for this.

This means space in your environment, a cluttered environment clogs up your channel. I practice removing at least one thing a day from my environment to keep new energy coming in intuitively and money-wise.

And this means mental space. Limiting social media, putting down your phone and getting away from screens altogether and just doing nothing. As women we need at least 20 minutes a day to do nothing—nothing. When I first heard that I didn't even comprehend there was such a thing. We have to slow parts of our day down enough to have some mental space.

3. **Learning to deeply connect.** My garden and learning plant medicine was a quickening of learning how to connect for me. Being in nature, growing plants and following the cycles of the sun, moon and your menstrual cycle are ways to do this.

Asking for help from your divine team, spirit guides and angels helps you connect with the help available and help facilitate expanding your intuition. They are there waiting, you just have to ask so they have permission to help you.

Create a daily practice around listening. Mediate. Channel through writing. Just intend to listen and clearly receive guidance. You can start to ask yes or no questions, then reverse the question to check the guidance. Approach connecting with curiosity and play. Try different ways, experiment.

In a world tearing itself apart to be reborn, it's crucial you activate and operate from your intuition, the highest intelligence we as feminine leaders can embody. You are here for a reason and meant to lead from the heart.

Breathe deeply and connect. The bigness of your journey awaits.

ABOUT THE AUTHOR

Shannon Van Den Berg is an International Best-Selling Author, Feminine Leadership Mentor, and the CEO and Founder of Kiva Publishing. She provides a platform for women leaders to share their story and message globally. She is the creator of *"Fierce as Fuck: Unleashing the Wild Woman Within,"* a whole life upgrade program for mom entrepreneurs.

Shannon specializes in guiding moms to break free from the limitations keeping them stuck in their life and business. She supports her clients to activate their inner Creatrix so they can cultivate an epic life and unlock deeper levels of service and wealth in their business.

Her work is a bespoke fusion of intuitive self-healing, embodiment practices, mindset work and channeled activations that quantum leap you into the bigness of your soul purpose so you can call in higher levels of impact, income and activate your feminine leadership.

She lives on her ranch in the sacred Four Corners area of Hesperus, Colorado with her husband and four boys.

If you are a mom in business, and want to share your story with the world and create massive visibility, credibility and expression in your business, you are invited to apply to contribute to Kiva Publishing's upcoming multi-author book, Magdalene Rising: Feminine Leaders Who are Guided by Her Fierce and Unconditional Wisdom.

Website: *www.shannonvandenberg.com*
Facebook: *https://www.facebook.com/ groups/divinefeminineleaderssanctum*
Instagram: *www.instagram.com/shannonvandenberg_*

TRUDY MALINS

EX-ME

Before I begin, I want to let you know that for the longest time I thought that I did not have any intuition and therefore I must be broken. I was broken. It's that simple. However, I have connected with my inner self and restored the link, and I am ready to fly. So, here goes:

I grew up as a devout Catholic. Lots of rules to live by; giving responsibility over to God and walking through life with blind faith. Everything is forgiven as long as you repent, go to Church on Sunday, receive Holy Communion and take Confession regularly. Nothing wrong with that. I had no reason to question my faith, as it was there to keep me on the straight and narrow path that would eventually lead me to the Kingdom of God, after going to purgatory to cleanse me of my sins! Happy me, happy family. What a lovely facade.

My father sexually abused me for years. It was easy for him since my mother had an evening job, leaving him free to do what he wanted with me. He had a day job that left my mother free to look after my siblings and me throughout the day. This arrangement of opposite working hours lasted until we moved from Clapham to Thornton Heath.

The new job my grandfather helped my father find and our change of location did not end the abuse. It just meant that my father had to put more effort into changing his situation to facilitate his end game. It made me wary and guarded around new people. Not really a surprise. His manipulation knew no bounds. He managed to split loyalties between me, my brother and sister and my mother. I could see that he treated my sister differently. He had a little nickname for her, but none for me or my brother. She was always the first child he greeted when he returned home from work, and the first child considered for an outing. Stuff like that. His real intention was to keep her apart from our mother, so that she was not on mother's radar. This way, my sister would be willing to be with my father as he loved her the most, and the wedge he put between her and my mother made her more dependent on him. This did not work with me. Maybe he did not try as hard because he knew that a younger sister would want to emulate the older one.

Although he did not destroy the bond or love I had for my mother, there was obviously a certain amount of secrecy involved. Looking back, secrecy, or rather being closed-mouth, is something that I have struggled with throughout my life. I have relied on the safety of the facade that "everything is alright." Turn the other way, no one can see what you do not allow them to see, smile big and everyone is willing to accept the illusion. When I talked to my mother, as a child and as an adult, I had to carefully choose not just my words but my thoughts too to censor my conversation.

Well, I managed to create a very safe box for myself. It was not a very practical one, but one in which I felt safe. My father had taught me to follow the instructions of adults blindly. My faith reinforced this. As one of the Ten Commandments tell us, "honour thy mother and father." Where do you go from there? All the bad things lived outside my box; this kept the inside of my box comfortable. I knew what I liked to do. I knew how to keep smiling and make everyone think life was good. I thought that when my father left (I think I was about 10 years old), life would get better. It did not. Instead, I felt even more afraid. He would turn up at random school open evenings and leave notes or pictures on my desk. When I saw them, I would shake, and spend the day looking over my shoulder. At the time, I would not have been able to tell why I felt this way. Reflection tells me a lot. I felt the freedom from his heavy presence. His notes and drawings felt that he could reach me and do whatever he wanted with me any time he liked. I felt his presence for days after. My friends could never understand why I would become quiet and withdrawn. I did not tell them either.

He left. That was the end. I would not have to deal with him again. He moved on with another family anyway. This sent me into confusion and jealousy. He had other girls now, so he did not need me anymore. It was hard for a short time, even though he had not managed to destroy my relationship with my mother—she managed that all on her own later on in my life—the devastation he caused between my sister and mother left my sister in a terrible place. You would think that we would become a closer family unit when my father left. Not so much. The facade was a good one though.

My parents' marriage was not a happy one. My father had numerous affairs and treated my mother like a second-class citizen. Happy families on the outside when they went to parties but at home, he was full of anger, suspicion and accusations that my mother was sleeping around. I suppose he was deflecting his own guilt onto her. She did eventually succumb and have an affair—the result of which was my little brother. She paid heavily for that truth. He beat her badly that night and left shortly after. Anyway, when he left all that pressure and heaviness should have gone with him. Well, it didn't. It was replaced by something different, and I think left me with longer lasting damage.

Do not get me wrong, we had some good times, but there was always an edge to them. When would the bubble burst? When would my mother get angry, leading to an argument? That sounds a bit harsh, but that's just how it was. Married life was not easy for my mother, but our lives became worse after my father left.

Well, either with or without my father around I had become resilient and very good at creating a happy life illusion for everyone to see. I still do that now. Although, now I manage to take a breath and step back. This does not mean to say that I stomp around in a bad mood, wailing and moaning, when I see my friends! It means my friends allow me to have a moment and help me find solutions. I have found that is a much better way of connecting with people and dealing with problems. No one likes a superhero mum with a picture perfect life. Not only that, it's unattainable, unrealistic and probably not much fun!

So, we all had to grow up. The childhood that I had was long gone. With the addition of my little brother, there was now an extra responsibility for all of us. My older brother was now the man of the house, and had to learn how to fix things, change plugs, handle wallpaper, and paint. Bear in mind, he was only 14 years old. My sister and I cleaned, cooked and helped with the baby when mother was either having a night out, or working nights and evenings as a barmaid.

This is not so bad—or so it seems. My mother's temper grew. Maybe fear and frustration because of her full responsibility. Her anger was always evident after I had visited my grandparents. For me, they were great: a place to go in the school holidays, and someone to cuddle and be showered in unconditional love. For my mother they were not so helpful. They did not drive, and the whole cultural background that children look after their parents weighed heavily on her. My aunts and uncles also saw my mother and our house as a place of refuge when their lives at home were not going well. This caused friction for my mother and her parents too. I think maybe there also was a bit of jealously hanging around. We received the love she so desperately wanted and felt that she was not getting. Also, I spoke with Granny a lot. She was interested in what I thought and what I had to say and how I was coping with school. This was something my mother was not able to do, either emotionally or time wise.

Having grandparents who were giving eased so much. It also planted the seed that not all adults want something in return. Their love was there, mine for the taking, no agenda, and no fuss. Just free.

There was hope! I also tucked this away deep in my brain, hoping that any children I would have in the future would be lucky enough to have grandparents like mine. Hoping against hope that in the face of all the adversity, my mother would be able to put it all aside and enjoy the product of all her hard work. Her grandchildren.

It dawned on me that not all families were like mine. When I made friends in senior

school and then met with their parents, I found that they were really good people and seemed to be genuine. Parents that did not fight with you but had discussions instead was a rather alien concept. Cracks were beginning to appear in my safely constructed box. So, I began to let my guard down. Slowly. My friends eventually found out that home life sucked. Not all the time, but a lot of the time. I could not go out with my friends if there was an opportunity for my little brother to come along. You know the type of thing, going swimming, lying about his age so he could get in free. That was probably more because she could not afford for the two of us to go but did not want to say no to me. Taking him to the park with me, little things like that. My friends were so good they went along with it. I was indeed blessed. As I got older, we did different things like clubbing—no ID required back in the day—or house parties. I worried about how I was going to get home. Mum would be working so could not collect me. When could, it would be at 2 or 3 am. I was a bit of a party girl but I did not want to stay out late at a party, mainly because that's when "naughtiness" between the boys and girls would happen. I was still a strict catholic. Also, the thought of having sex sent me into a spiral of fear, unsurprisingly. Although by this stage, I had pushed all memories of the abuse *waaaay* down deep, so much so I could not understand why I was not curious about sex but scared. So, my friend's dad always picked us up. It did not matter where we were or what time we needed collecting. There he was. Smiling and happy that we had a good time. No fuss, no moaning, no agenda. You would think that my mother would be happy that I was safe. Oh, no, it made her mad. It was very confusing. She did not want the responsibility but got mad when someone else stepped up.

What my friend's dad did for me struck a deep cord within me. That's how I wanted to be with my children. In fact I am. Even though my oldest daughter and her boyfriend can drive, my husband and I are always willing to drop off or collect them. It was the same when my girls were at gymnastics; if someone needed help we were there, no questions asked. This unfortunately led to being used by others, a lot. I used my gut to defend and protect my children daily, but when it came to me, I ignored that little voice and pushed away my gut feeling. I was such a people pleaser. My mother's mood swings and my father's abuse had taught me to mould myself into whatever was required. I have learnt to listen to that voice and rely on my gut instinct. It's only taken me 53 years!

Life moves on, but I was coming more and more in contact with people that had good boundaries and models of behaviour. Phillip, then boyfriend and now husband, really threw me for a loop. My friends' families, Phillip's family and people that I worked with. Some along the way pushed my buttons and sent me running for my battered, cracked and bruised box.

I joined the Police Force in December 1987. That job appealed to my need for order and rules. The law is after all Black and White. Right and Wrong. Or so I thought. My training at Hendon Centre prepared me for my role as a Police Officer. However, what I was not prepared for was the prejudice I received from a few officers when I was placed on division. My forte for becoming invisible came in handy. I did not realise that I had this little trick up my sleeve.

Let me explain. When my parents' divorce became final, it meant that within the eyes of the church, any relationship my mother had that may lead to marriage would be rejected. Divorce is not allowed. The only way for a catholic to re-marry is if the marriage ended due to death. You know the line, "till death us do part." The only other way is to have the marriage annulled. It's a long and difficult process. The church wants to know the ins and outs of a bats arse. Well, forms were

completed and sent to whoever and wherever they needed to go. An annulment means the slate is wiped clean. You are nice and clean, fresh to start all over again. Stop; there is a problem—or should I say three problems? That's right: me, my brother and my sister. Where did that leave us? We were the products of that marriage. You cannot wipe us out. We are very much alive and kicking. Did that make us invisible? I did not realise how much that one decision affected me. Even as I tried to make myself invisible in my new job, it's only now I can see how it made me feel and hopefully today can stop that old pattern of behaviour.

Okay, back to my job as a police officer. At training school, you feel so empowered. All this knowledge and confidence in a classroom is easy. Taking exams is easy. Teachers who can break it down for you, supporting your understanding and areas of difficulty, surround you. Everyone around you wants the same thing: to make a difference. Colour, age, where you are from did not register on the radar. Everyone had life experience and it was all good.

Not so true for the people that I started my working life with. A few of them just like my mother and father eroded my sense of self-worth. Two officers just picked and picked at whatever I did. It was not good enough; I had made the wrong decision, or written up a crime wrong. Two people stood up for me and put them both in their place. Those two acts woke the sleeping dragon. From that day forward, I became vocal. If I did not know the answer, I asked the question. If I disagreed with something I was being asked to do, I opened my mouth. Life certainly became easier for me as a police officer. I left on medical grounds in 1998. Total devastation. I had to find a new path and I did. Phillip and I decided to start a family.

With all that had happened in my life, both as an adult and a child, you will be forgiven for thinking that I would be one bad ass mother. You would be wrong. I had been shown so much compassion and support from friends, their families and my new family that it should have been easy. All of my insecurities around my mother came flooding back. I was hoping that she would turn into the grandmother I had. Nope. My girls did have an amazing grandmother in their lives so it's not all bad.

The one regret that I have is that I allowed my mother to treat my kids so badly. I made such huge leaps in my quest for self-improvement but fell at the first hurdle. That little voiced was silenced and my gut ignored. All I wanted was that dream I had hidden away when I was a little girl. Sadly, I put my children on that sacrificial alter.

Everything that I had learnt, all that I had taught my girls about not letting others trample over you stood for nothing.

Things came to a head with my mother. The voice I was trying to tune out was getting louder and louder. My girls and my husband echoed that voice. So, I put on my big girl knickers and refused to feed my mother's outrageous behaviour. As soon as I decided, I felt lighter. I knew that it had to be done but I really did not want to crush the hopes and dreams of a little girl. In reality, that was exactly what I was doing to my girls. I remembered how it felt when someone goes into bat for you. I remembered that day as a police officer when I allowed my dragon its freedom. I need to be true to me and mine. It's hard. but I have learnt to take a breath, feel the light and listen to my inner voice. I have found it's a much nicer way to live. My family think so too.

I need to remember every day that although actions speak louder than words, if my actions are not aligned with my integrity, my words and actions are empty. I have lived with narcissistic parents; they have shaped me and allowed me to become visible. For that, I am thankful. So that's why this chapter is titled Ex-Me. Like Ex-partners, we do not want them in our lives. I do not want the old me to come back. I love the new and improved me.

ABOUT THE AUTHOR

Trudy Malins served as a police officer for 12 years until circumstances led her to move on. She has a passion for reading, writing and crochet. Her working life took many turns—one she enjoyed was working with children as a gymnastics coach. Her passion led her to open a pre-school. She is married to Phil and has two girls.

Trudy contributed to this book with the intention to show others that despite their circumstances, we can all trust our intuition, and although we may not always use it, it is always available to us.

Trudy is now happily retired and indulges in travelling with her husband in their motor home while knitting, crocheting and writing.

Website: *www.cuddlebuddies.uk*
Facebook: *www.facebook.com/Cuddle-Buddies-100451208716469*

ABOUT THE ART OF GRACE PUBLISHING HOUSE

A two-time best-selling author, a successful business woman both on- and off-line, Brigid Holder is the founder and CEO of The Art of Grace Publishing House.

After a successful corporate career and accounting under her belt, Brigid created a successful traditional business, that she still operates alongside her husband. Spending a number of years as Mothers Mentor and a Business Coach only to discover her passion for story telling and hence founding the publishing company.

Brigid is now on a mission to share the stories of women with the aim to grant permission to other women to change their lives.

Brigid lives on a small farm in the rural town of Cootamundra NSW Australia with her two boys and husband.

Facebook: www.facebook.com/brigid.holder
Email: brigid@brigidholder.com

Printed in Great Britain
by Amazon

62183812R00190